BUREAU FOR PARANORMAL • RESEARCH AND DEFENSE •

B.P.R.D. HELL ON EARTH:
THE REIGN OF THE BLACK FLAME

created by MIKE MIGNOLA

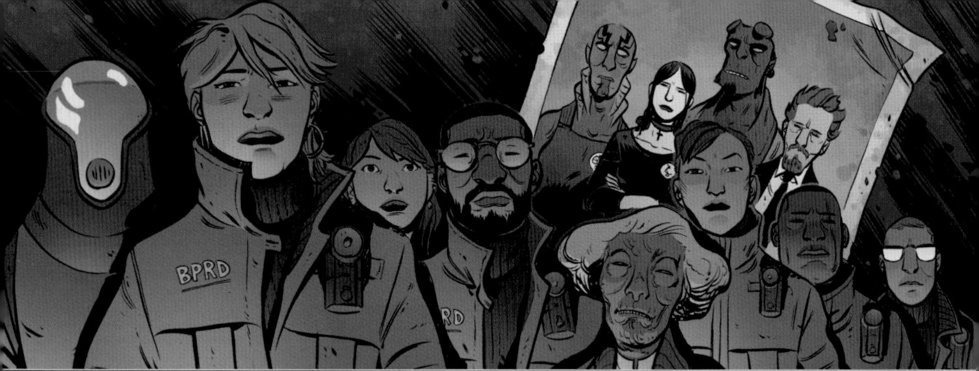
BPRD

To stop the Black Flame's attempt to raise a new race of man, Liz Sherman lit a fire in the underground city of Agartha that nearly cracked the world in two. Though the Black Flame was destroyed, new threats continue to crawl out of the earth. After Agartha, Liz went missing, and Abe Sapien was shot by the young psychic Fenix. Now Abe has disappeared, and the B.P.R.D. has joined forces with the Russian Special Sciences Service to deal with the worldwide crisis. Neither group knows that the current increase in devastation was caused by the rebirth of the Black Flame.

MIKE MIGNOLA'S

B.P.R.D.™ HELL ON EARTH

THE REIGN OF THE BLACK FLAME

story by **MIKE MIGNOLA** and **JOHN ARCUDI**

art by **JAMES HARREN**

colors by **DAVE STEWART**

letters by **CLEM ROBINS**

cover art by **MIKE MIGNOLA** with **DAVE STEWART**

chapter break art by **RAFAEL ALBUQUERQUE**
with **DAVE STEWART**

editor **SCOTT ALLIE**   associate editor **DANIEL CHABON**

assistant editor **SHANTEL LAROCQUE**   collection designer **AMY ARENDTS**

publisher **MIKE RICHARDSON**

DarkHorse.com   Hellboy.com

B.P.R.D.™ Hell on Earth Volume 9: The Reign of the Black Flame

This book collects *B.P.R.D. Hell on Earth* #115–#119.

Published by Dark Horse Books
A division of Dark Horse Comics, Inc.
10956 SE Main Street
Milwaukie, OR 97222

THE REIGN OF THE BLACK FLAME

CHAPTER ONE

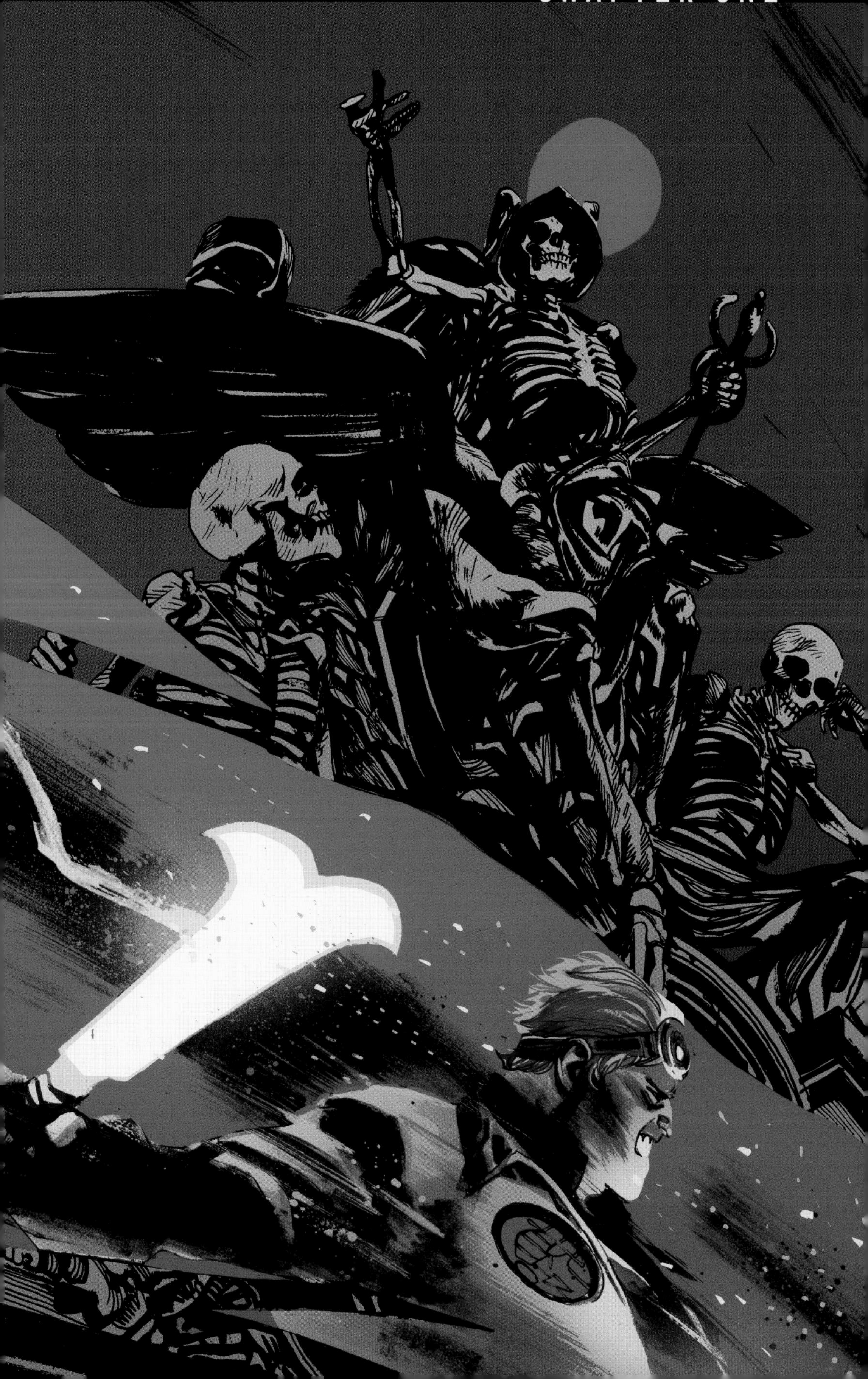

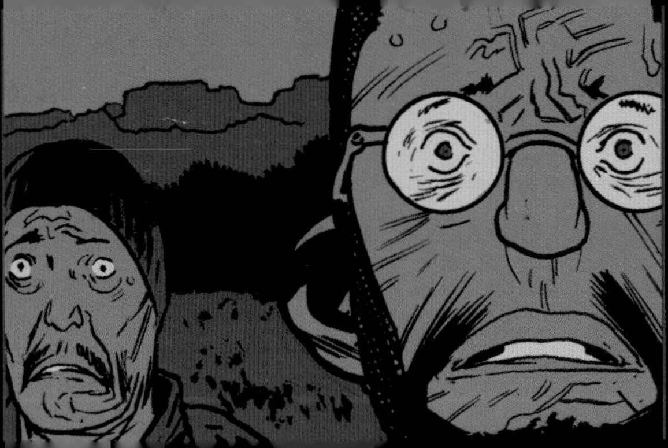

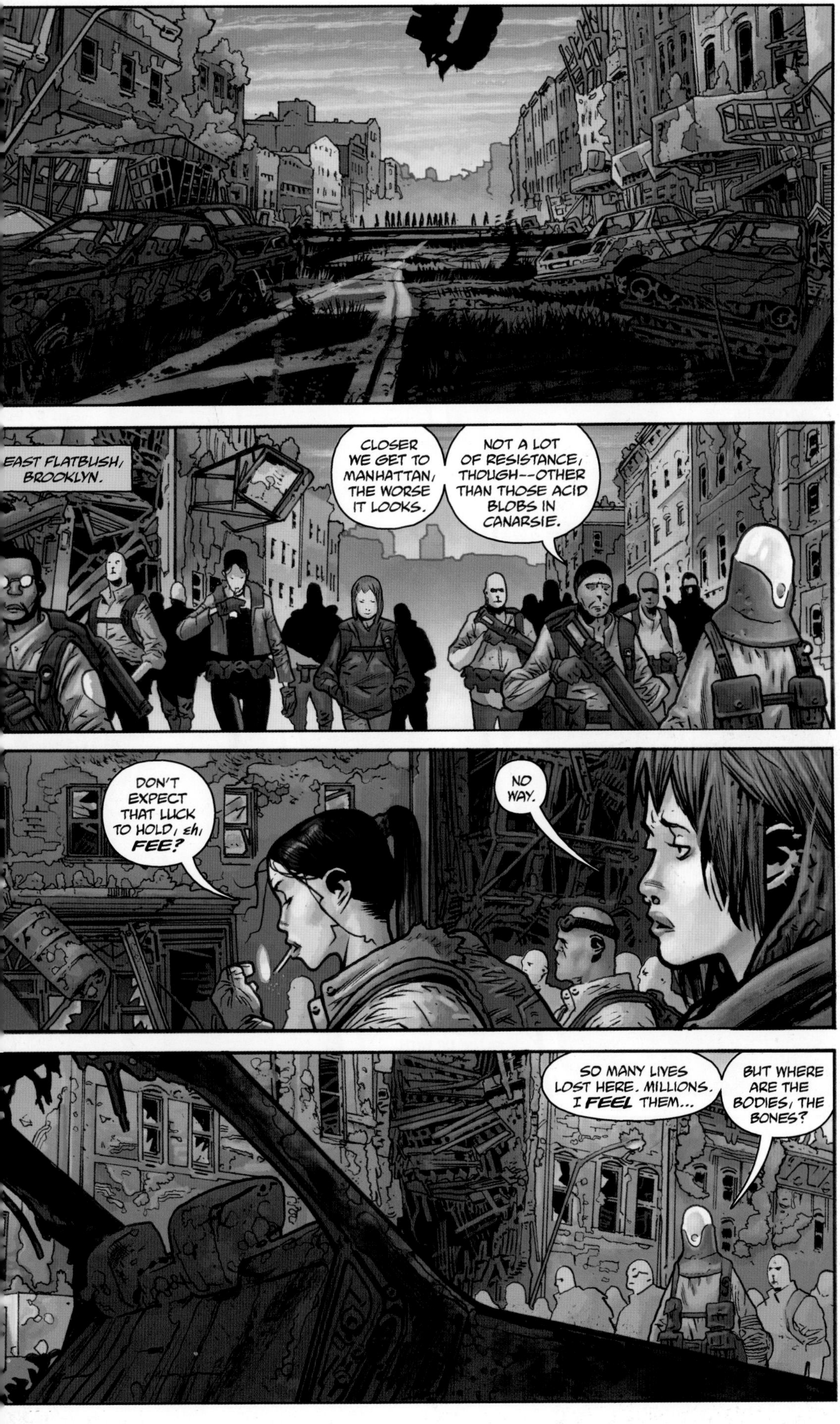
EAST FLATBUSH, BROOKLYN.
CLOSER WE GET TO MANHATTAN, THE WORSE IT LOOKS.
NOT A LOT OF RESISTANCE, THOUGH--OTHER THAN THOSE ACID BLOBS IN CANARSIE.
DON'T EXPECT THAT LUCK TO HOLD, eh, FEE?
NO WAY.
SO MANY LIVES LOST HERE. MILLIONS. I FEEL THEM...
BUT WHERE ARE THE BODIES, THE BONES?

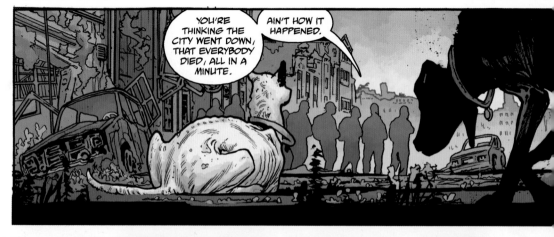

YOU'RE THINKING THE CITY WENT DOWN, THAT EVERYBODY DIED, ALL IN A MINUTE.

AIN'T HOW IT HAPPENED.

LAST FEW DAYS I'VE BEEN GETTING THESE IMAGES OF PEOPLE HUNTED IN THE STREETS--LIKE FOR WEEKS.

HOSPITALS FILLIN' UP WITH THE SICK. LOT OF BODIES STILL THERE.

TOWARDS T END, THOUSA TRIED TO J BAIL BY BO *THERE* YOUR ANSWE

UH-HUH. THAT, AND I'D SAY A LOT OF CANS OF DOG FOOD HAVEN'T BEEN OPENED AROUND HERE LATELY.

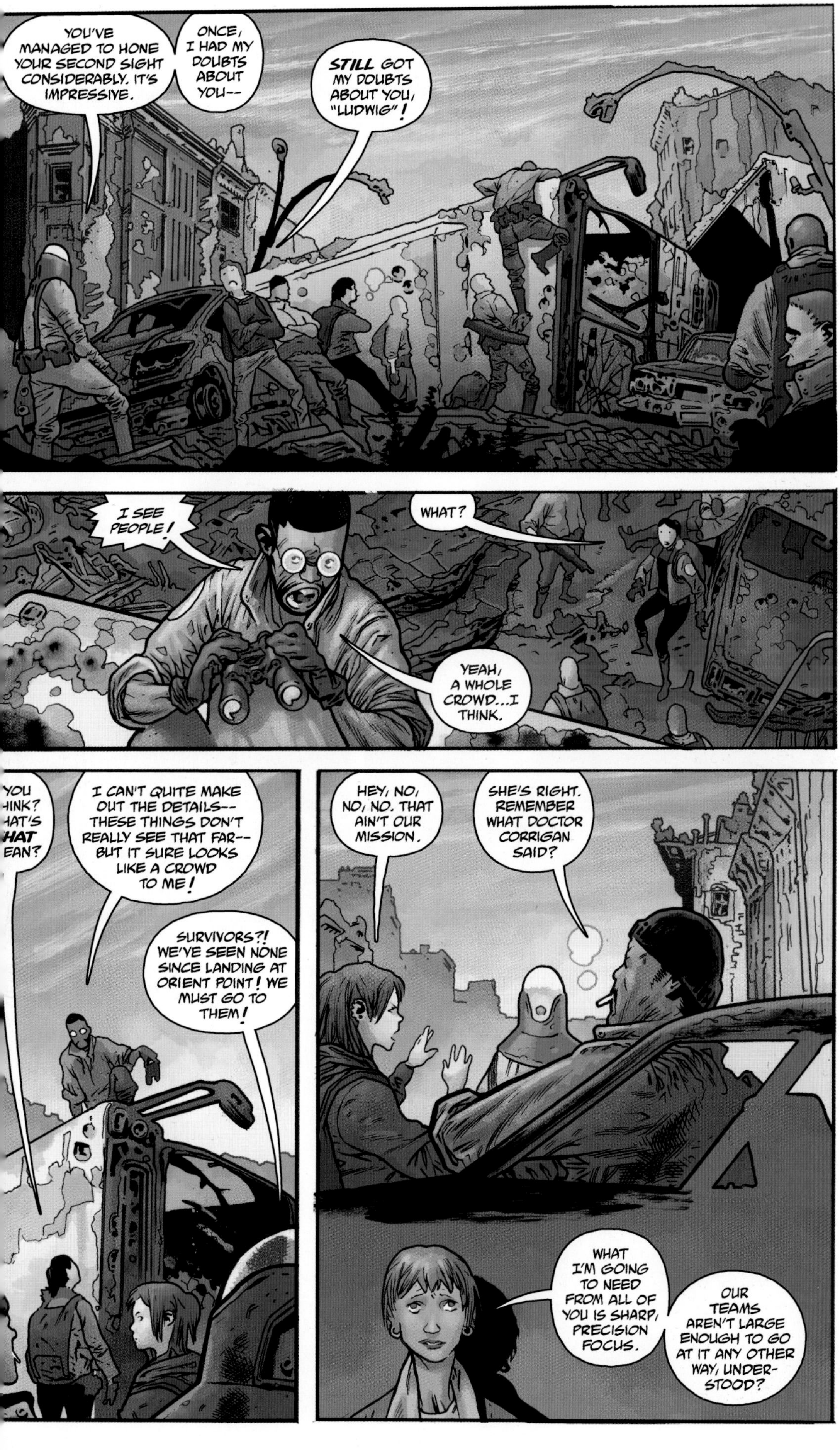
YOU'VE MANAGED TO HONE YOUR SECOND SIGHT CONSIDERABLY. IT'S IMPRESSIVE.
ONCE, I HAD MY DOUBTS ABOUT YOU--
STILL GOT MY DOUBTS ABOUT YOU, "LUDWIG"!
I SEE PEOPLE!
WHAT?
YEAH, A WHOLE CROWD...I THINK.
YOU HINK? HAT'S HAT EAN?
I CAN'T QUITE MAKE OUT THE DETAILS-- THESE THINGS DON'T REALLY SEE THAT FAR-- BUT IT SURE LOOKS LIKE A CROWD TO ME!
SURVIVORS?! WE'VE SEEN NONE SINCE LANDING AT ORIENT POINT! WE MUST GO TO THEM!
HEY, NO, NO, NO. THAT AIN'T OUR MISSION.
SHE'S RIGHT. REMEMBER WHAT DOCTOR CORRIGAN SAID?
WHAT I'M GOING TO NEED FROM ALL OF YOU IS SHARP, PRECISION FOCUS.
OUR TEAMS AREN'T LARGE ENOUGH TO GO AT IT ANY OTHER WAY, UNDER-STOOD?

NO DISTRACTIONS. PANYA WILL HELP WITH THAT.

SHE'LL BE HEF OFFSHORE, HELF FENIX AMPLIFY SECOND SIGHT. OUGHT TO HELP AVOID A LOT TROUBLE.

WE'VE RUN A LOT OF DRILLS, AND IT'S BEEN GOING GREAT.

ASSUMING THEIR *THETA WAVES* CAN PENETRATE THE "MANHATTAN WALL"-- BECAUSE OUR RADIOS CAN'T--IT OUGHT TO BE A HUGE ADVANTAGE.

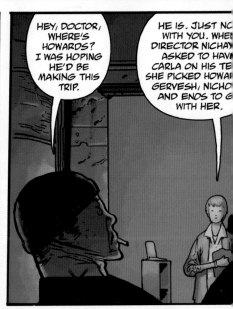

HEY, DOCTOR, WHERE'S HOWARDS? I WAS HOPING HE'D BE MAKING THIS TRIP.

HE IS. JUST NC WITH YOU. WHEN DIRECTOR NICHAY ASKED TO HAVE CARLA ON HIS TE SHE PICKED HOWAF GERVESH, NICHO AND ENOS TO G WITH HER.

SINCE THEY'RE COMING IN OVER LAND THROUGH *NEW JERSEY*, THEY'LL HAVE AN A.P.C., AND A TANK OR TWO.

DOESN'T REALLY SOUND FAIR, YOU SNEAKING OVER TO LONG ISLAND IN A COUPLE OF SKIFFS--THEN ON FOOT THE REST OF THE WAY--WHILE THEY RIDE IN WITH ARMOR, BUT REMEMBER ONE THING.

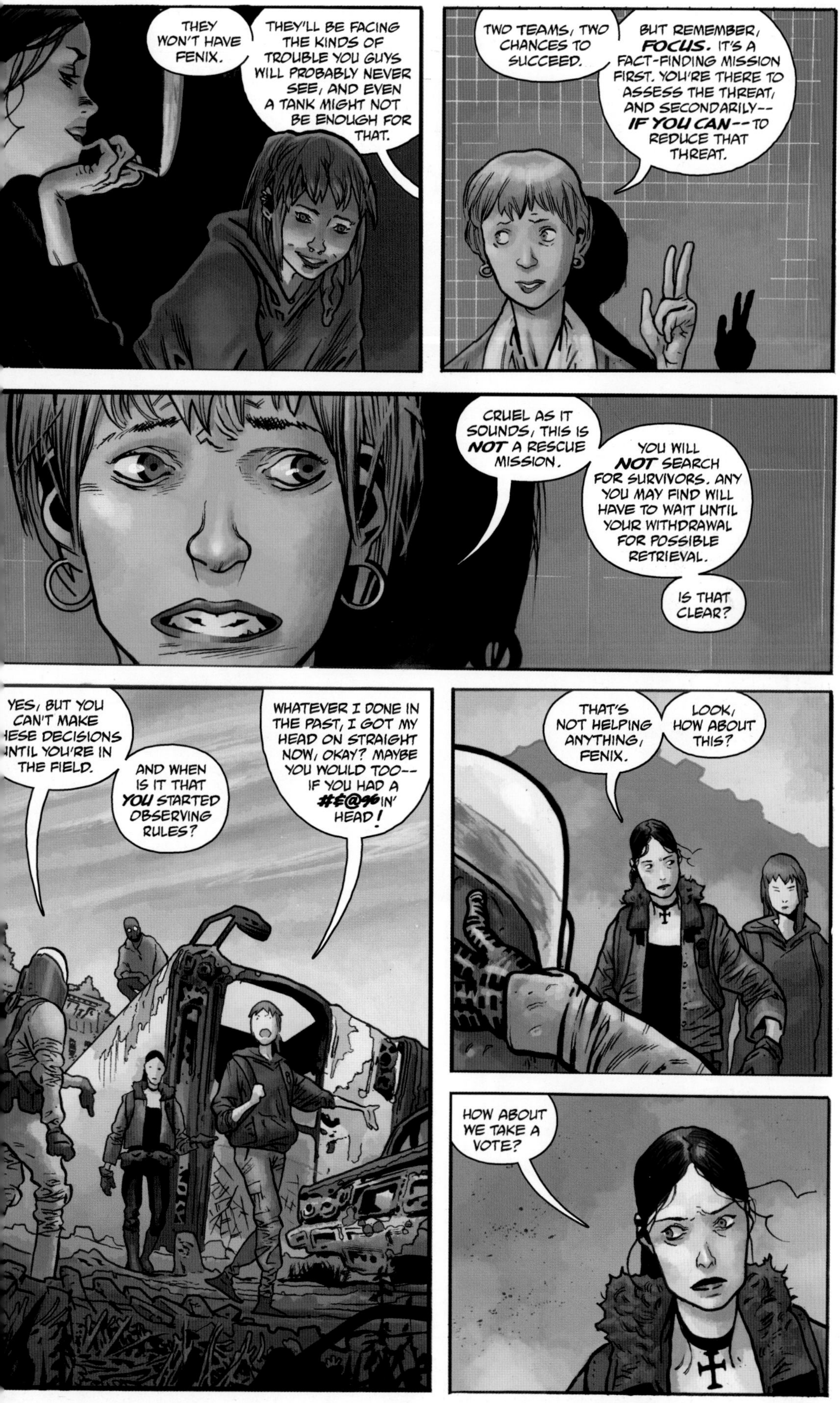
THEY WON'T HAVE FENIX.
THEY'LL BE FACING THE KINDS OF TROUBLE YOU GUYS WILL PROBABLY NEVER SEE, AND EVEN A TANK MIGHT NOT BE ENOUGH FOR THAT.
TWO TEAMS, TWO CHANCES TO SUCCEED.
BUT REMEMBER, FOCUS. IT'S A FACT-FINDING MISSION FIRST. YOU'RE THERE TO ASSESS THE THREAT, AND SECONDARILY-- IF YOU CAN--TO REDUCE THAT THREAT.
CRUEL AS IT SOUNDS, THIS IS NOT A RESCUE MISSION.
YOU WILL NOT SEARCH FOR SURVIVORS. ANY YOU MAY FIND WILL HAVE TO WAIT UNTIL YOUR WITHDRAWAL FOR POSSIBLE RETRIEVAL.
IS THAT CLEAR?
YES, BUT YOU CAN'T MAKE HESE DECISIONS UNTIL YOU'RE IN THE FIELD.
AND WHEN IS IT THAT YOU STARTED OBSERVING RULES?
WHATEVER I DONE IN THE PAST, I GOT MY HEAD ON STRAIGHT NOW, OKAY? MAYBE YOU WOULD TOO-- IF YOU HAD A #€@%IN' HEAD!
THAT'S NOT HELPING ANYTHING, FENIX.
LOOK, HOW ABOUT THIS?
HOW ABOUT WE TAKE A VOTE?

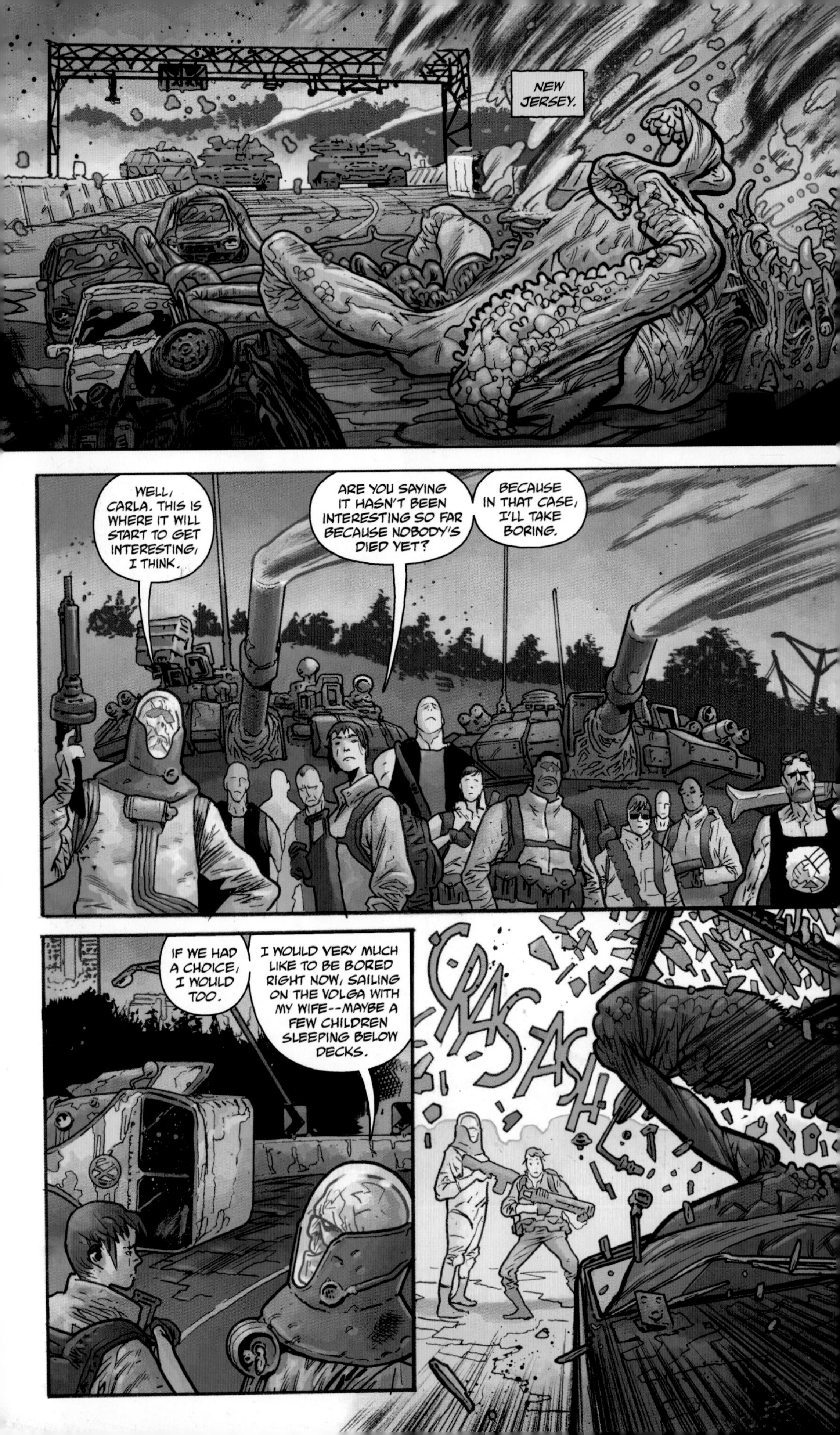
NEW JERSEY.
WELL, CARLA. THIS IS WHERE IT WILL START TO GET INTERESTING, I THINK.
ARE YOU SAYING IT HASN'T BEEN INTERESTING SO FAR BECAUSE NOBODY'S DIED YET?
BECAUSE IN THAT CASE, I'LL TAKE BORING.
IF WE HAD A CHOICE, I WOULD TOO.
I WOULD VERY MUCH LIKE TO BE BORED RIGHT NOW, SAILING ON THE VOLGA WITH MY WIFE--MAYBE A FEW CHILDREN SLEEPING BELOW DECKS.
CRASSASH

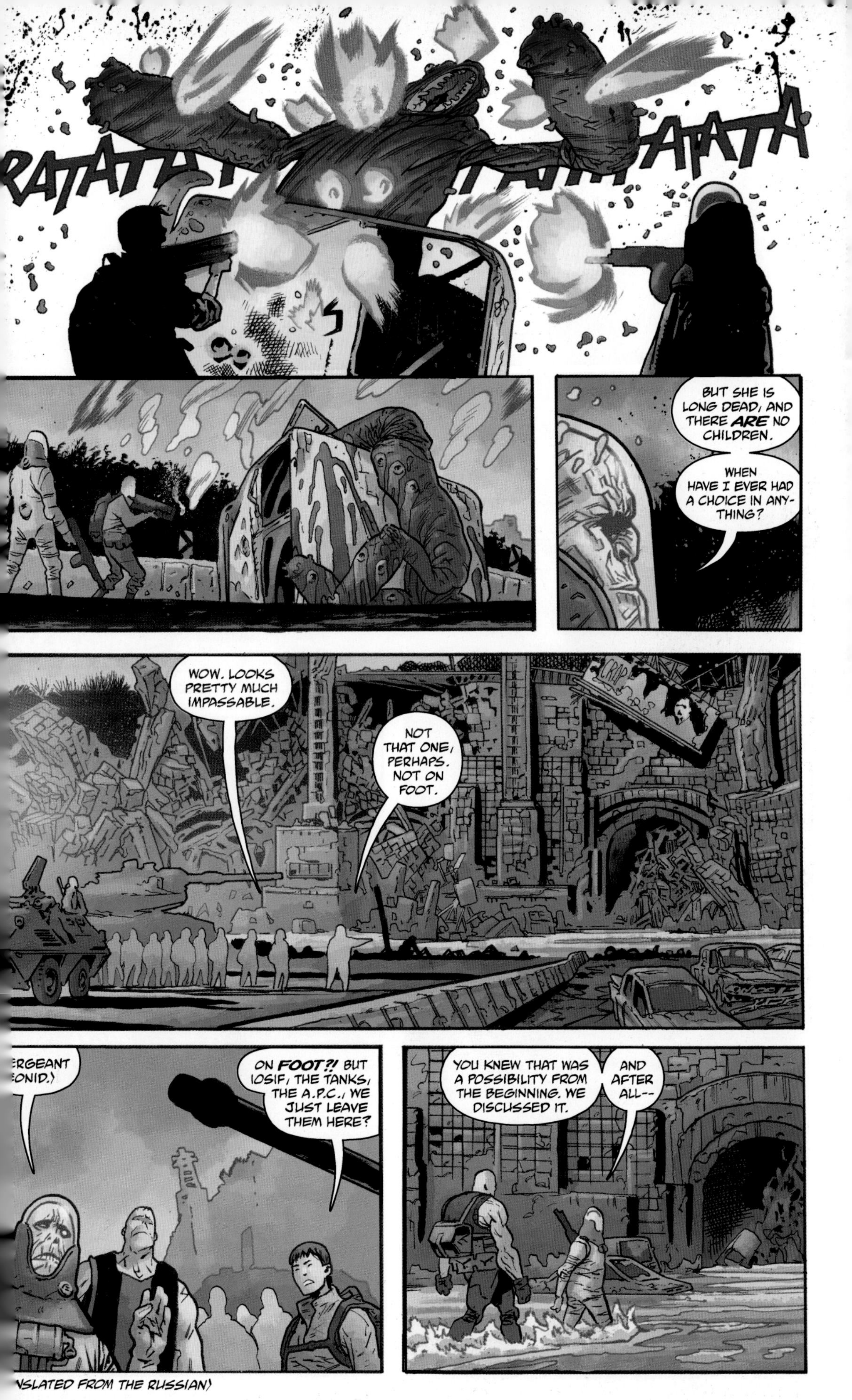

RATATAT
TATATA
BUT SHE IS LONG DEAD, AND THERE ***ARE*** NO CHILDREN.
WHEN HAVE I EVER HAD A CHOICE IN ANY-THING?
WOW. LOOKS PRETTY MUCH IMPASSABLE.
NOT THAT ONE, PERHAPS. NOT ON FOOT.
ERGEANT EONID.)
ON ***FOOT?!*** BUT IOSIF, THE TANKS, THE A.P.C., WE JUST LEAVE THEM HERE?
YOU KNEW THAT WAS A POSSIBILITY FROM THE BEGINNING. WE DISCUSSED IT.
AND AFTER ALL--
NSLATED FROM THE RUSSIAN)

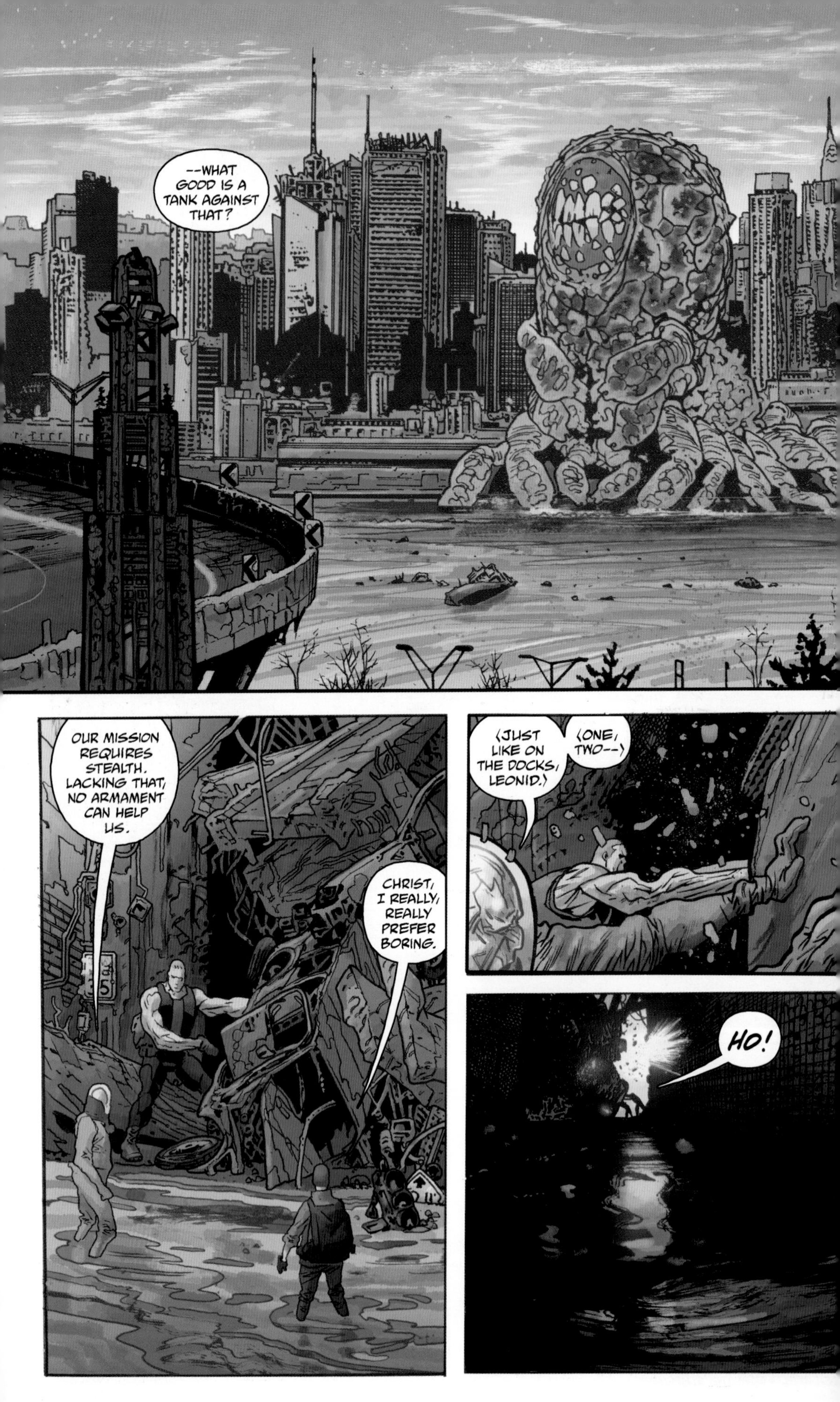
--WHAT GOOD IS A TANK AGAINST THAT?
OUR MISSION REQUIRES STEALTH. LACKING THAT, NO ARMAMENT CAN HELP US.
CHRIST, I REALLY, REALLY PREFER BORING.
‹JUST LIKE ON THE DOCKS, LEONID.›
‹ONE, TWO--›
HO!

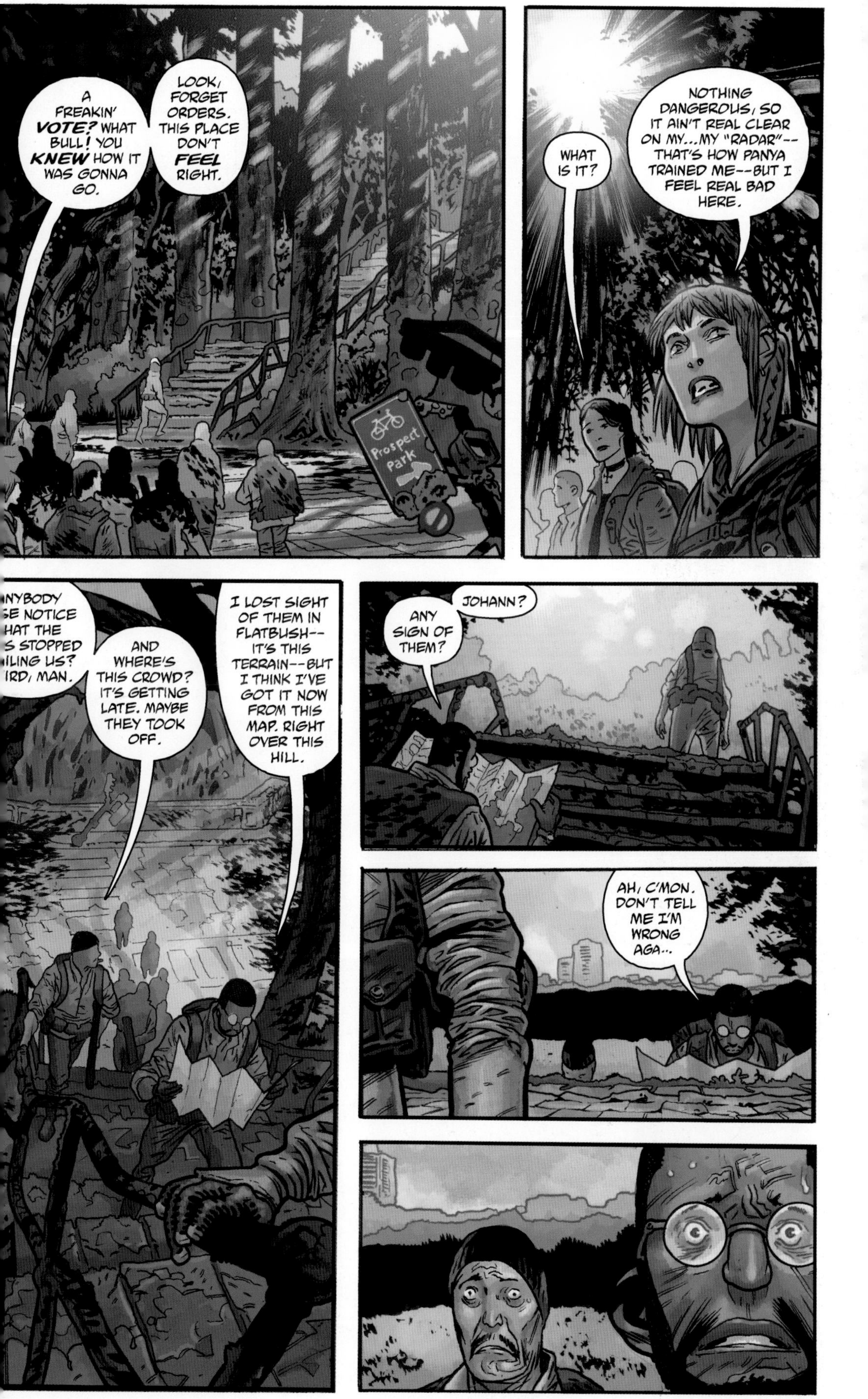
A FREAKIN' **VOTE?** WHAT BULL! YOU **KNEW** HOW IT WAS GONNA GO.
LOOK, FORGET ORDERS. THIS PLACE DON'T **FEEL** RIGHT.
Prospect Park
WHAT IS IT?
NOTHING DANGEROUS, SO IT AIN'T REAL CLEAR ON MY...MY "RADAR"--THAT'S HOW PANYA TRAINED ME--BUT I FEEL REAL BAD HERE.
NYBODY SE NOTICE HAT THE S STOPPED ILING US? IRD, MAN.
AND WHERE'S THIS CROWD? IT'S GETTING LATE. MAYBE THEY TOOK OFF.
I LOST SIGHT OF THEM IN FLATBUSH--IT'S THIS TERRAIN--BUT I THINK I'VE GOT IT NOW FROM THIS MAP. RIGHT OVER THIS HILL.
JOHANN?
ANY SIGN OF THEM?
AH, C'MON. DON'T TELL ME I'M WRONG AGA...

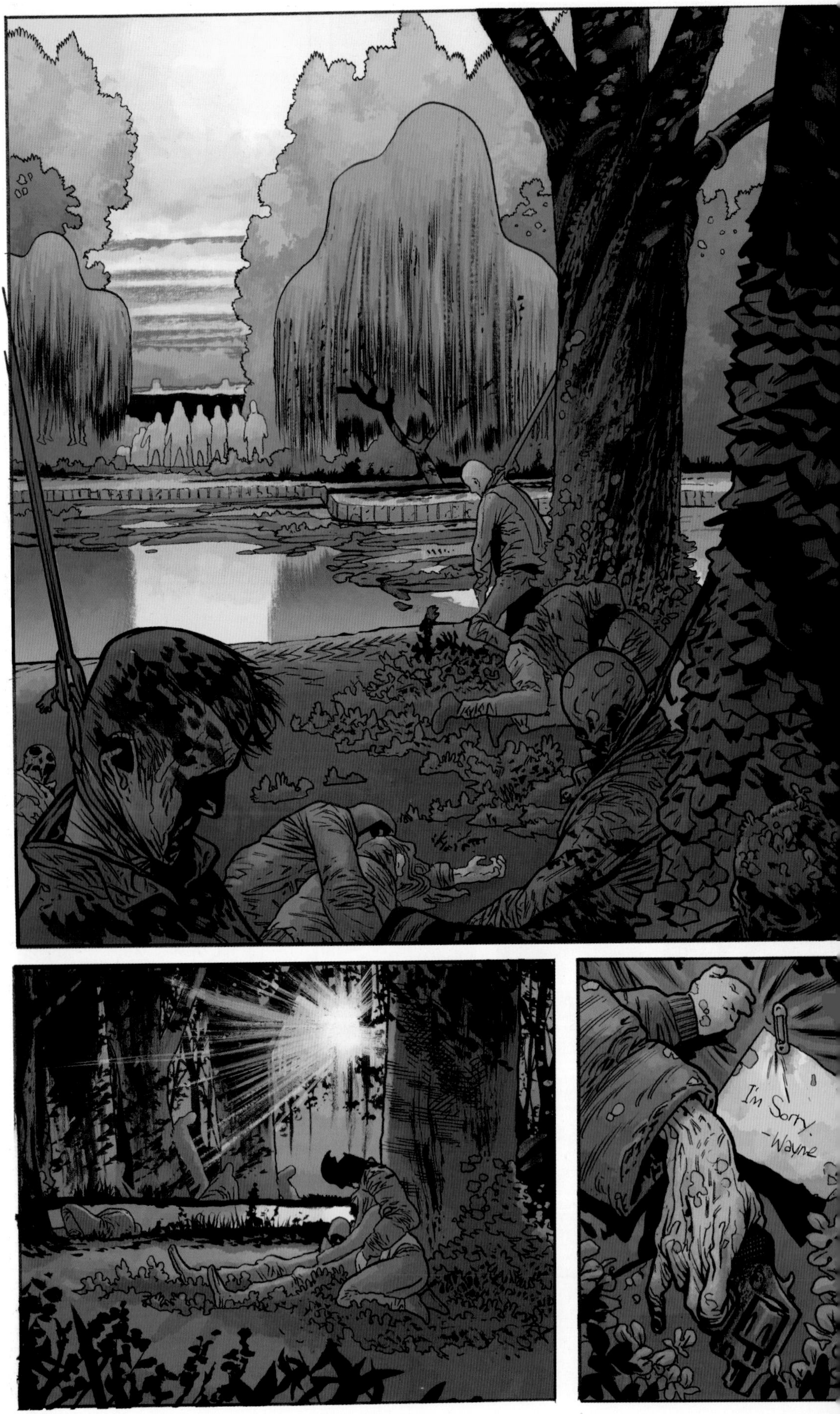
I'm Sorry.
-Wayne

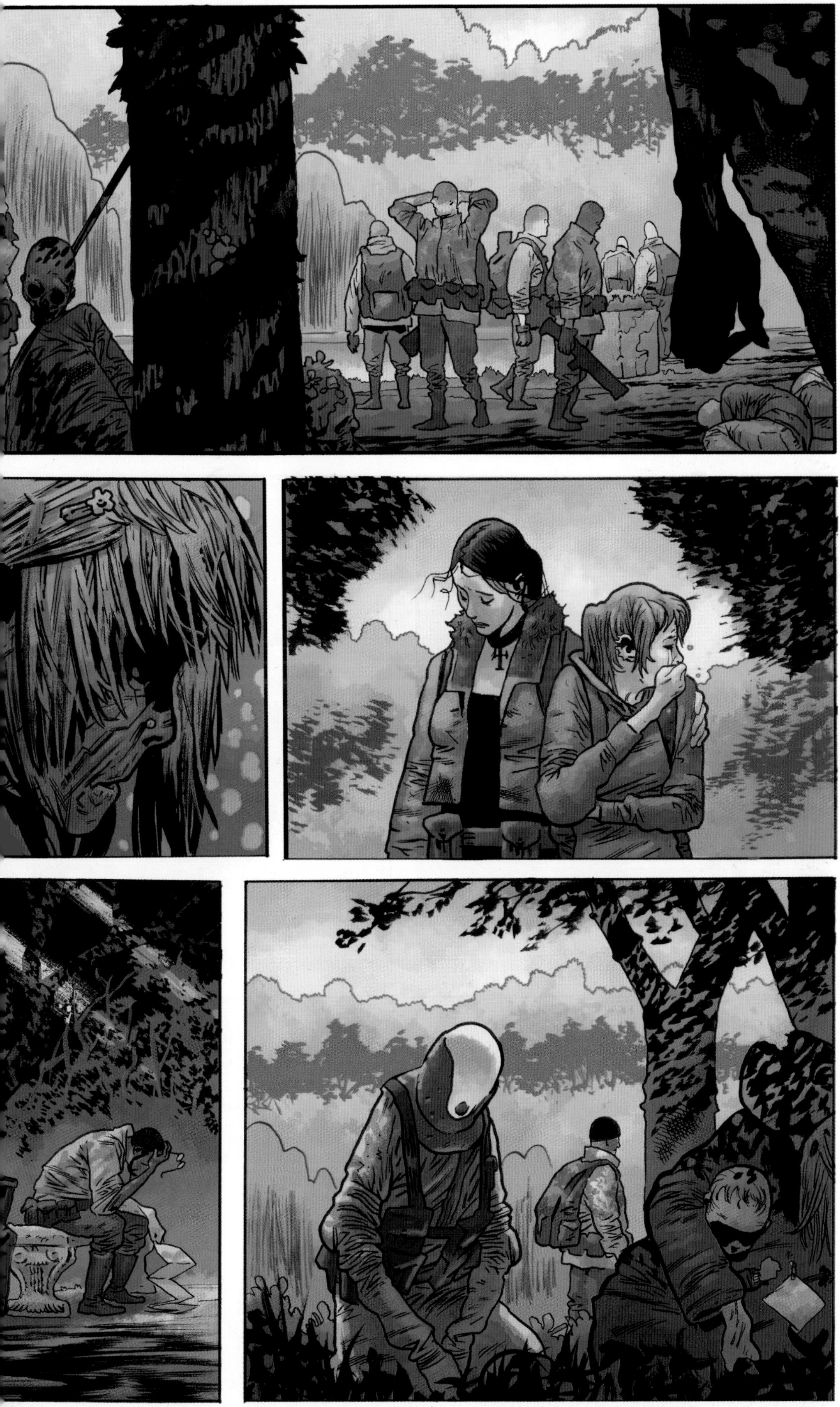

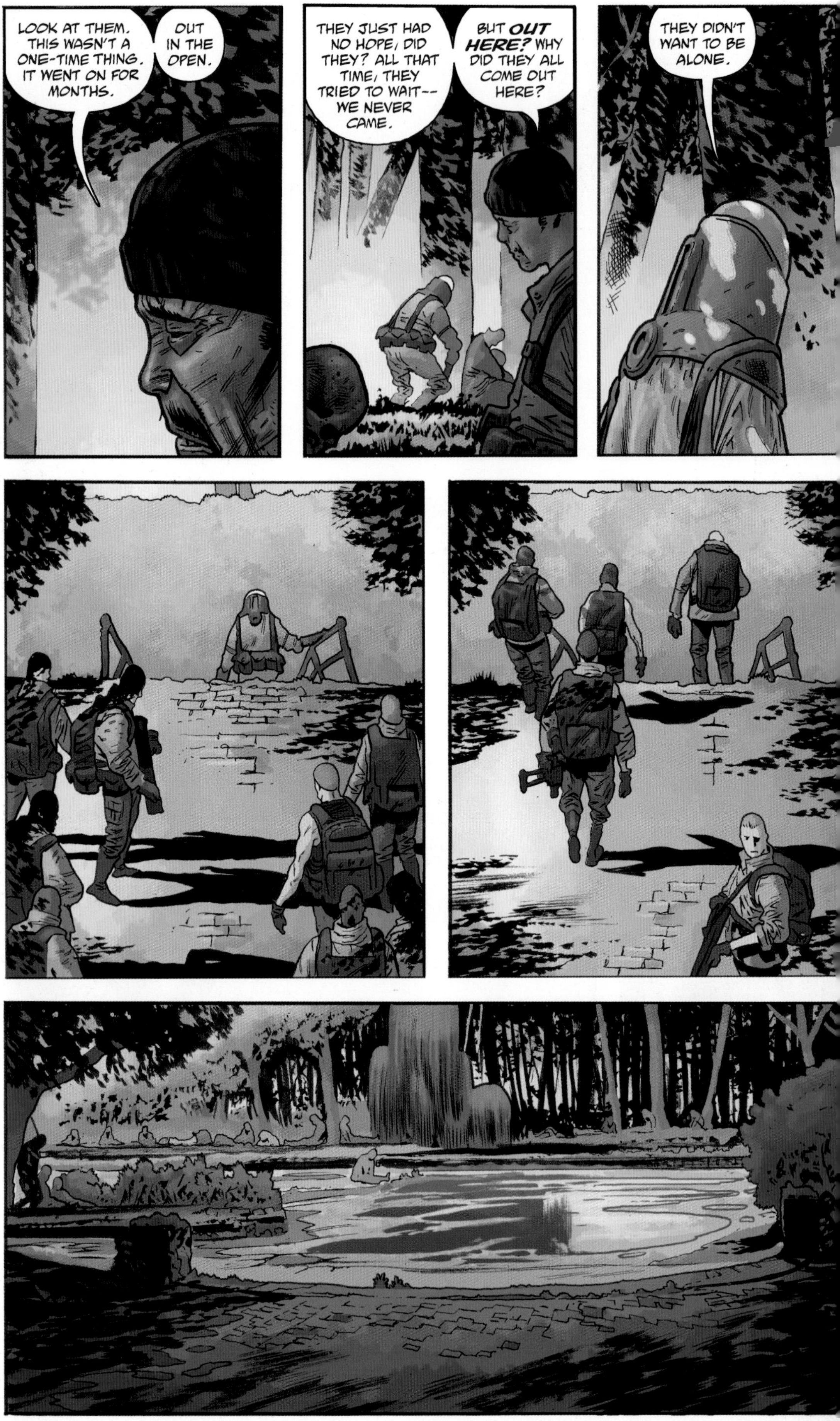
LOOK AT THEM. THIS WASN'T A ONE-TIME THING. IT WENT ON FOR MONTHS.
OUT IN THE OPEN.
THEY JUST HAD NO HOPE, DID THEY? ALL THAT TIME, THEY TRIED TO WAIT-- WE NEVER CAME.
BUT OUT HERE? WHY DID THEY ALL COME OUT HERE?
THEY DIDN'T WANT TO BE ALONE.

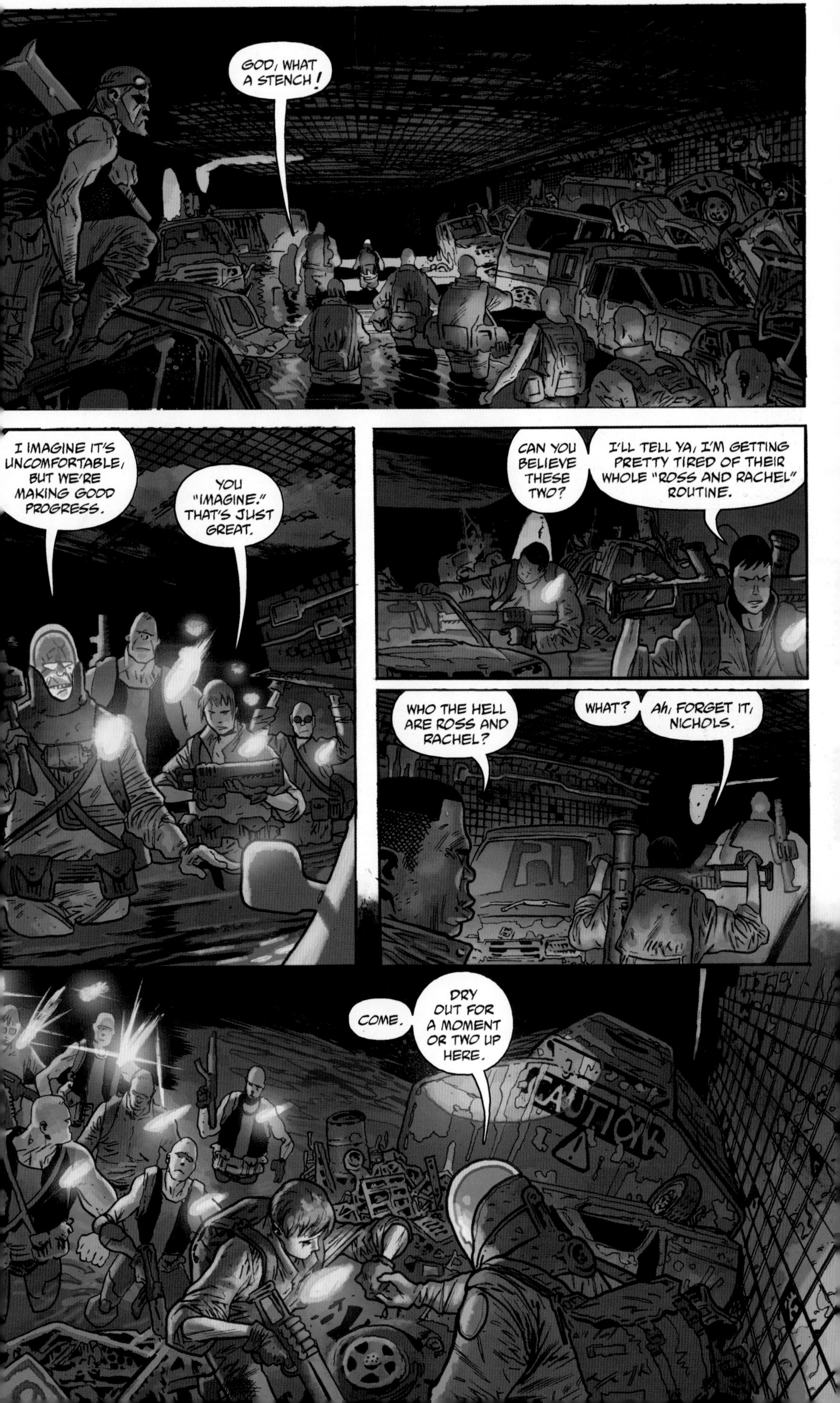
GOD, WHAT A STENCH!
I IMAGINE IT'S UNCOMFORTABLE, BUT WE'RE MAKING GOOD PROGRESS.
YOU "IMAGINE." THAT'S JUST GREAT.
CAN YOU BELIEVE THESE TWO?
I'LL TELL YA, I'M GETTING PRETTY TIRED OF THEIR WHOLE "ROSS AND RACHEL" ROUTINE.
WHO THE HELL ARE ROSS AND RACHEL?
WHAT?
AH, FORGET IT, NICHOLS.
COME.
DRY OUT FOR A MOMENT OR TWO UP HERE.
CAUTION

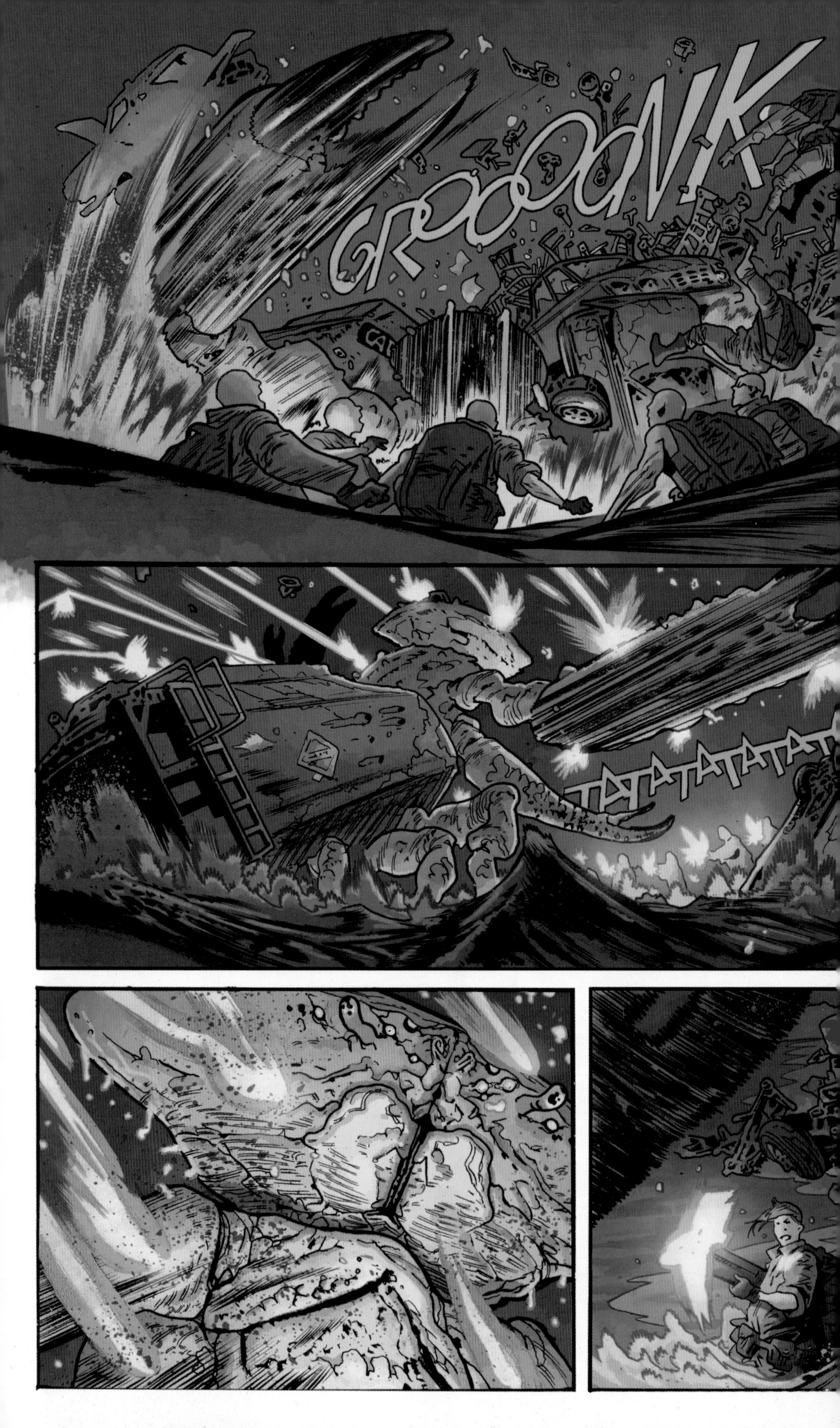
GROOOONK
TATATATATAT

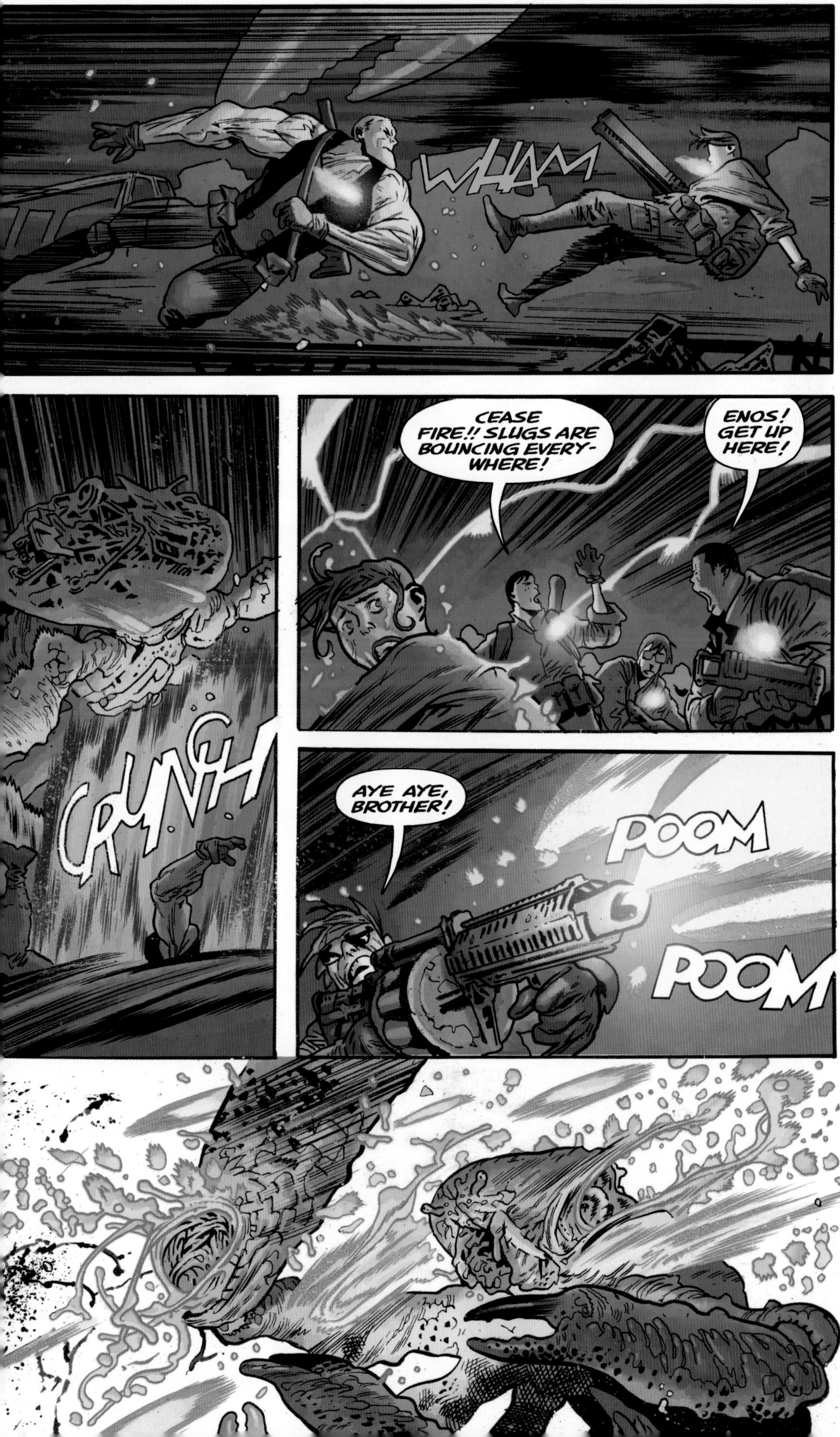
WHAM
CRUNCH
CEASE FIRE!! SLUGS ARE BOUNCING EVERY-WHERE!
ENOS! GET UP HERE!
AYE AYE, BROTHER!
POOM
POOM

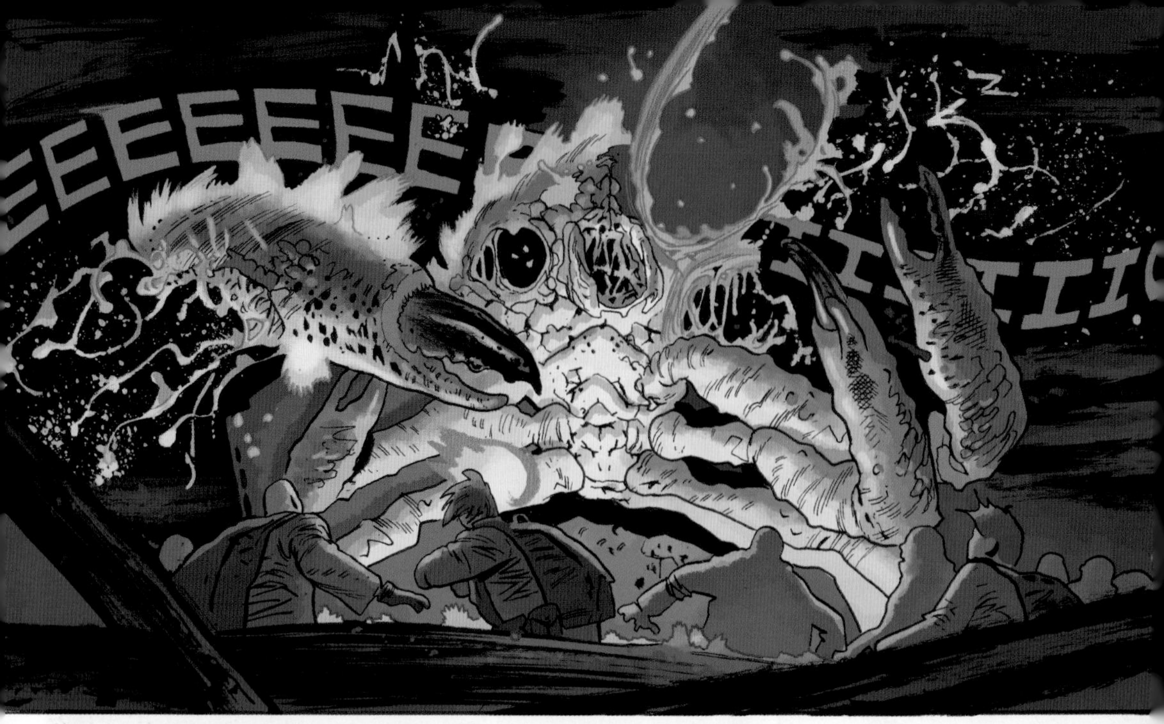

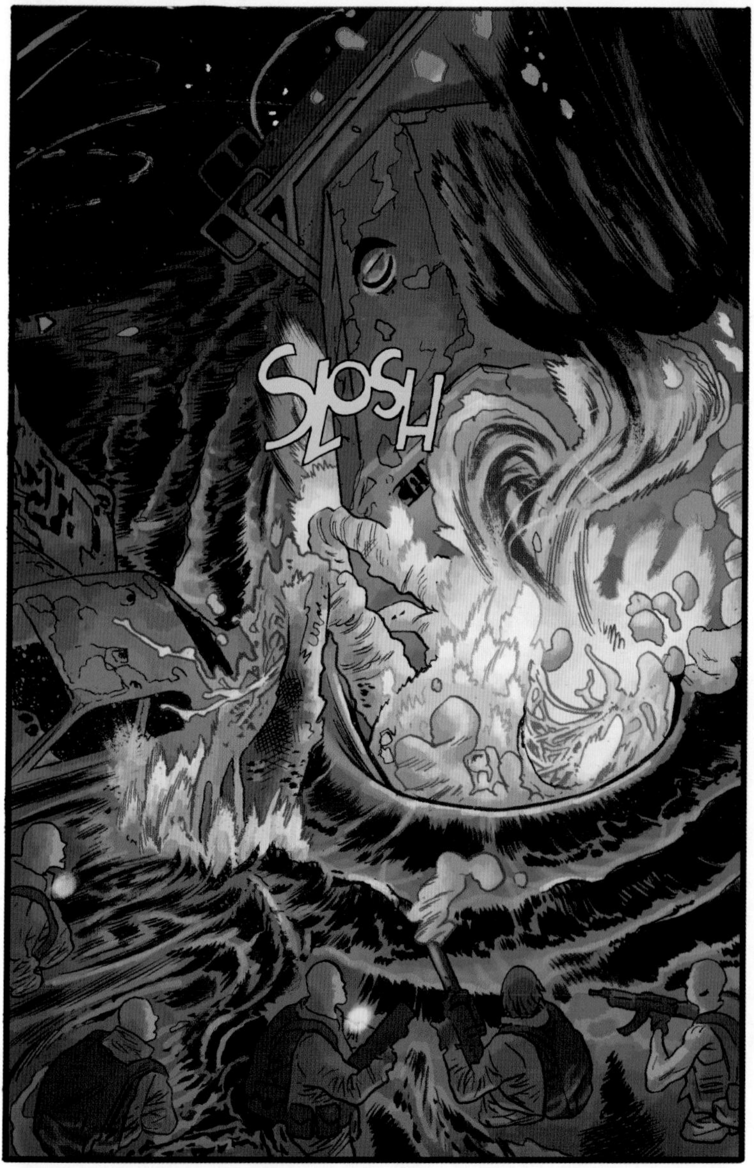
SLOSH

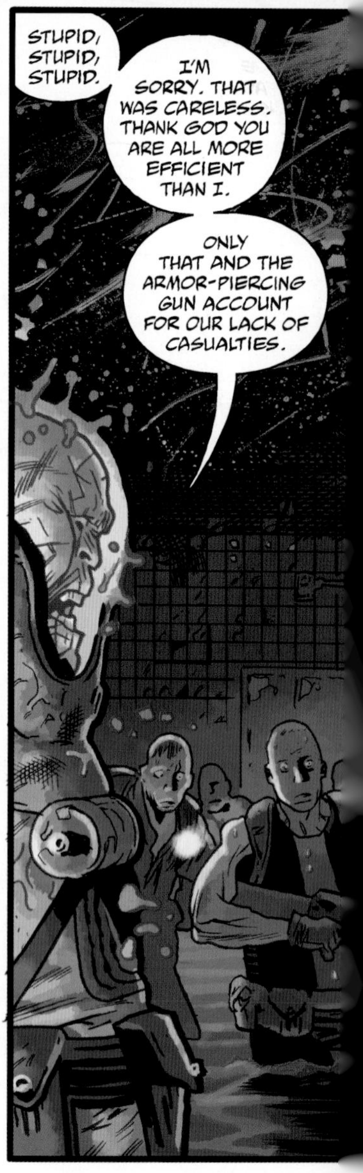
STUPID, STUPID, STUPID.
I'M SORRY. THAT WAS CARELESS. THANK GOD YOU ARE ALL MORE EFFICIENT THAN I.
ONLY THAT AND THE ARMOR-PIERCING GUN ACCOUNT FOR OUR LACK OF CASUALTIES.

WHAT DO YOU MEAN "LACK" OF CASUALTIES? WHAT ABOUT LEONID?

SERGEANT, ARE YOU ALL RIGHT?

DA.

!

COME. I SEE LIGHT AHEAD, BUT WE MUST HURRY.

BUT *CAUTION* THIS TIME!

HOW THE HELL...

AM I CRAZY? SHOULDN'T THAT GUY BE DEAD?

THEY MAKE 'EM TOUGH IN RUSSIA, I GUESS.

AND EVEN WHEN THEY *DO* DIE, THEY STILL SEEM TO HANG AROUND. BUT DON'T FORGET--

--WE GOT OUR OWN SUPERMAN!

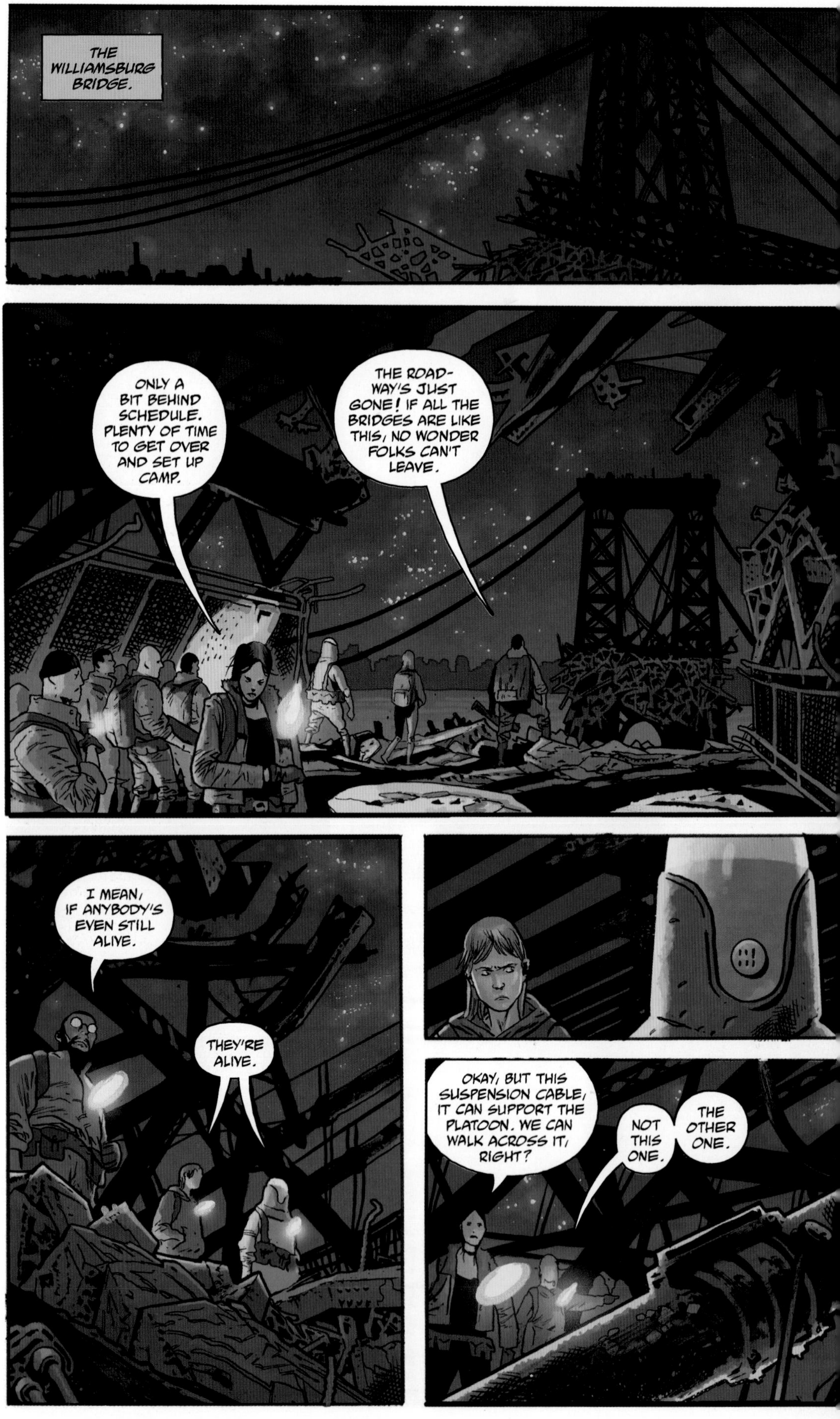
THE WILLIAMSBURG BRIDGE.
ONLY A BIT BEHIND SCHEDULE. PLENTY OF TIME TO GET OVER AND SET UP CAMP.
THE ROAD-WAY'S JUST GONE! IF ALL THE BRIDGES ARE LIKE THIS, NO WONDER FOLKS CAN'T LEAVE.
I MEAN, IF ANYBODY'S EVEN STILL ALIVE.
THEY'RE ALIVE.
OKAY, BUT THIS SUSPENSION CABLE, IT CAN SUPPORT THE PLATOON. WE CAN WALK ACROSS IT, RIGHT?
NOT THIS ONE.
THE OTHER ONE.

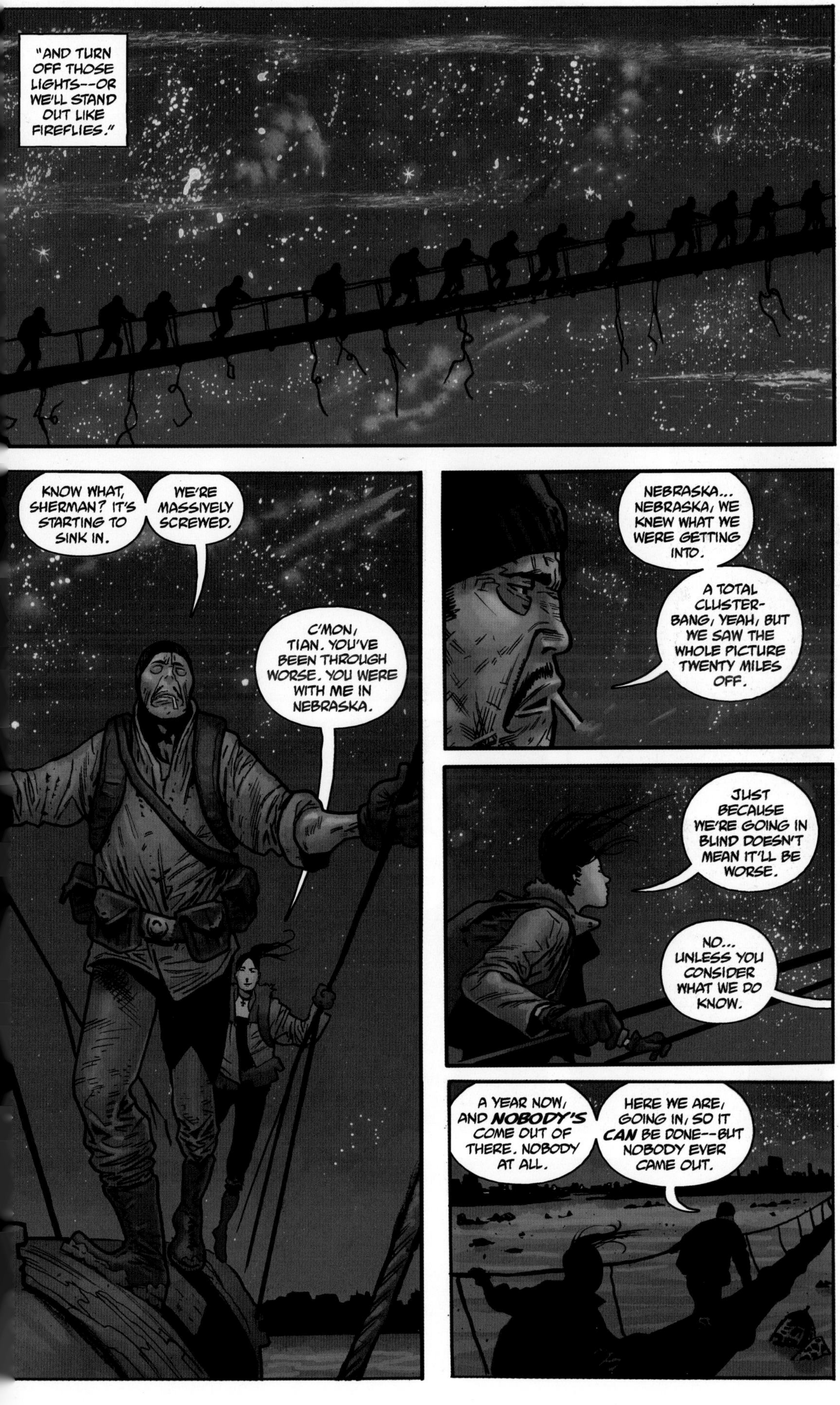
"AND TURN OFF THOSE LIGHTS--OR WE'LL STAND OUT LIKE FIREFLIES."
KNOW WHAT, SHERMAN? IT'S STARTING TO SINK IN.
WE'RE MASSIVELY SCREWED.
C'MON, TIAN. YOU'VE BEEN THROUGH WORSE. YOU WERE WITH ME IN NEBRASKA.
NEBRASKA... NEBRASKA, WE KNEW WHAT WE WERE GETTING INTO.
A TOTAL CLUSTER-BANG, YEAH, BUT WE SAW THE WHOLE PICTURE TWENTY MILES OFF.
JUST BECAUSE WE'RE GOING IN BLIND DOESN'T MEAN IT'LL BE WORSE.
NO... UNLESS YOU CONSIDER WHAT WE DO KNOW.
A YEAR NOW, AND **NOBODY'S** COME OUT OF THERE. NOBODY AT ALL.
HERE WE ARE, GOING IN, SO IT **CAN** BE DONE--BUT NOBODY EVER CAME OUT.

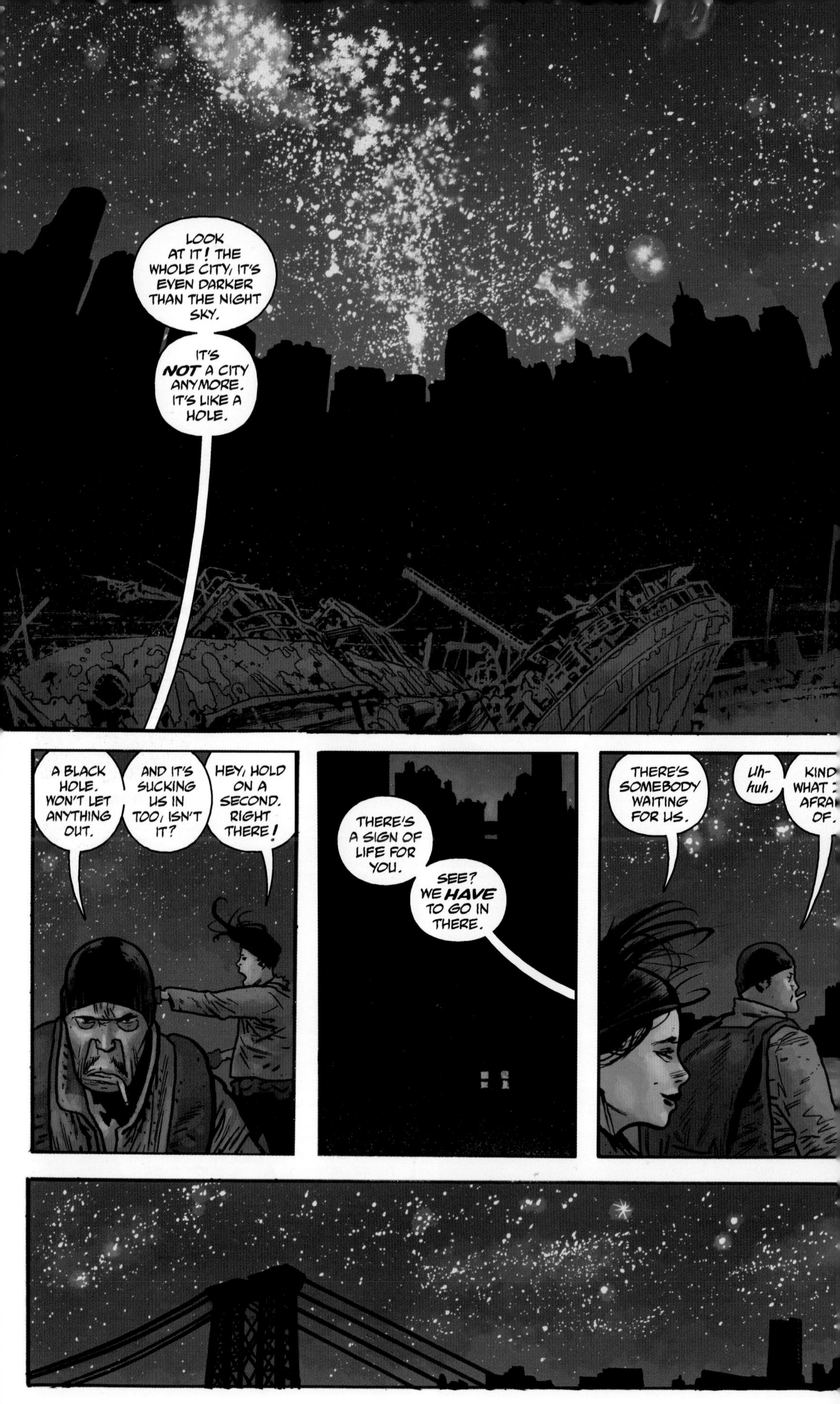
LOOK AT IT! THE WHOLE CITY, IT'S EVEN DARKER THAN THE NIGHT SKY.
IT'S NOT A CITY ANYMORE. IT'S LIKE A HOLE.
A BLACK HOLE. WON'T LET ANYTHING OUT.
AND IT'S SUCKING US IN TOO, ISN'T IT?
HEY, HOLD ON A SECOND. RIGHT THERE!
THERE'S A SIGN OF LIFE FOR YOU.
SEE? WE HAVE TO GO IN THERE.
THERE'S SOMEBODY WAITING FOR US.
Uh-huh.

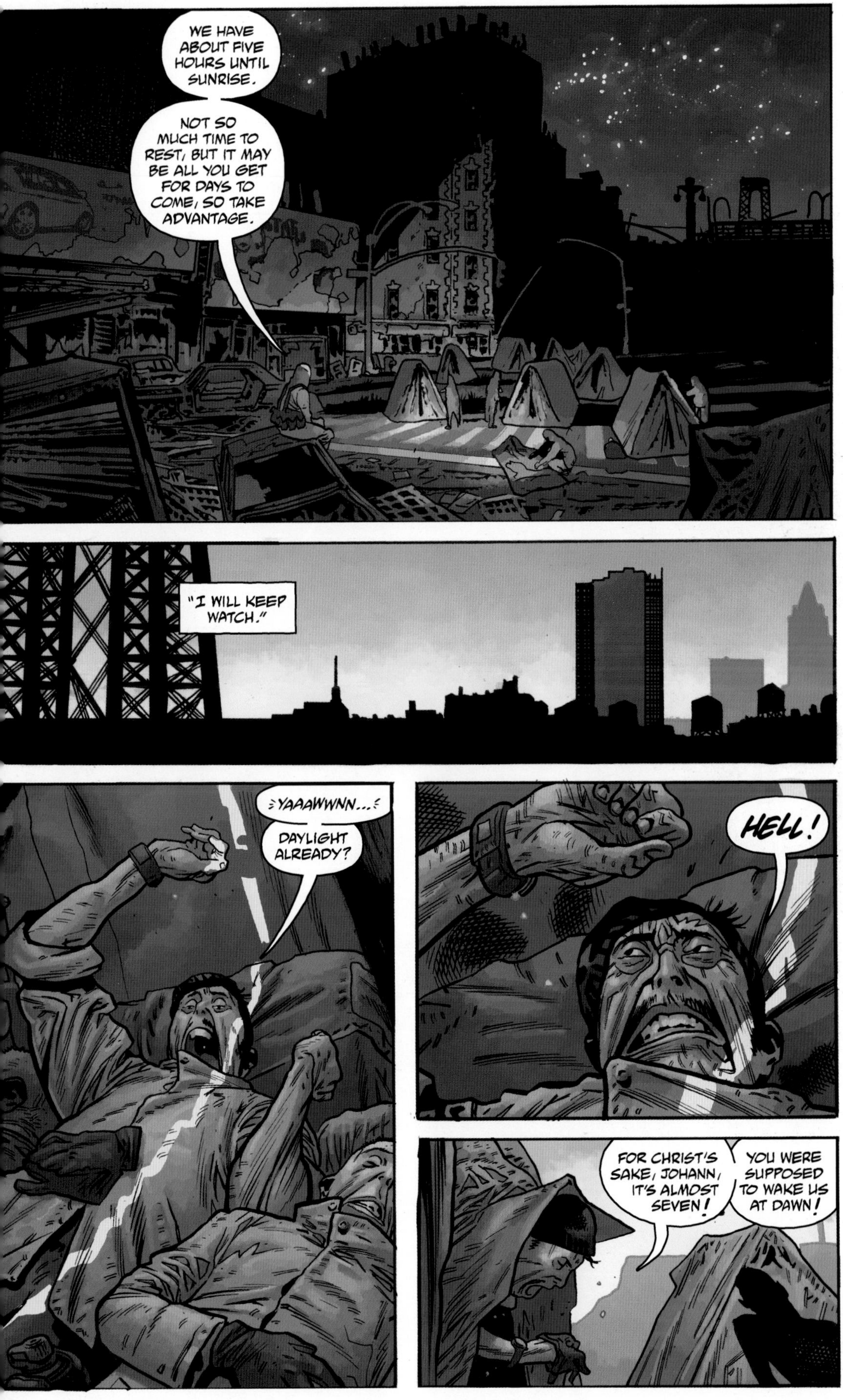
WE HAVE ABOUT FIVE HOURS UNTIL SUNRISE.
NOT SO MUCH TIME TO REST, BUT IT MAY BE ALL YOU GET FOR DAYS TO COME, SO TAKE ADVANTAGE.
"I WILL KEEP WATCH."
YAAAWWNN...
DAYLIGHT ALREADY?
HELL!
FOR CHRIST'S SAKE, JOHANN, IT'S ALMOST SEVEN!
YOU WERE SUPPOSED TO WAKE US AT DAWN!

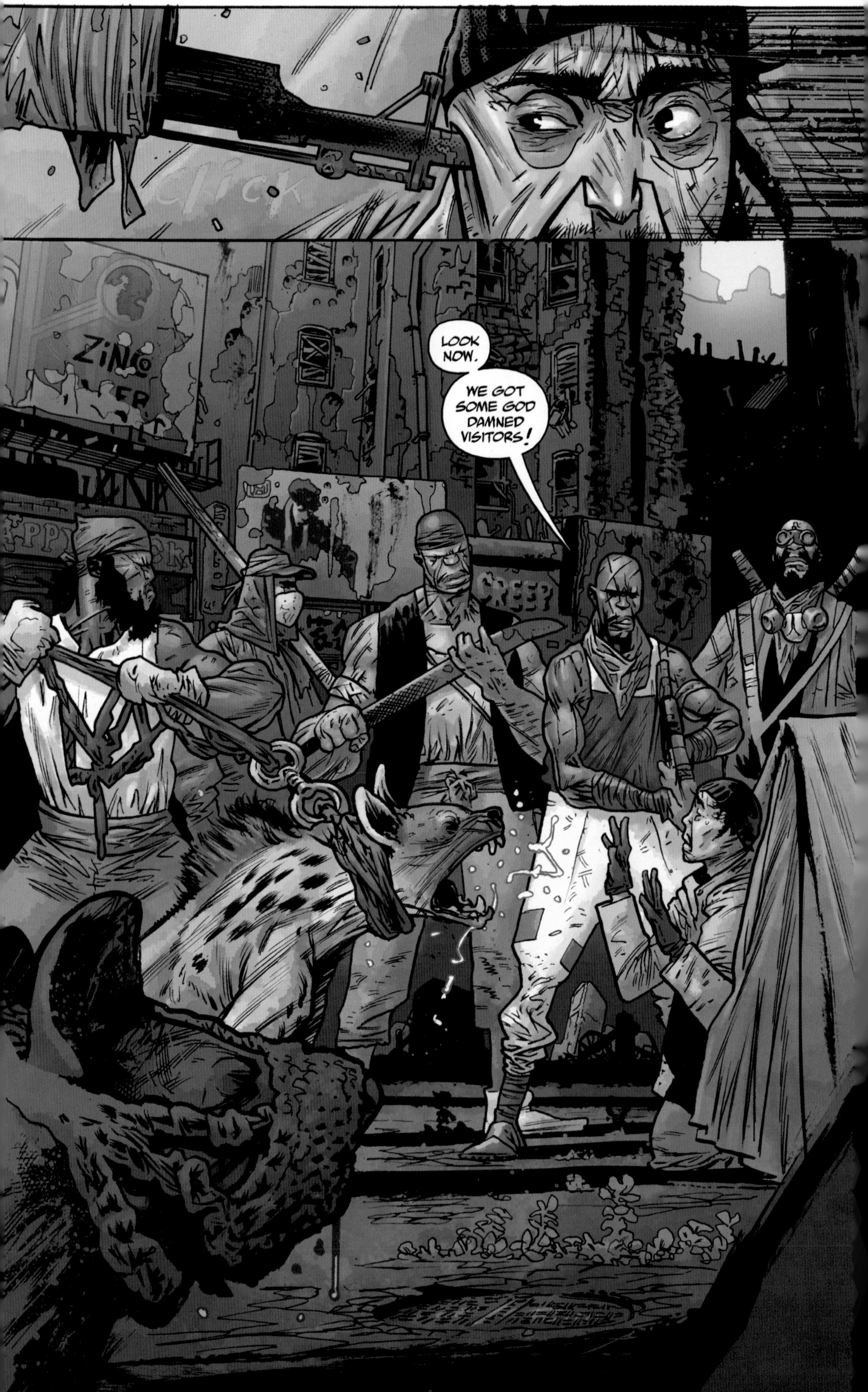
CLICK
LOOK NOW.
WE GOT SOME GOD DAMNED VISITORS!

THE REIGN OF THE BLACK FLAME
CHAPTER TWO

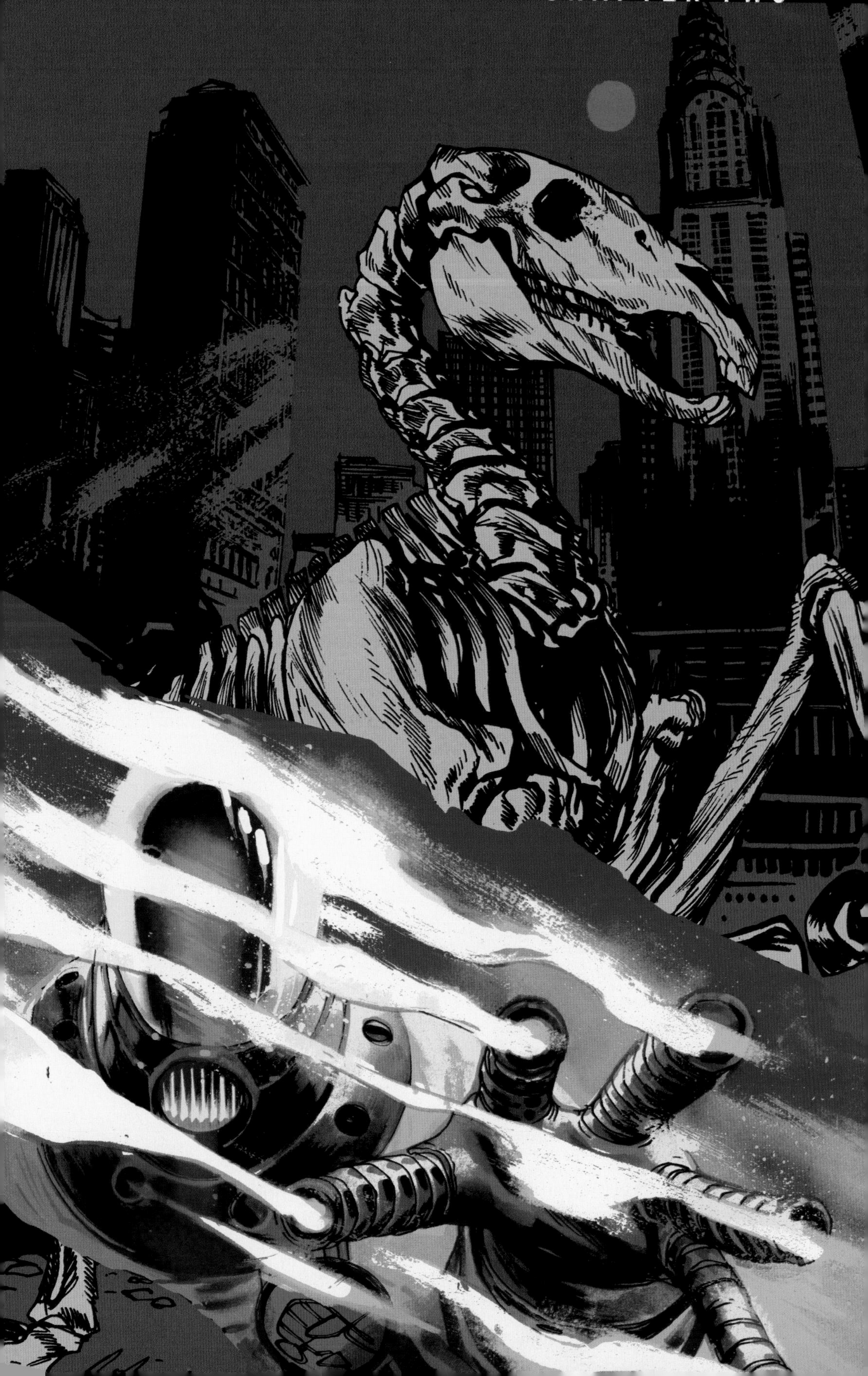

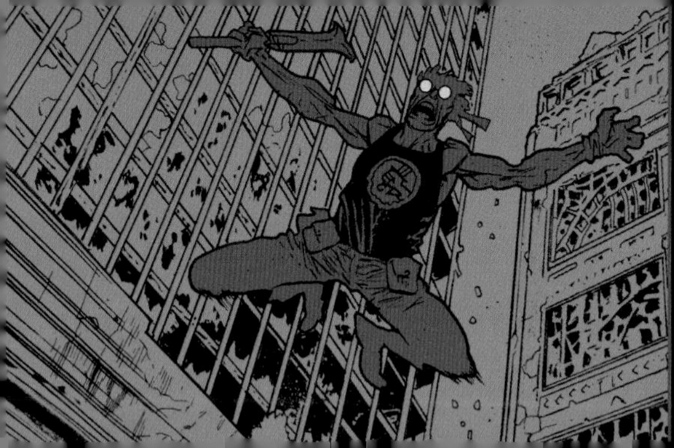

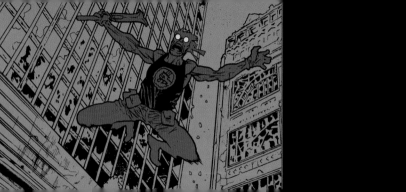

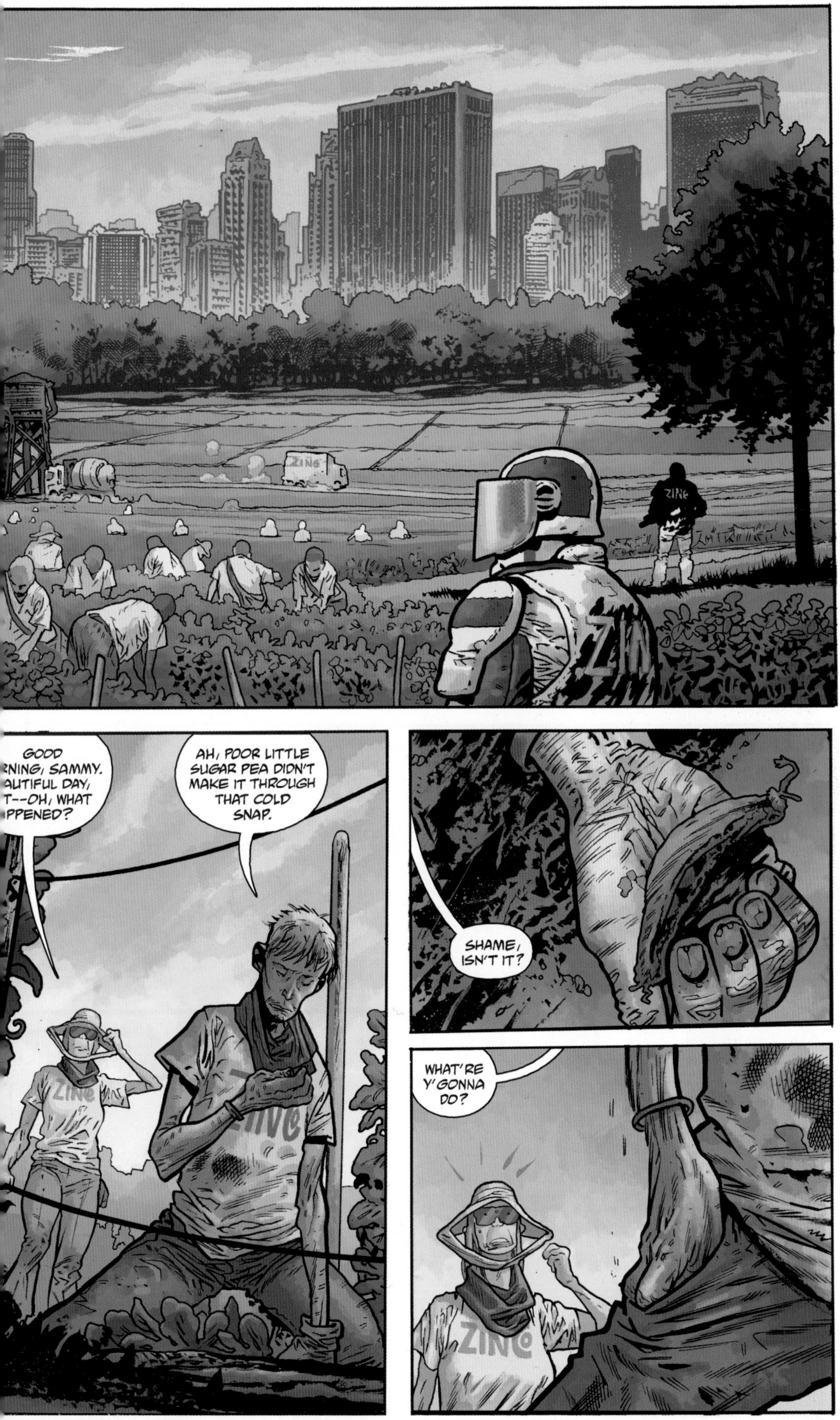
ZINC
ZINC
ZINC
GOOD
RNING, SAMMY.
AUTIFUL DAY,
T--OH, WHAT
PPENED?
AH, POOR LITTLE
SUGAR PEA DIDN'T
MAKE IT THROUGH
THAT COLD
SNAP.
SHAME,
ISN'T IT?
WHAT'RE
Y'GONNA
DO?
ZINC
ZINC
ZINC

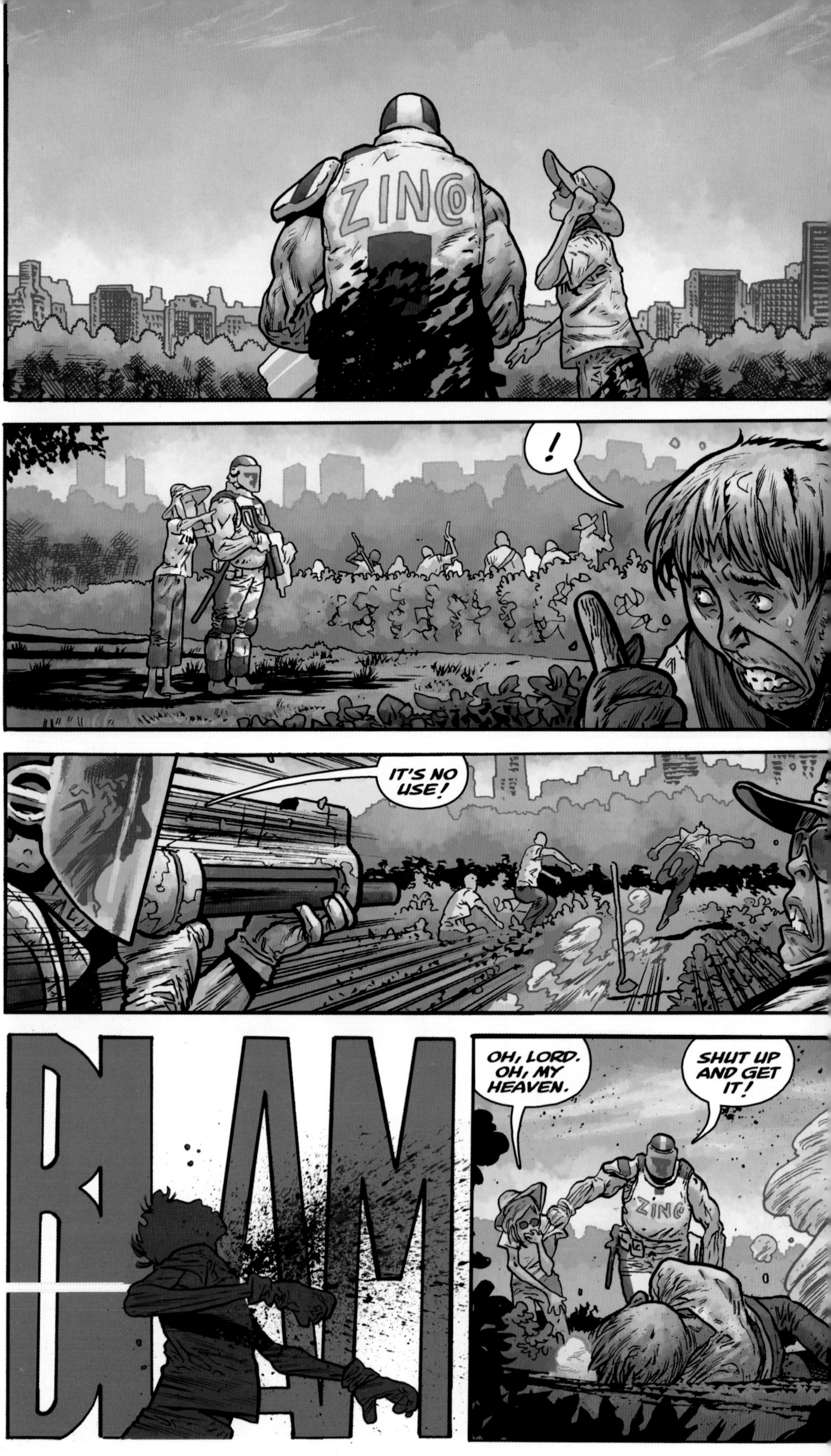
ZINO
!
IT'S NO USE!
BLAM
OH, LORD. OH, MY HEAVEN.
SHUT UP AND GET IT!
ZINO

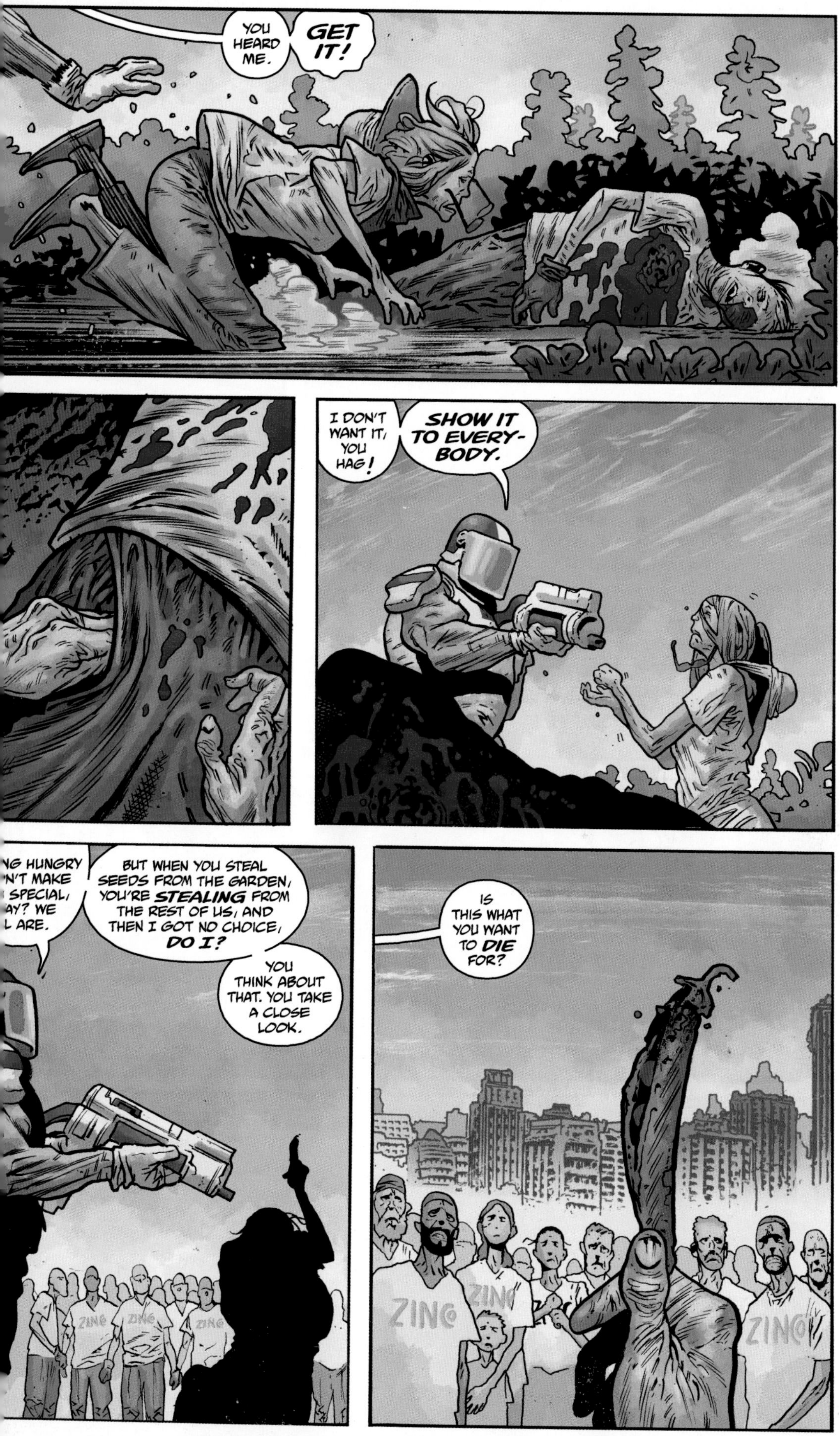
YOU HEARD ME.
GET IT!
I DON'T WANT IT, YOU HAG!
SHOW IT TO EVERY-BODY.
NG HUNGRY N'T MAKE SPECIAL, AY? WE L ARE.
BUT WHEN YOU STEAL SEEDS FROM THE GARDEN, YOU'RE STEALING FROM THE REST OF US, AND THEN I GOT NO CHOICE, DO I?
YOU THINK ABOUT THAT. YOU TAKE A CLOSE LOOK.
IS THIS WHAT YOU WANT TO DIE FOR?
ZINC
ZINC
ZINC
ZINC
ZINC

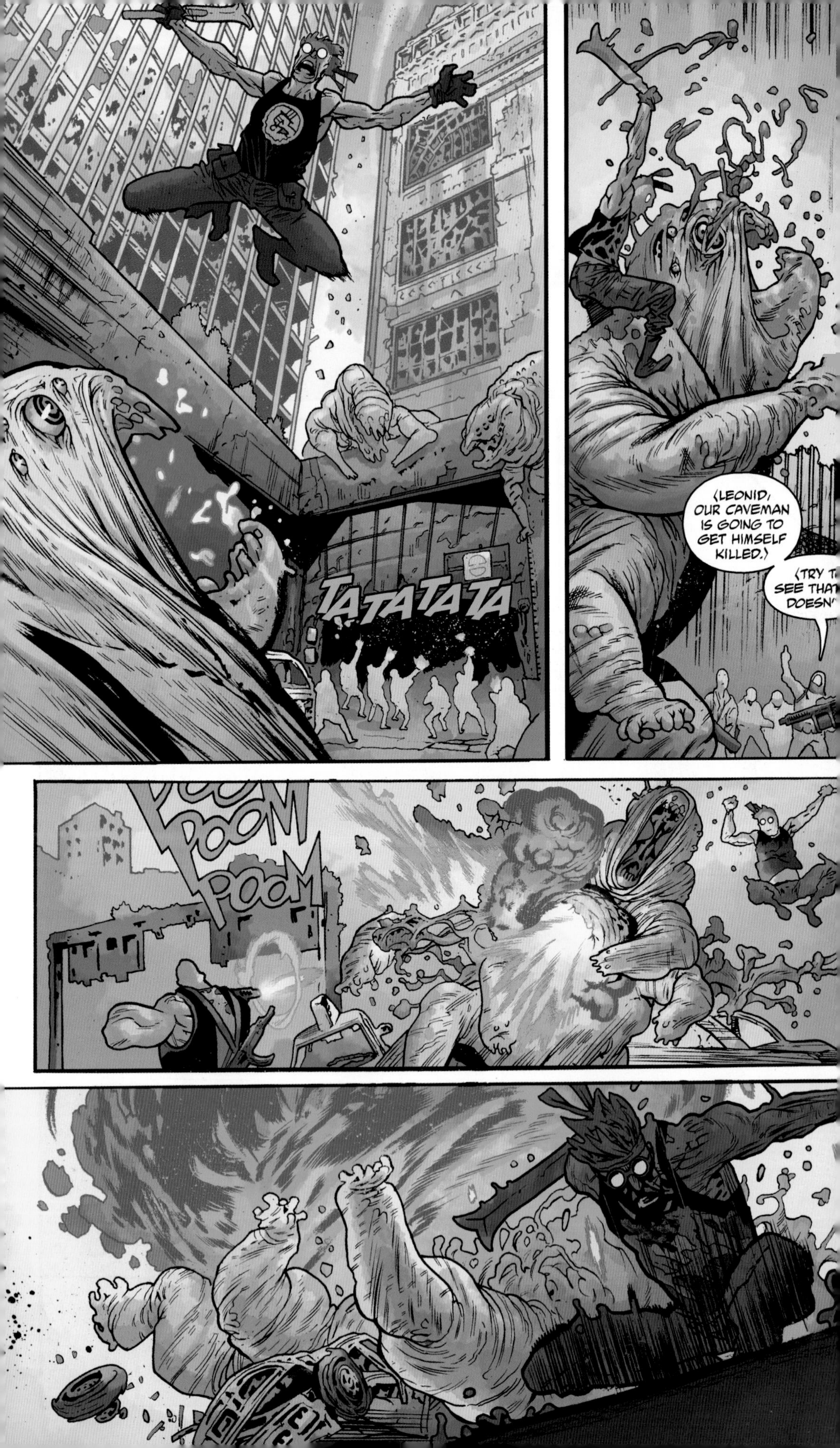
TATATATA
⟨LEONID, OUR CAVEMAN IS GOING TO GET HIMSELF KILLED.⟩
⟨TRY T SEE THAT DOESN'
POOM POOM
POOM

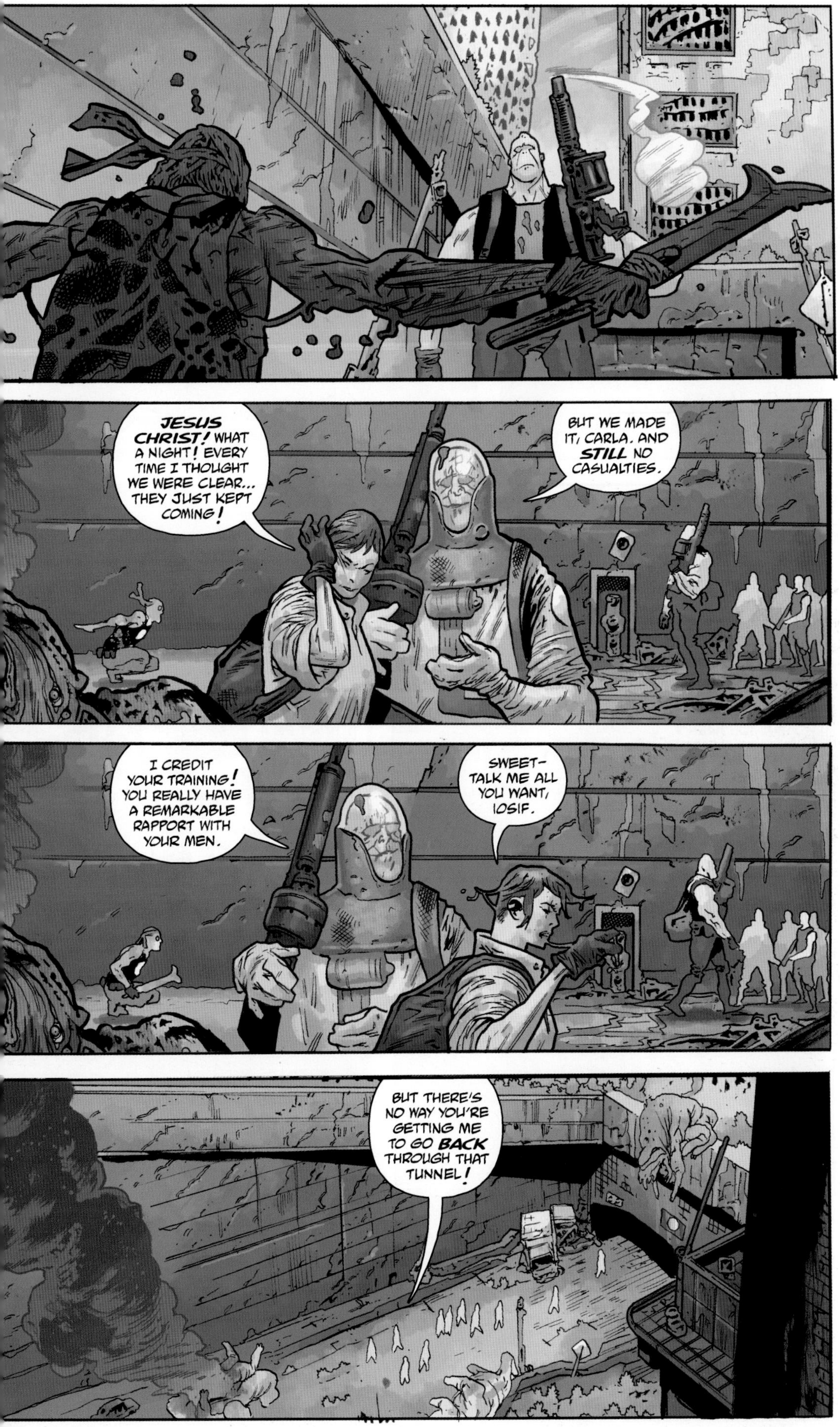
JESUS CHRIST! WHAT A NIGHT! EVERY TIME I THOUGHT WE WERE CLEAR... THEY JUST KEPT COMING!
BUT WE MADE IT, CARLA. AND STILL NO CASUALTIES.
I CREDIT YOUR TRAINING! YOU REALLY HAVE A REMARKABLE RAPPORT WITH YOUR MEN.
SWEET-TALK ME ALL YOU WANT, IOSIF.
BUT THERE'S NO WAY YOU'RE GETTING ME TO GO BACK THROUGH THAT TUNNEL!

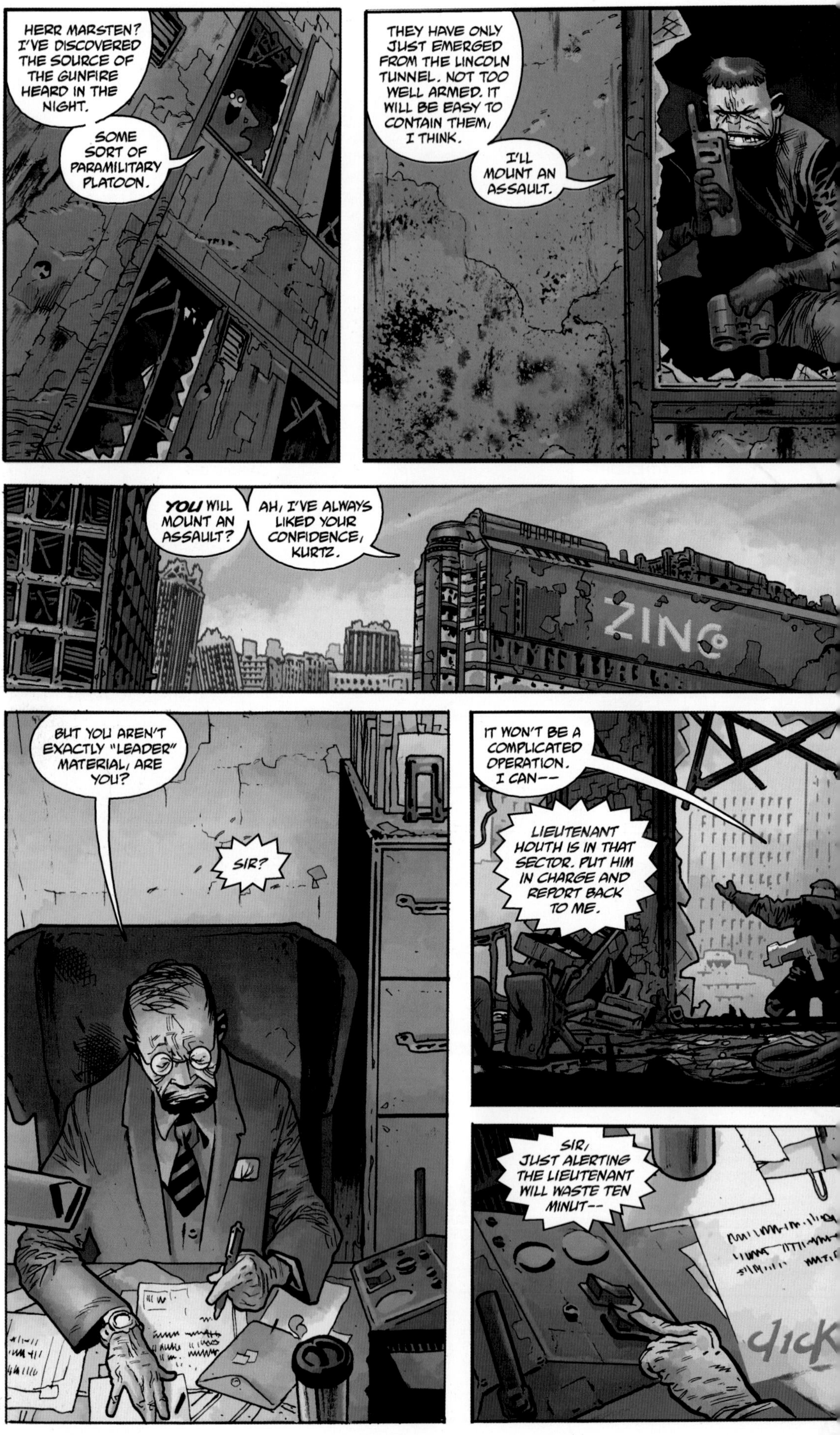
HERR MARSTEN? I'VE DISCOVERED THE SOURCE OF THE GUNFIRE HEARD IN THE NIGHT.
SOME SORT OF PARAMILITARY PLATOON.
THEY HAVE ONLY JUST EMERGED FROM THE LINCOLN TUNNEL. NOT TOO WELL ARMED. IT WILL BE EASY TO CONTAIN THEM, I THINK.
I'LL MOUNT AN ASSAULT.
YOU WILL MOUNT AN ASSAULT?
AH, I'VE ALWAYS LIKED YOUR CONFIDENCE, KURTZ.
ZINC
BUT YOU AREN'T EXACTLY "LEADER" MATERIAL, ARE YOU?
SIR?
IT WON'T BE A COMPLICATED OPERATION. I CAN--
LIEUTENANT HOUTH IS IN THAT SECTOR. PUT HIM IN CHARGE AND REPORT BACK TO ME.
SIR, JUST ALERTING THE LIEUTENANT WILL WASTE TEN MINUT--
click

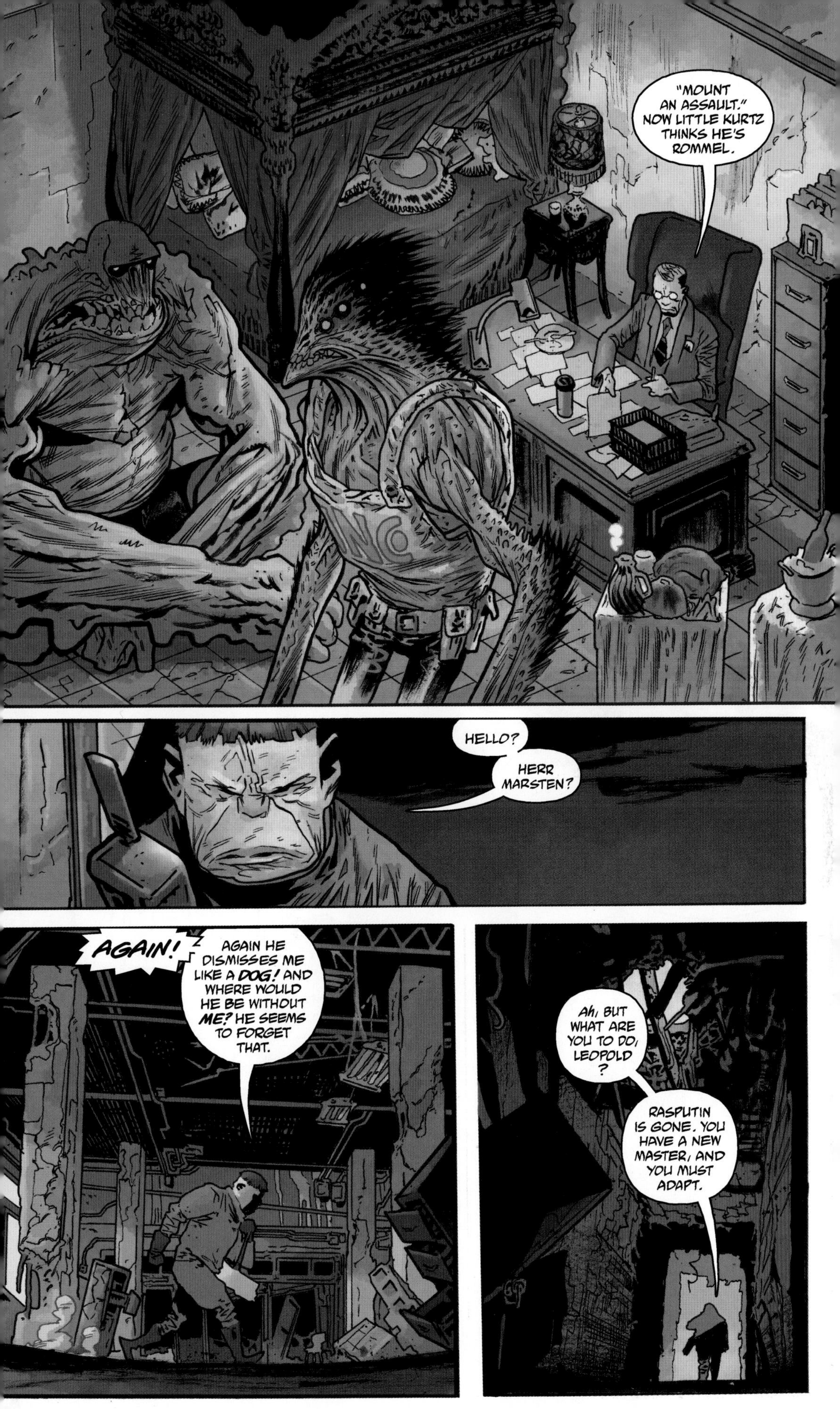

"MOUNT AN ASSAULT." NOW LITTLE KURTZ THINKS HE'S ROMMEL.
HELLO?
HERR MARSTEN?
AGAIN!
AGAIN HE DISMISSES ME LIKE A DOG! AND WHERE WOULD HE BE WITHOUT ME? HE SEEMS TO FORGET THAT.
Ah, BUT WHAT ARE YOU TO DO, LEOPOLD?
RASPUTIN IS GONE. YOU HAVE A NEW MASTER, AND YOU MUST ADAPT.

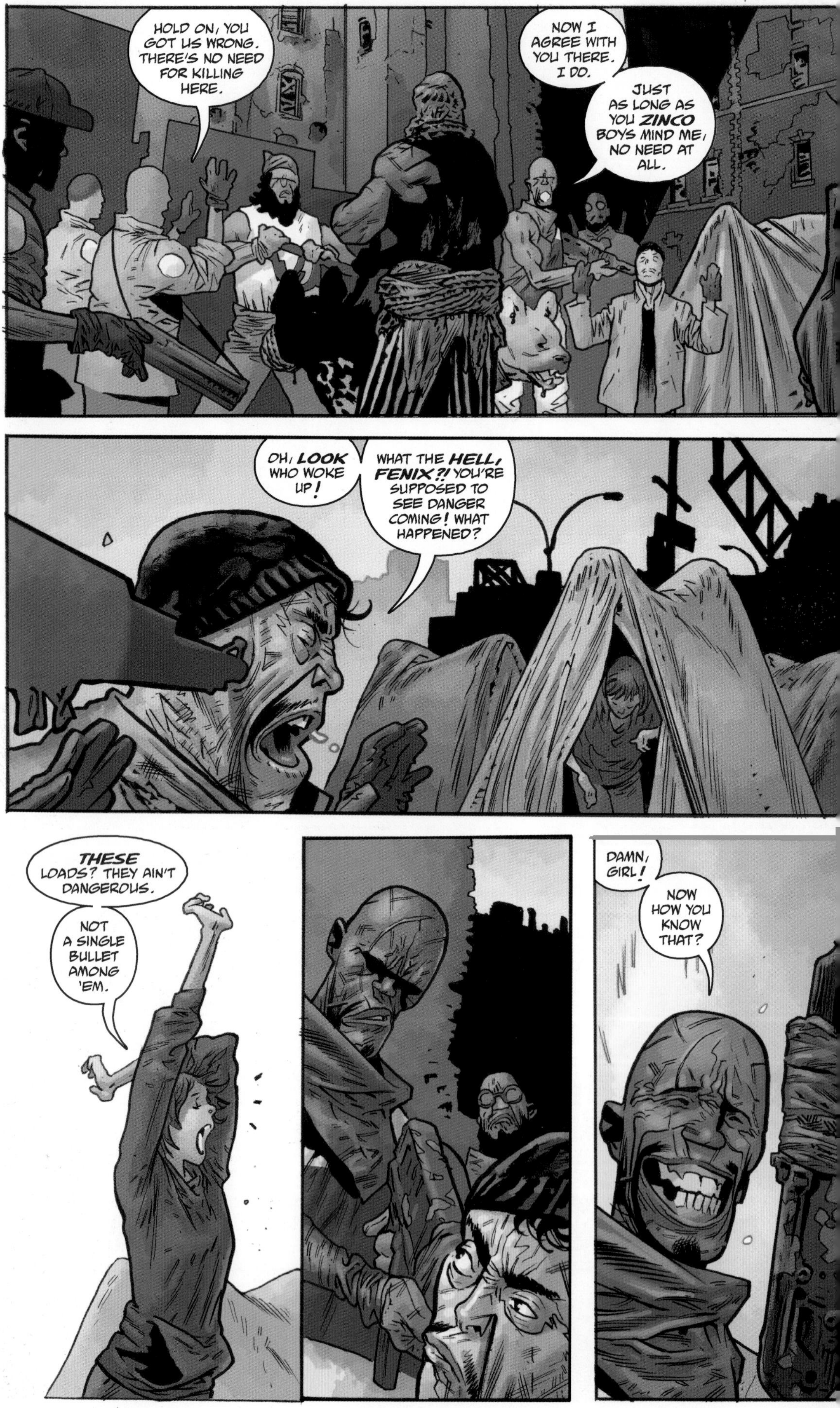
HOLD ON, YOU GOT US WRONG. THERE'S NO NEED FOR KILLING HERE.
NOW I AGREE WITH YOU THERE. I DO.
JUST AS LONG AS YOU ZINCO BOYS MIND ME, NO NEED AT ALL.
OH, LOOK WHO WOKE UP!
WHAT THE HELL, FENIX?! YOU'RE SUPPOSED TO SEE DANGER COMING! WHAT HAPPENED?
THESE LOADS? THEY AIN'T DANGEROUS.
NOT A SINGLE BULLET AMONG 'EM.
DAMN, GIRL!
NOW HOW YOU KNOW THAT?

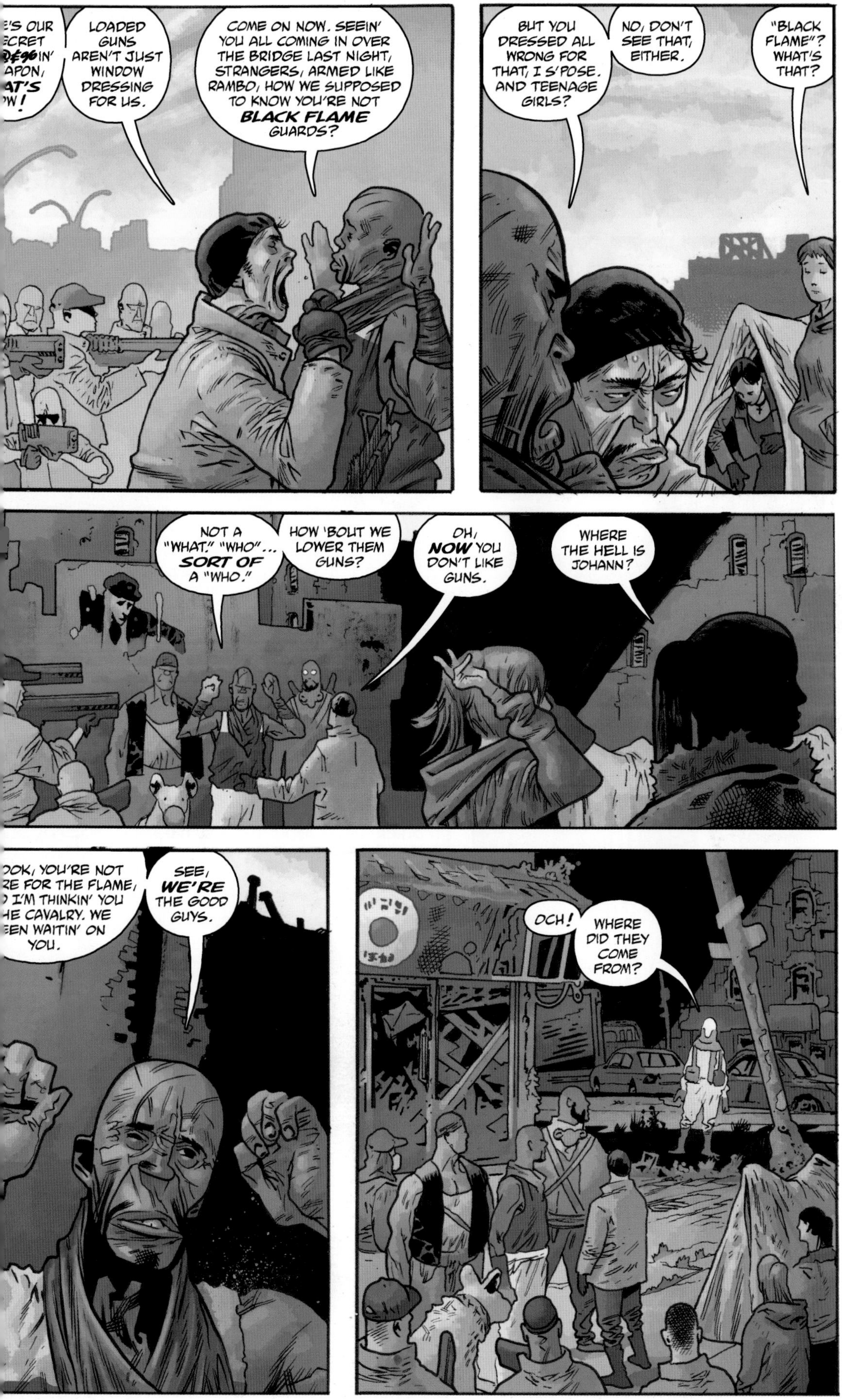
E'S OUR CRET IN' APON, AT'S W!
LOADED GUNS AREN'T JUST WINDOW DRESSING FOR US.
COME ON NOW. SEEIN' YOU ALL COMING IN OVER THE BRIDGE LAST NIGHT, STRANGERS, ARMED LIKE RAMBO, HOW WE SUPPOSED TO KNOW YOU'RE NOT **BLACK FLAME** GUARDS?
BUT YOU DRESSED ALL WRONG FOR THAT, I S'POSE. AND TEENAGE GIRLS?
NO, DON'T SEE THAT, EITHER.
"BLACK FLAME"? WHAT'S THAT?
NOT A "WHAT." "WHO"... **SORT OF** A "WHO."
HOW 'BOUT WE LOWER THEM GUNS?
OH, **NOW** YOU DON'T LIKE GUNS.
WHERE THE HELL IS JOHANN?
OOK, YOU'RE NOT RE FOR THE FLAME, I'M THINKIN' YOU HE CAVALRY. WE EEN WAITIN' ON YOU.
SEE, **WE'RE** THE GOOD GUYS.
OCH!
WHERE DID THEY COME FROM?

DON'T YOU THINK YOU'RE OVER-REACTING?

WE'VE BEEN TASKED WITH AN IMPORTANT DUTY--RIDDING THE NEW ORDER OF ANY TIES TO A REGIME OF MURDEROUS RACISM.

WE'RE A MERITOCRACY, AS IT SHOULD BE, AND YOUR NOSTALGIA IS MISPLACED HERE.

I THINK YOU MISINTERRPET MY MELANCHOLY.

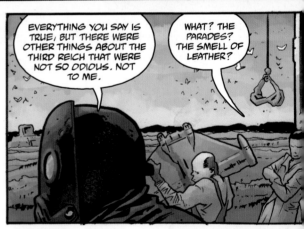

EVERYTHING YOU SAY IS TRUE, BUT THERE WERE OTHER THINGS ABOUT THE THIRD REICH THAT WERE NOT SO ODIOUS. NOT TO ME.

WHAT? THE PARADES? THE SMELL OF LEATHER?

NO. NOT LEATHER.

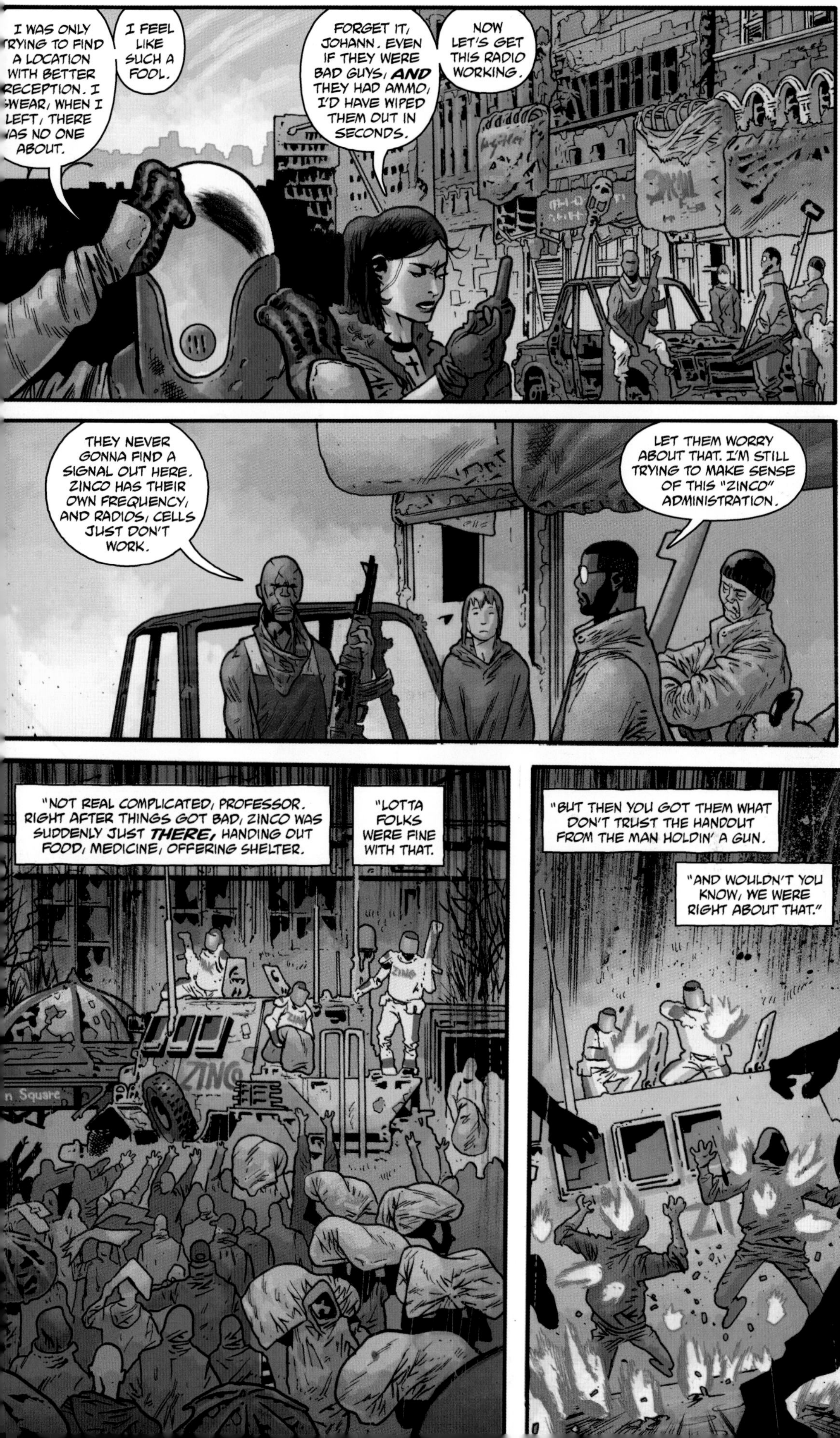
I WAS ONLY TRYING TO FIND A LOCATION WITH BETTER RECEPTION. I SWEAR, WHEN I LEFT, THERE WAS NO ONE ABOUT.
I FEEL LIKE SUCH A FOOL.
FORGET IT, JOHANN. EVEN IF THEY WERE BAD GUYS, **AND** THEY HAD AMMO, I'D HAVE WIPED THEM OUT IN SECONDS.
NOW LET'S GET THIS RADIO WORKING.
THEY NEVER GONNA FIND A SIGNAL OUT HERE. ZINCO HAS THEIR OWN FREQUENCY, AND RADIOS, CELLS JUST DON'T WORK.
LET THEM WORRY ABOUT THAT. I'M STILL TRYING TO MAKE SENSE OF THIS "ZINCO" ADMINISTRATION.
"NOT REAL COMPLICATED, PROFESSOR. RIGHT AFTER THINGS GOT BAD, ZINCO WAS SUDDENLY JUST ***THERE,*** HANDING OUT FOOD, MEDICINE, OFFERING SHELTER.
"LOTTA FOLKS WERE FINE WITH THAT.
n Square
"BUT THEN YOU GOT THEM WHAT DON'T TRUST THE HANDOUT FROM THE MAN HOLDIN' A GUN.
"AND WOULDN'T YOU KNOW, WE WERE RIGHT ABOUT THAT."

SO THEY GOT JUST ABOUT EVERYBODY IN, LIKE, *DORMITORIES,* WORKIN' IN GARDENS AND WHATNOT.

YOU KNOW, MAKING OUT LIKE THEY TAKING CARE OF 'EM, BUT REALLY JUST USIN' 'EM. JUST SLAVES, REALLY.

AND YOUR GROUP, YOU'RE THE REBELS.

"REBELS"? NO, NO.

RESISTANC. THAT'S A BETTE WORD, RIGH PROFESSO

THIS *BLACK FLAME.* WHAT ABOUT HIM?

ONLY SEEN HIM ONCE, AND THAT'S GOOD WITH ME. NINE FEET TALL, BLACK AS BLUE, AND EVERYTHING AROUND HIM BURNS LIKE PAPER.

HOW COME I SAW THE ZINCO THUGS, BUT SOMETHING LIKE *THAT*...I JUST CAN'T GET A READ ON HIM. THERE'S LIKE THIS *BLIND SPOT.*

DON'T GOTTA BE PSYCHIC TO FIND THE FLAME. I COULD SHOW YOU HIS FRONT DOOR.

"BUT THAT WON'T HELP YOU MUCH."

SCARLET TEAM TO INDIGO, SCARLET TO INDIGO, ARE YOU ON FREQUENCY?

ξZZZRACKLEξ TEAM THIS IS ξZZZξ HOLD Fξ ξZZZξ ECTOR NICHAYKO...

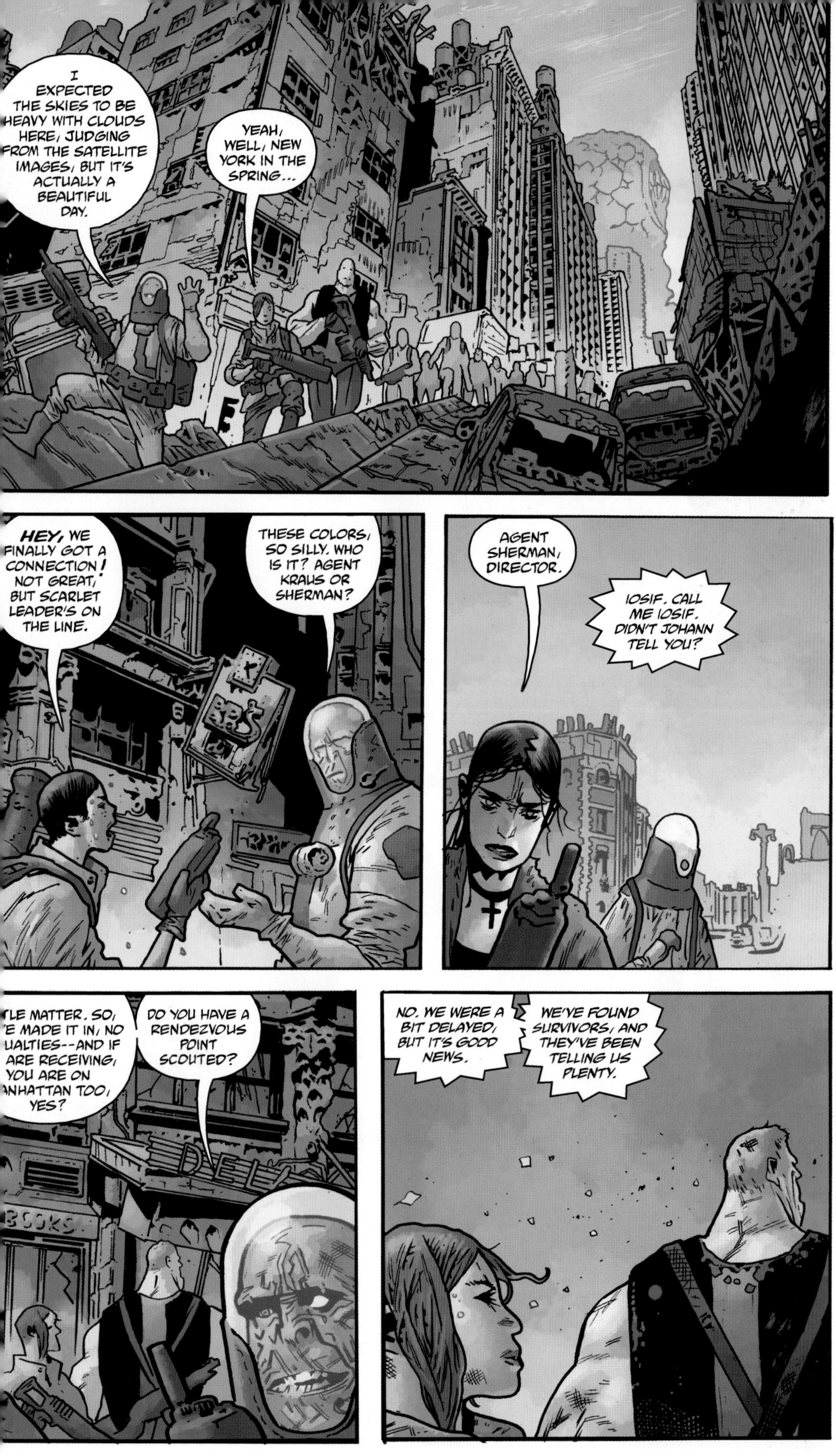
I EXPECTED THE SKIES TO BE HEAVY WITH CLOUDS HERE, JUDGING FROM THE SATELLITE IMAGES, BUT IT'S ACTUALLY A BEAUTIFUL DAY.
YEAH, WELL, NEW YORK IN THE SPRING...
HEY, WE FINALLY GOT A CONNECTION! NOT GREAT, BUT SCARLET LEADER'S ON THE LINE.
THESE COLORS, SO SILLY. WHO IS IT? AGENT KRAUS OR SHERMAN?
AGENT SHERMAN, DIRECTOR.
IOSIF. CALL ME IOSIF. DIDN'T JOHANN TELL YOU?
TLE MATTER. SO, 'E MADE IT IN, NO UALTIES--AND IF ARE RECEIVING, YOU ARE ON ANHATTAN TOO, YES?
DO YOU HAVE A RENDEZVOUS POINT SCOUTED?
NO. WE WERE A BIT DELAYED, BUT IT'S GOOD NEWS.
WE'VE FOUND SURVIVORS, AND THEY'VE BEEN TELLING US PLENTY.

!

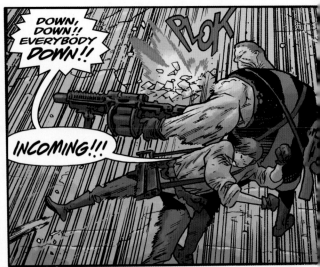

DOWN, DOWN!! EVERYBODY DOWN!!

INCOMING!!!

PLOK

TATATATAT TATATAT

THEY'RE ON BOTH SIDES!

TAKE THE RIGHT--EVERY-BODY TO THE RIGHT!

GERVESH-- THIRD FLOOR ACROSS THE STREET.

ON IT, CAP'N!

BAWHOOM

ACME

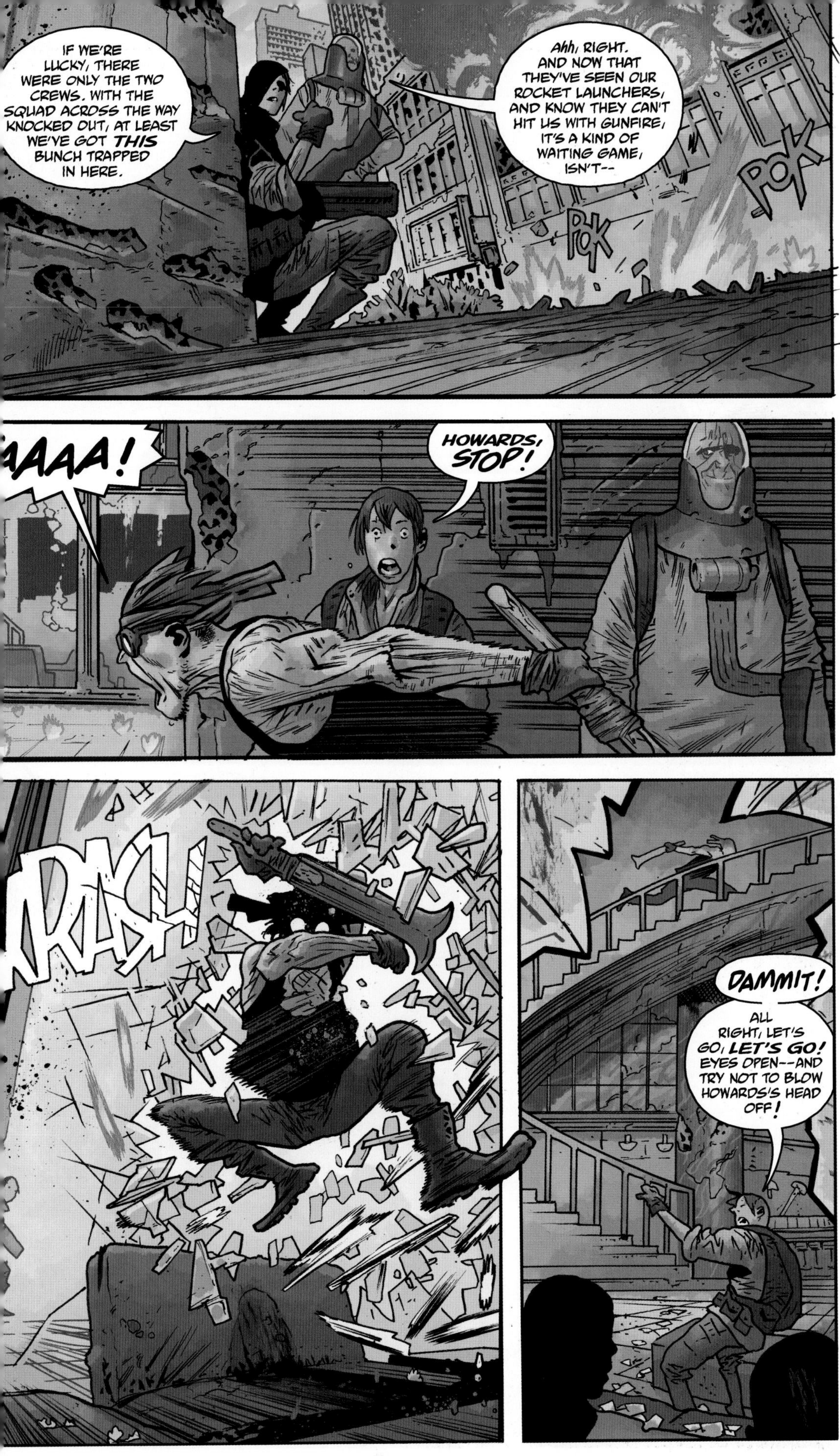
IF WE'RE LUCKY, THERE WERE ONLY THE TWO CREWS. WITH THE SQUAD ACROSS THE WAY KNOCKED OUT, AT LEAST WE'VE GOT THIS BUNCH TRAPPED IN HERE.
Ahh, RIGHT. AND NOW THAT THEY'VE SEEN OUR ROCKET LAUNCHERS, AND KNOW THEY CAN'T HIT US WITH GUNFIRE, IT'S A KIND OF WAITING GAME, ISN'T--
POK
POK
AAAA!
HOWARDS, STOP!
DAMMIT!
ALL RIGHT, LET'S GO, LET'S GO! EYES OPEN--AND TRY NOT TO BLOW HOWARDS'S HEAD OFF!

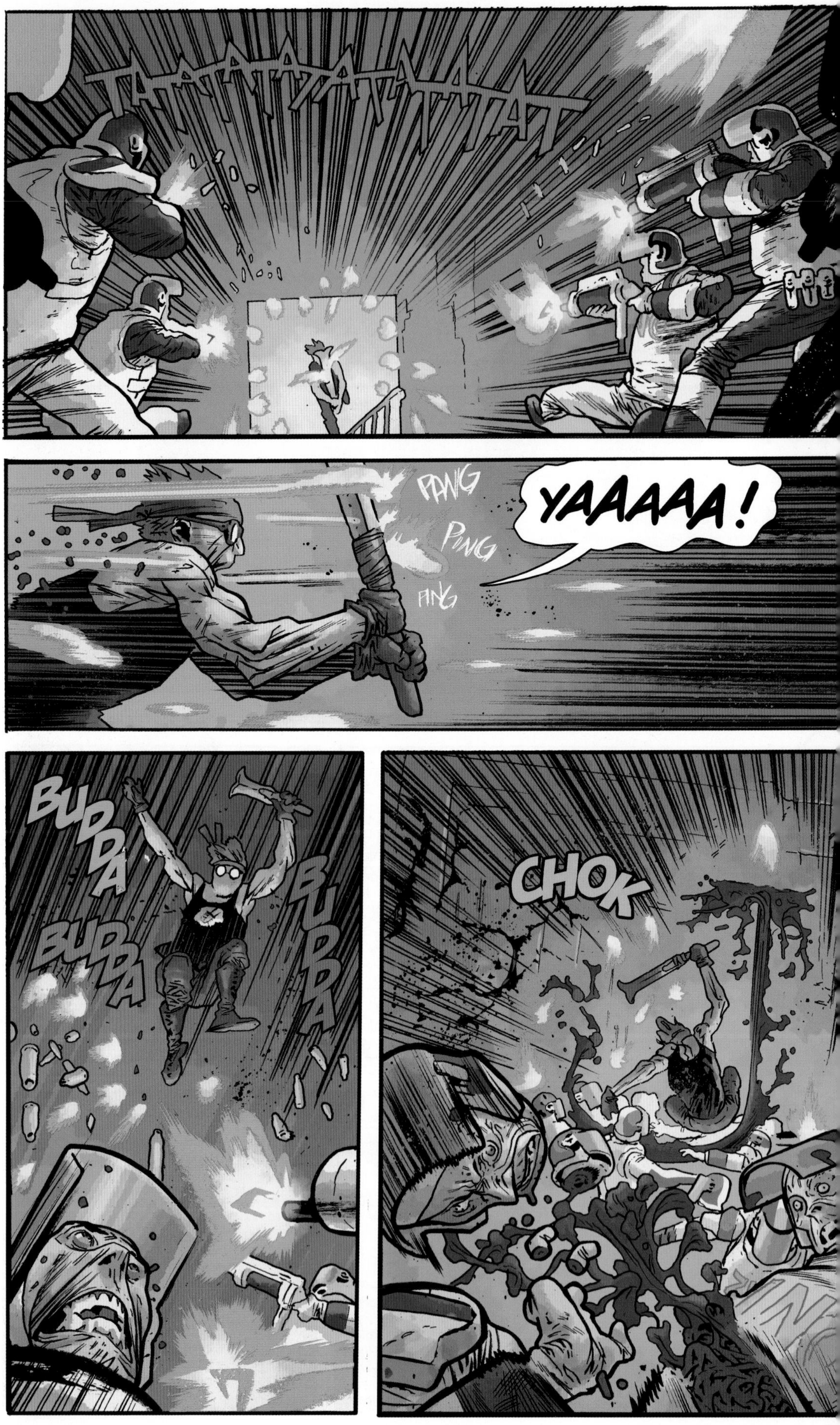
TATATATATATATAT
PANG
PING
PING
YAAAAA!
BUDDA
BUDDA
BUDDA
CHOK

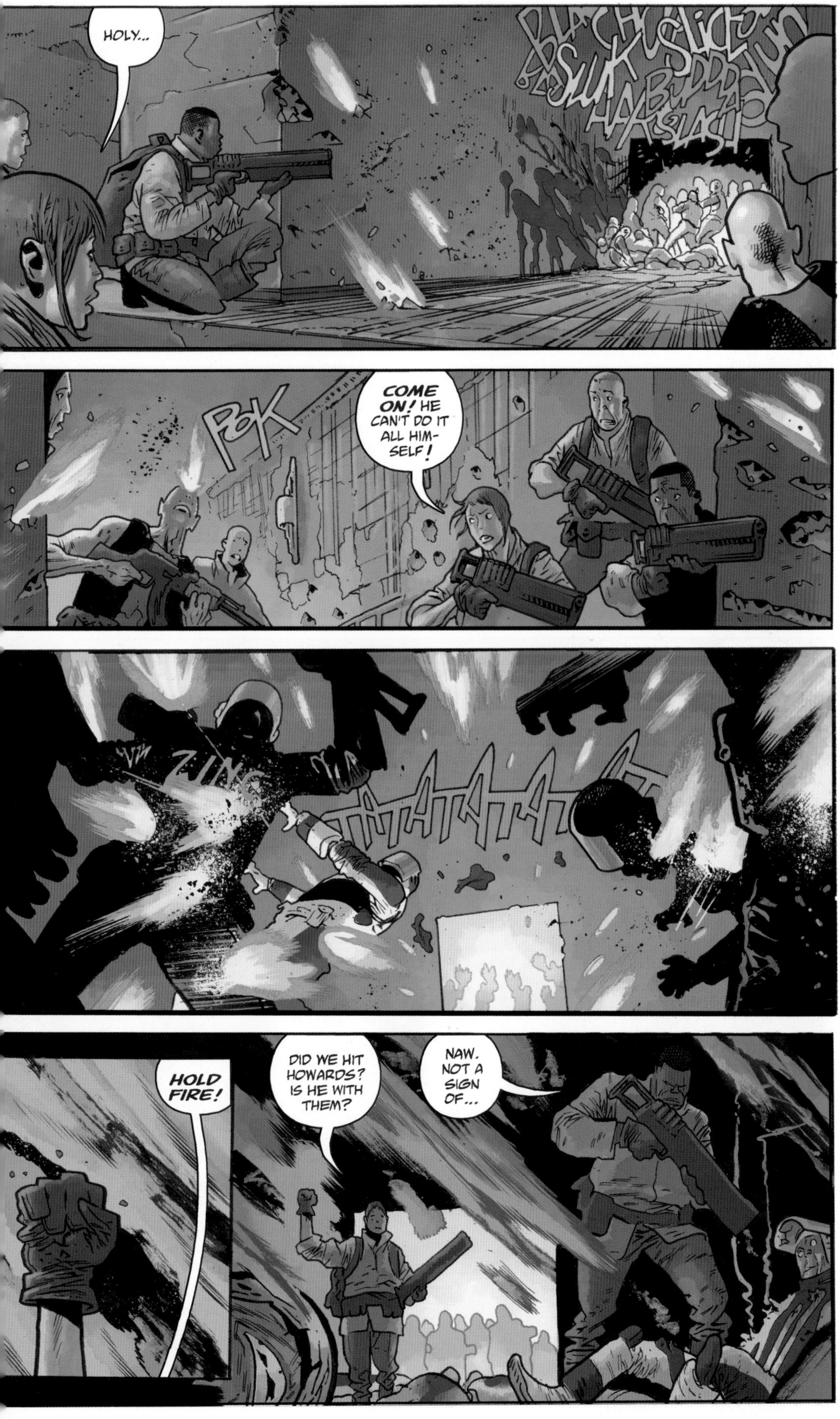
HOLY...
POK
COME ON! HE CAN'T DO IT ALL HIM-SELF!
ZING
HOLD FIRE!
DID WE HIT HOWARDS? IS HE WITH THEM?
NAW. NOT A SIGN OF...

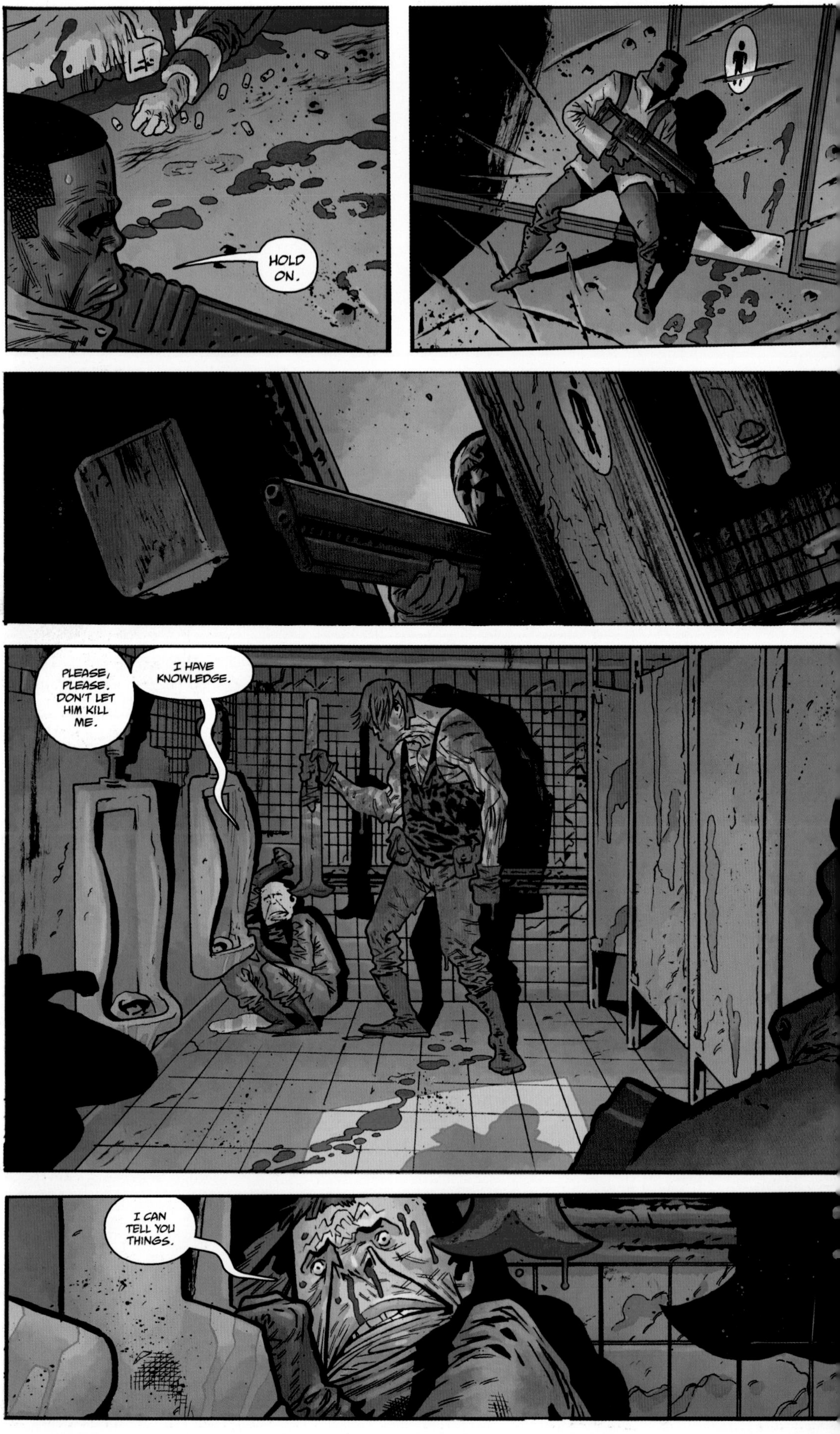
HOLD ON.
PLEASE, PLEASE. DON'T LET HIM KILL ME.
I HAVE KNOWLEDGE.
I CAN TELL YOU THINGS.

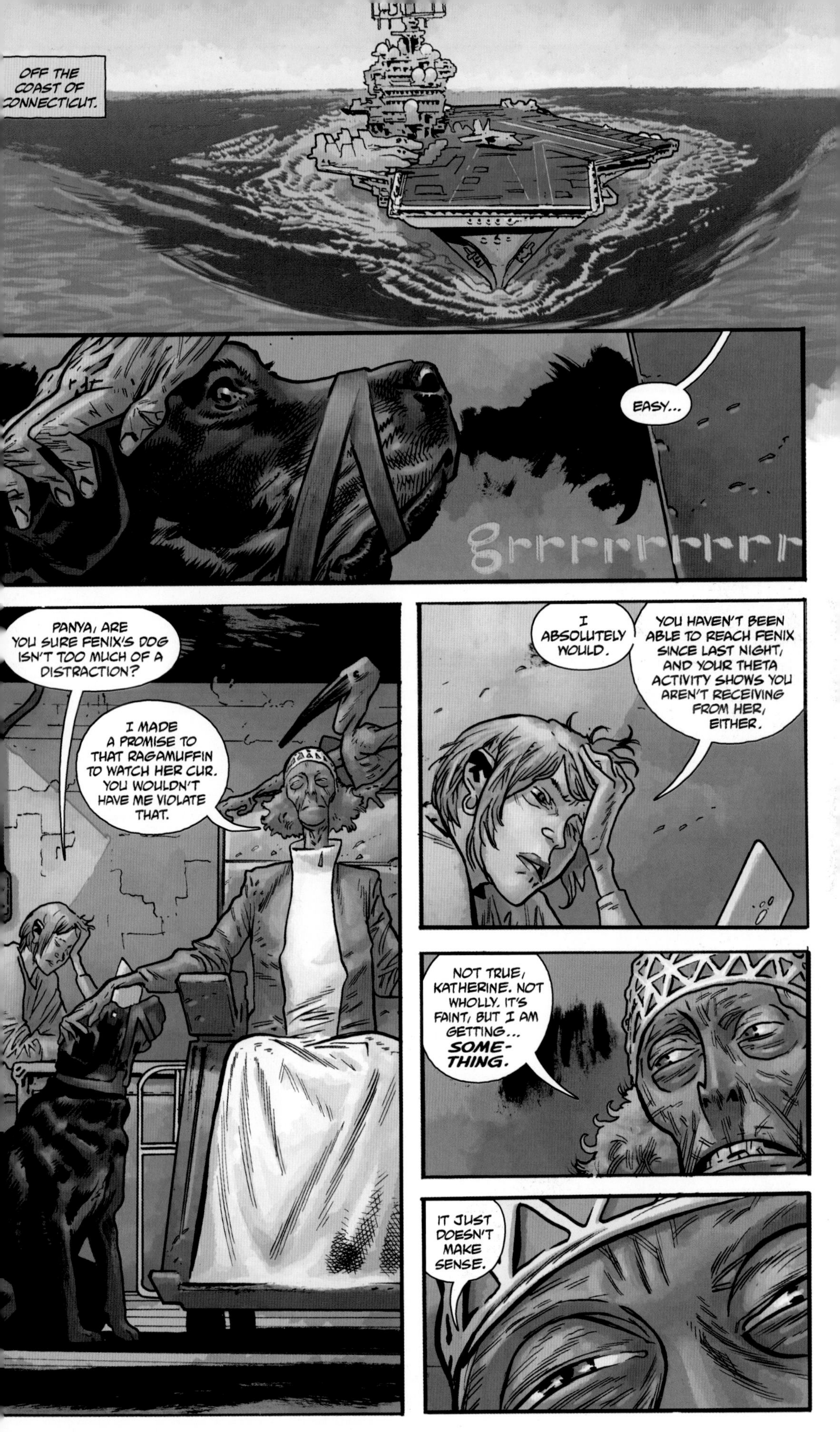
OFF THE COAST OF CONNECTICUT.
EASY...
grrrrrrrrrr
PANYA, ARE YOU SURE FENIX'S DOG ISN'T TOO MUCH OF A DISTRACTION?
I MADE A PROMISE TO THAT RAGAMUFFIN TO WATCH HER CUR. YOU WOULDN'T HAVE ME VIOLATE THAT.
I ABSOLUTELY WOULD.
YOU HAVEN'T BEEN ABLE TO REACH FENIX SINCE LAST NIGHT, AND YOUR THETA ACTIVITY SHOWS YOU AREN'T RECEIVING FROM HER, EITHER.
NOT TRUE, KATHERINE. NOT WHOLLY. IT'S FAINT, BUT I AM GETTING... SOME-THING.
IT JUST DOESN'T MAKE SENSE.

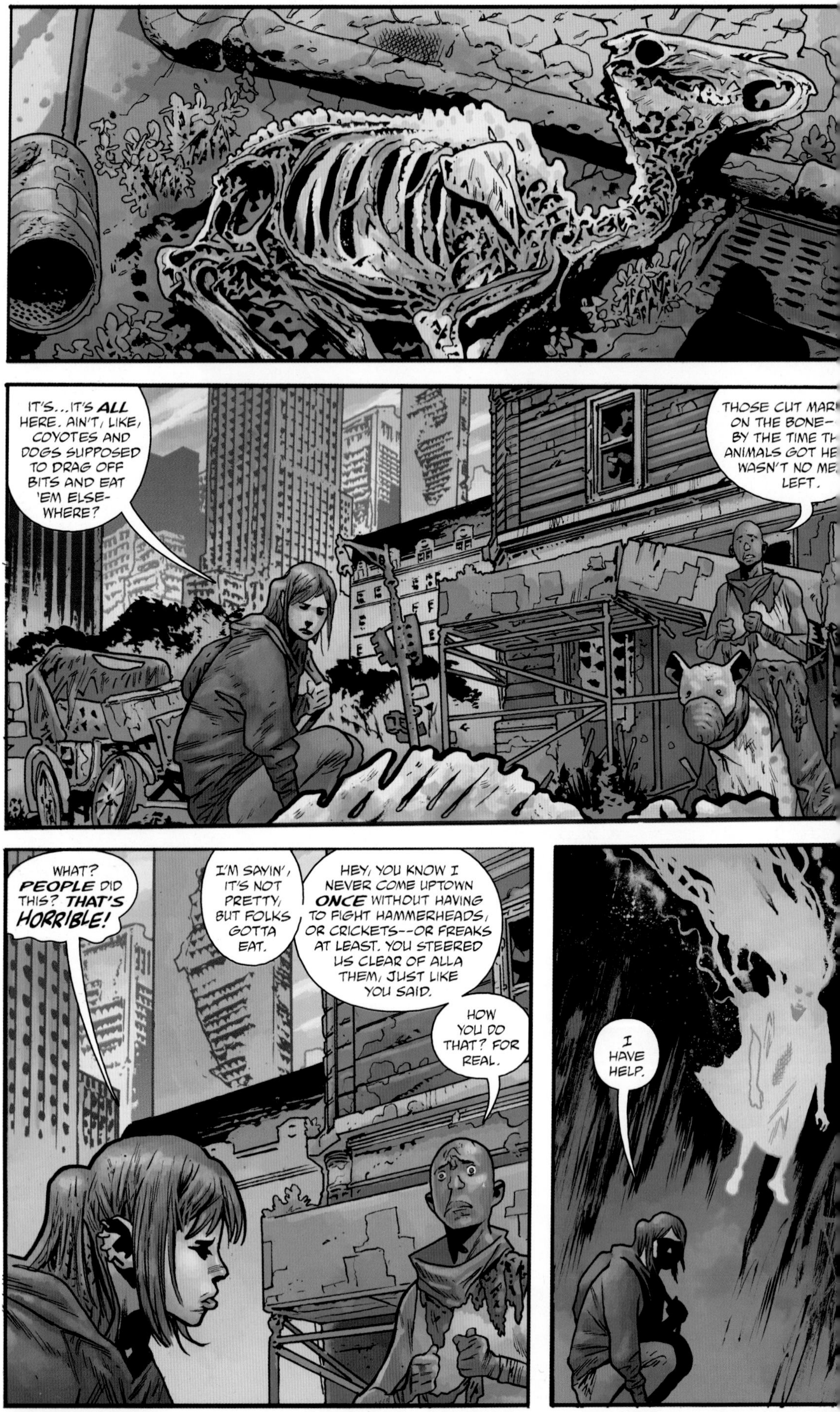

IT'S...IT'S ALL HERE. AIN'T, LIKE, COYOTES AND DOGS SUPPOSED TO DRAG OFF BITS AND EAT 'EM ELSE-WHERE?
THOSE CUT MAR ON THE BONE-- BY THE TIME TH ANIMALS GOT HE WASN'T NO ME LEFT.
WHAT? PEOPLE DID THIS? THAT'S HORRIBLE!
I'M SAYIN', IT'S NOT PRETTY, BUT FOLKS GOTTA EAT.
HEY, YOU KNOW I NEVER COME UPTOWN ONCE WITHOUT HAVING TO FIGHT HAMMERHEADS, OR CRICKETS--OR FREAKS AT LEAST. YOU STEERED US CLEAR OF ALLA THEM, JUST LIKE YOU SAID.
HOW YOU DO THAT? FOR REAL.
I HAVE HELP.

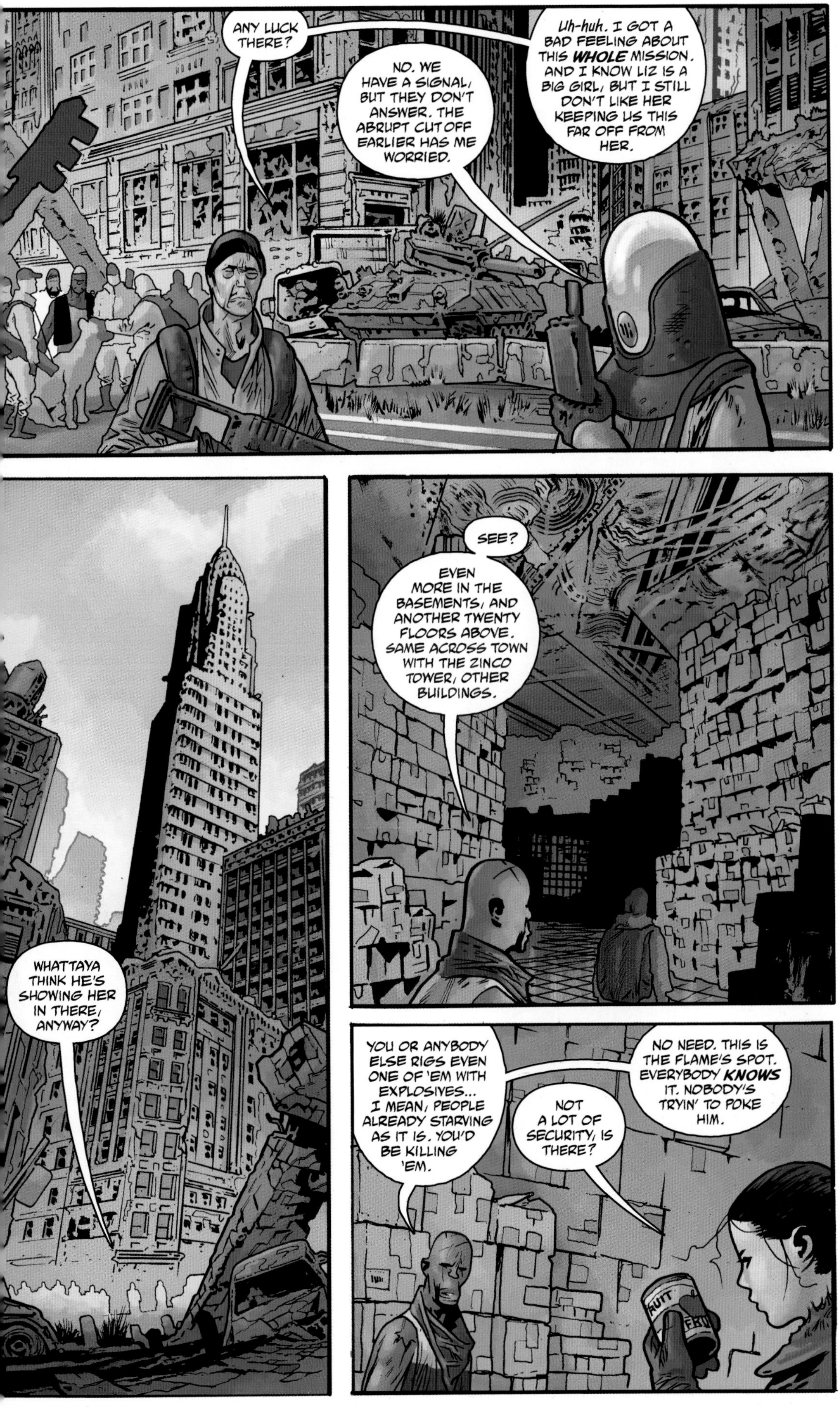
ANY LUCK THERE?
NO. WE HAVE A SIGNAL, BUT THEY DON'T ANSWER. THE ABRUPT CUTOFF EARLIER HAS ME WORRIED.
Uh-huh. I GOT A BAD FEELING ABOUT THIS WHOLE MISSION. AND I KNOW LIZ IS A BIG GIRL, BUT I STILL DON'T LIKE HER KEEPING US THIS FAR OFF FROM HER.
WHATTAYA THINK HE'S SHOWING HER IN THERE, ANYWAY?
SEE?
EVEN MORE IN THE BASEMENTS, AND ANOTHER TWENTY FLOORS ABOVE. SAME ACROSS TOWN WITH THE ZINCO TOWER, OTHER BUILDINGS.
YOU OR ANYBODY ELSE RIGS EVEN ONE OF 'EM WITH EXPLOSIVES... I MEAN, PEOPLE ALREADY STARVING AS IT IS. YOU'D BE KILLING 'EM.
NOT A LOT OF SECURITY, IS THERE?
NO NEED. THIS IS THE FLAME'S SPOT. EVERYBODY KNOWS IT. NOBODY'S TRYIN' TO POKE HIM.

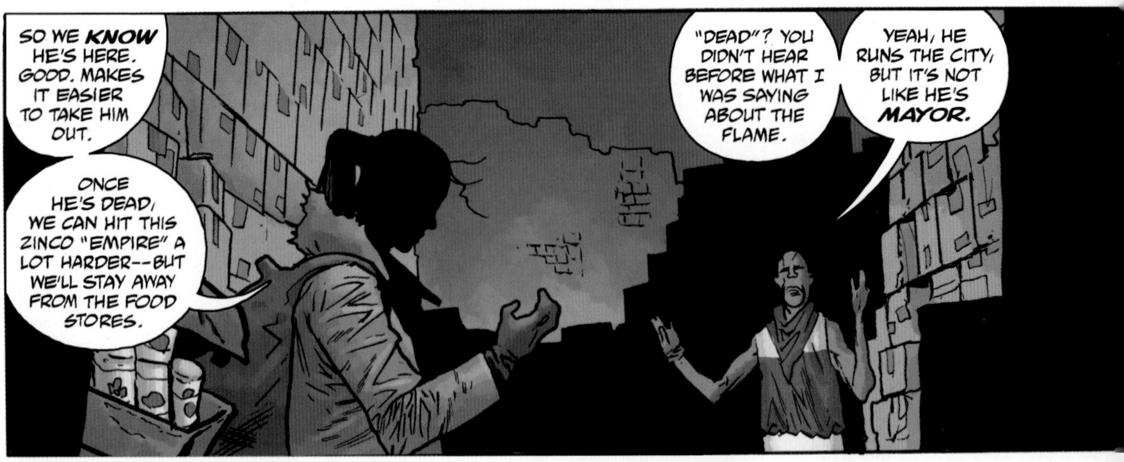
SO WE KNOW HE'S HERE. GOOD. MAKES IT EASIER TO TAKE HIM OUT.
ONCE HE'S DEAD, WE CAN HIT THIS ZINCO "EMPIRE" A LOT HARDER--BUT WE'LL STAY AWAY FROM THE FOOD STORES.
"DEAD"? YOU DIDN'T HEAR BEFORE WHAT I WAS SAYING ABOUT THE FLAME.
YEAH, HE RUNS THE CITY, BUT IT'S NOT LIKE HE'S MAYOR.

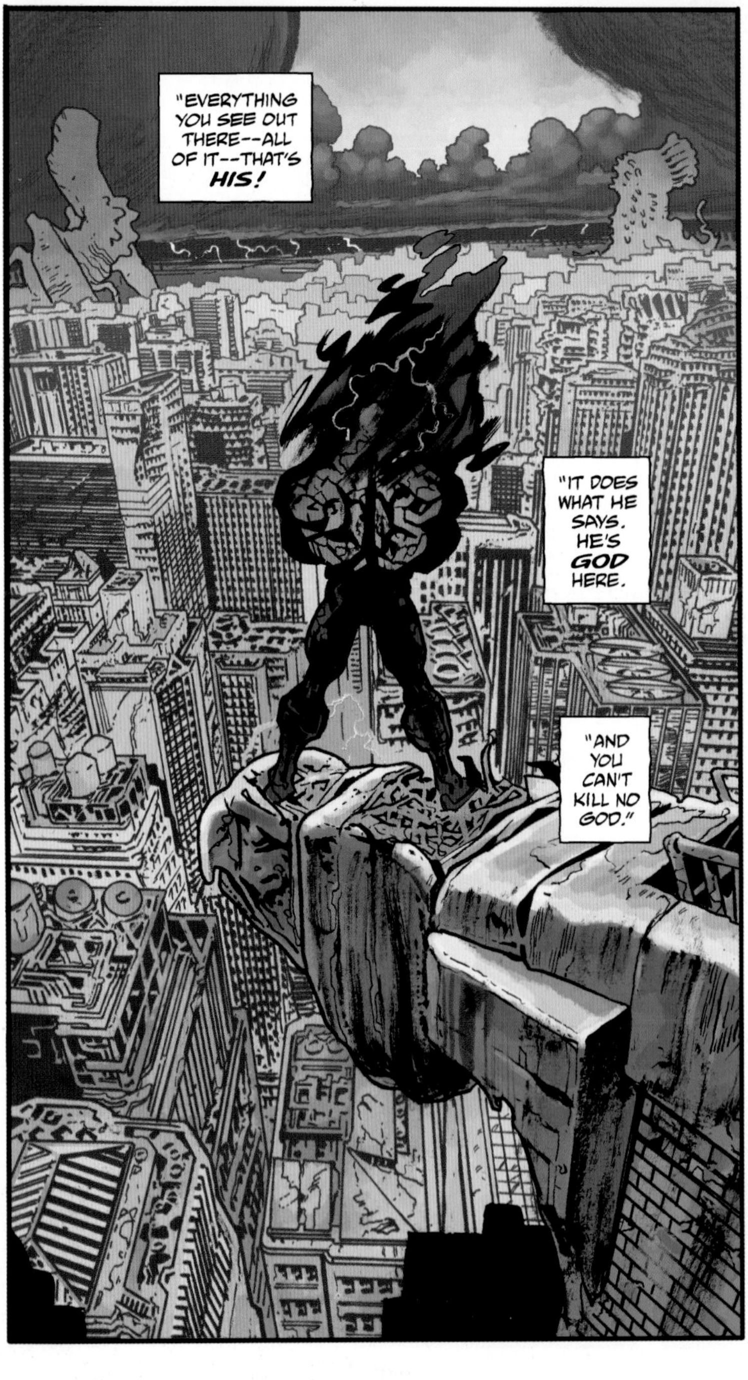
"EVERYTHING YOU SEE OUT THERE--ALL OF IT--THAT'S HIS!
"IT DOES WHAT HE SAYS. HE'S GOD HERE.
"AND YOU CAN'T KILL NO GOD."

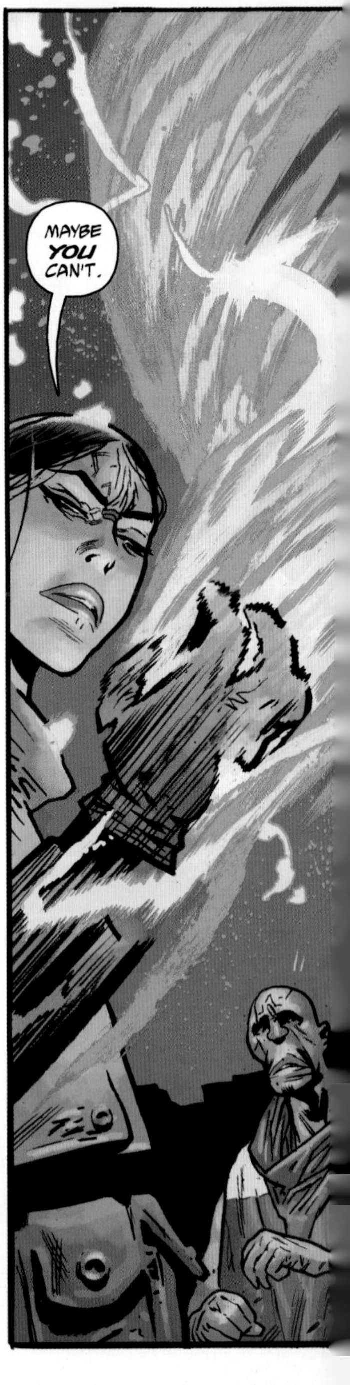
MAYBE YOU CAN'T.

THE REIGN OF THE BLACK FLAME

CHAPTER THREE

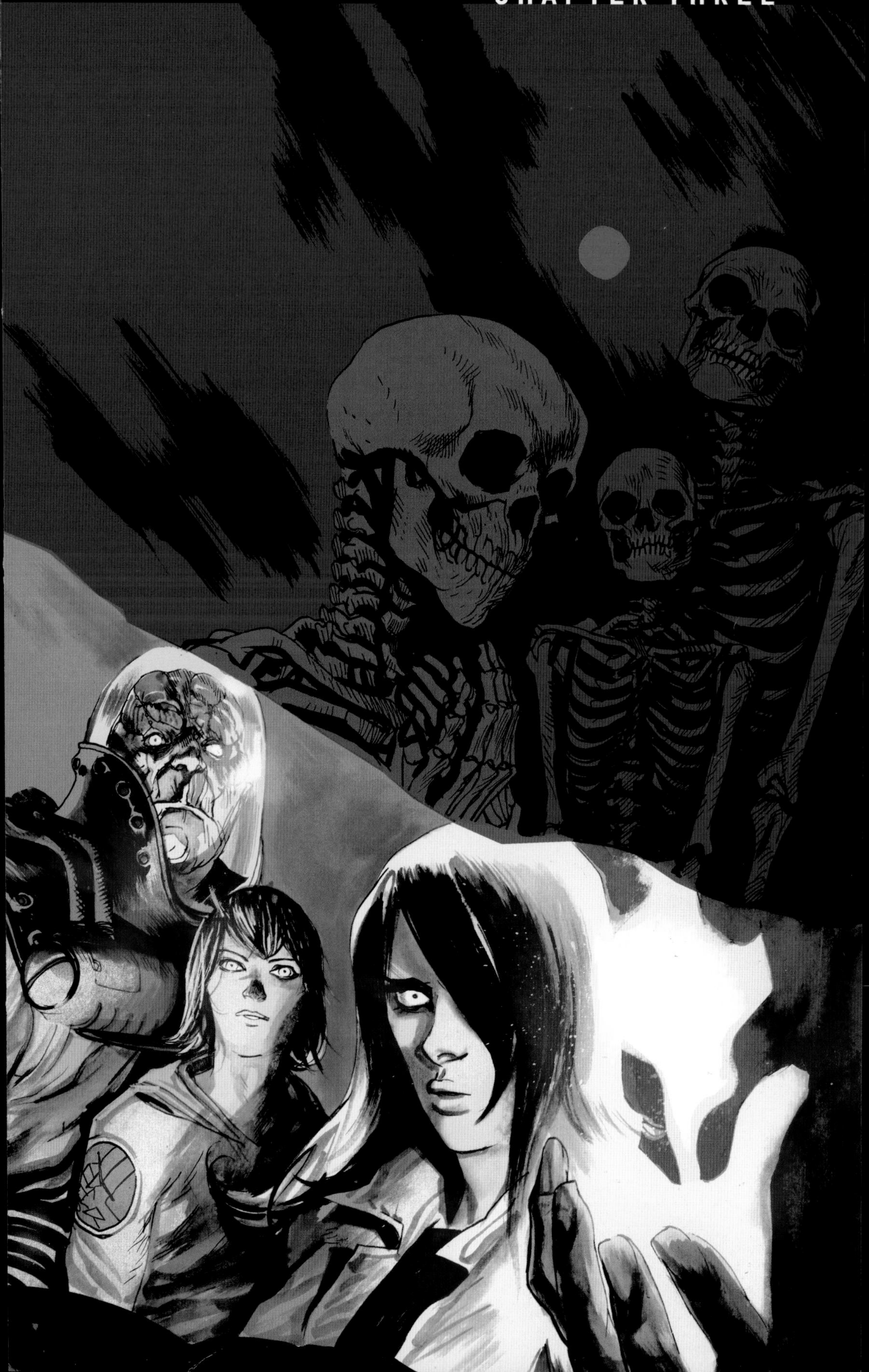

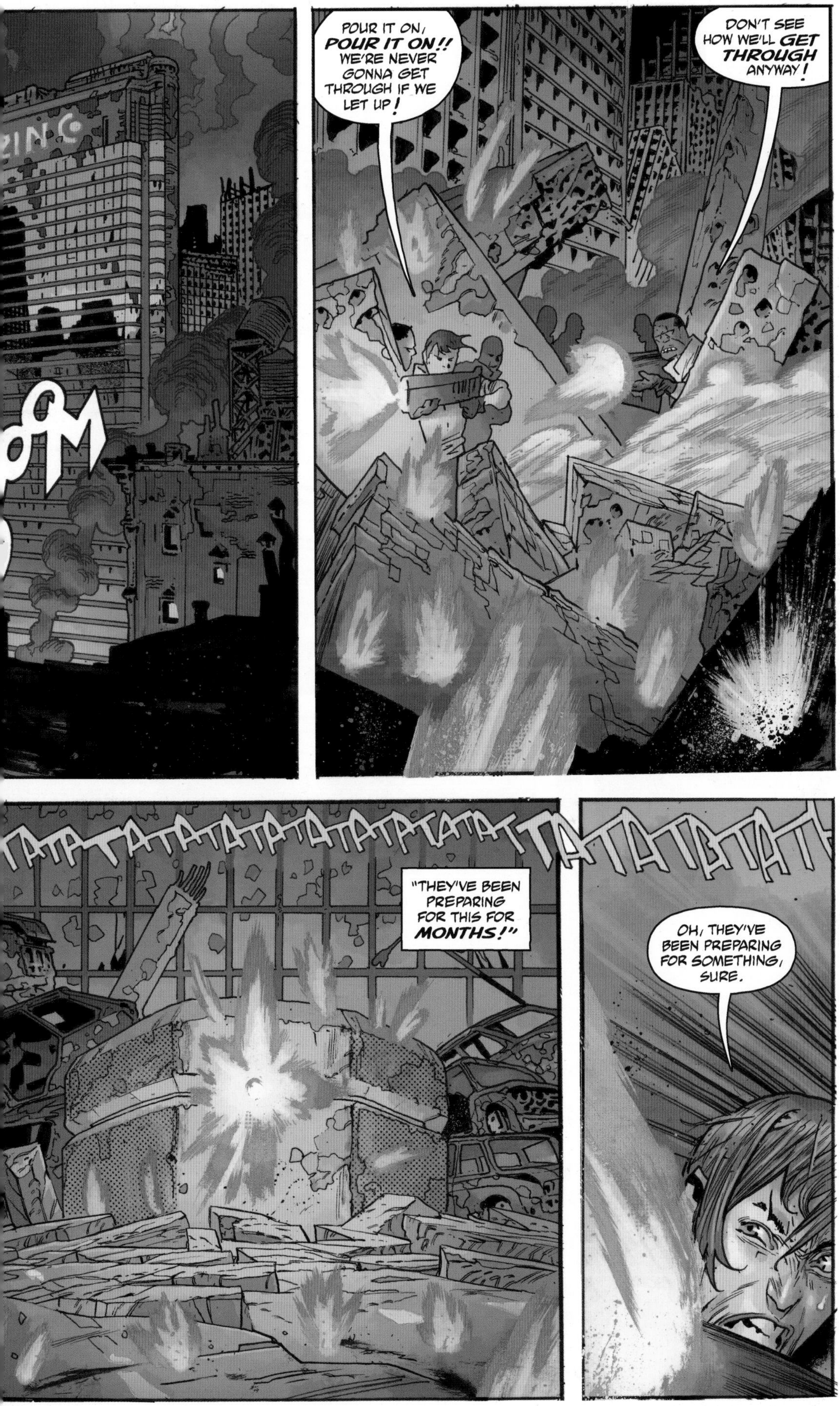

OOM
POUR IT ON, POUR IT ON!! WE'RE NEVER GONNA GET THROUGH IF WE LET UP!
DON'T SEE HOW WE'LL GET THROUGH ANYWAY!
TATATATATATATATATATATATATATATATATATATA
"THEY'VE BEEN PREPARING FOR THIS FOR MONTHS!"
OH, THEY'VE BEEN PREPARING FOR SOMETHING, SURE.

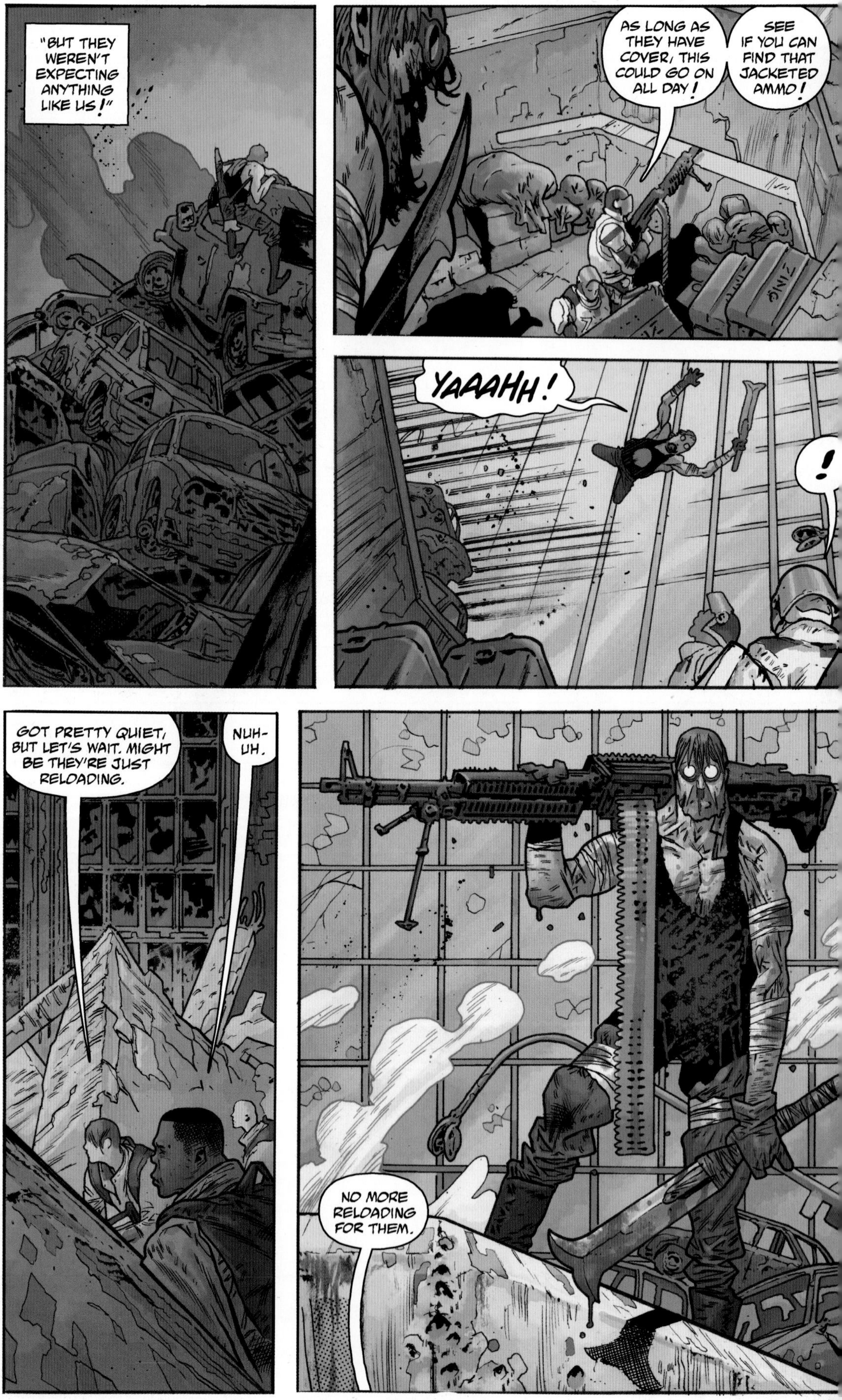
"BUT THEY WEREN'T EXPECTING ANYTHING LIKE US!"
AS LONG AS THEY HAVE COVER, THIS COULD GO ON ALL DAY!
SEE IF YOU CAN FIND THAT JACKETED AMMO!
YAAAHH!
!
GOT PRETTY QUIET, BUT LET'S WAIT. MIGHT BE THEY'RE JUST RELOADING.
NUH-UH.
NO MORE RELOADING FOR THEM.

COME ON, THIS ISN'T OVER!

KEEP MOVING, KEEP MOVING!

OKAY, IOSIF. YOU GOT YOUR DIVERSION.

I JUST HOPE YOU LIVE THROUGH THIS TO TESTIFY AT MY COURT-MARTIAL.

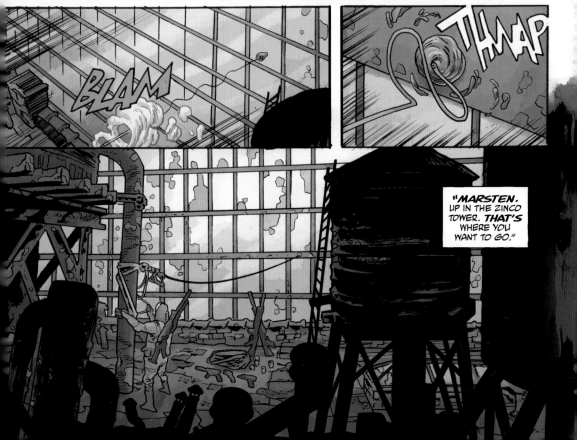

BLAM

THWAP

"MARSTEN. UP IN THE ZINCO TOWER. THAT'S WHERE YOU WANT TO GO."

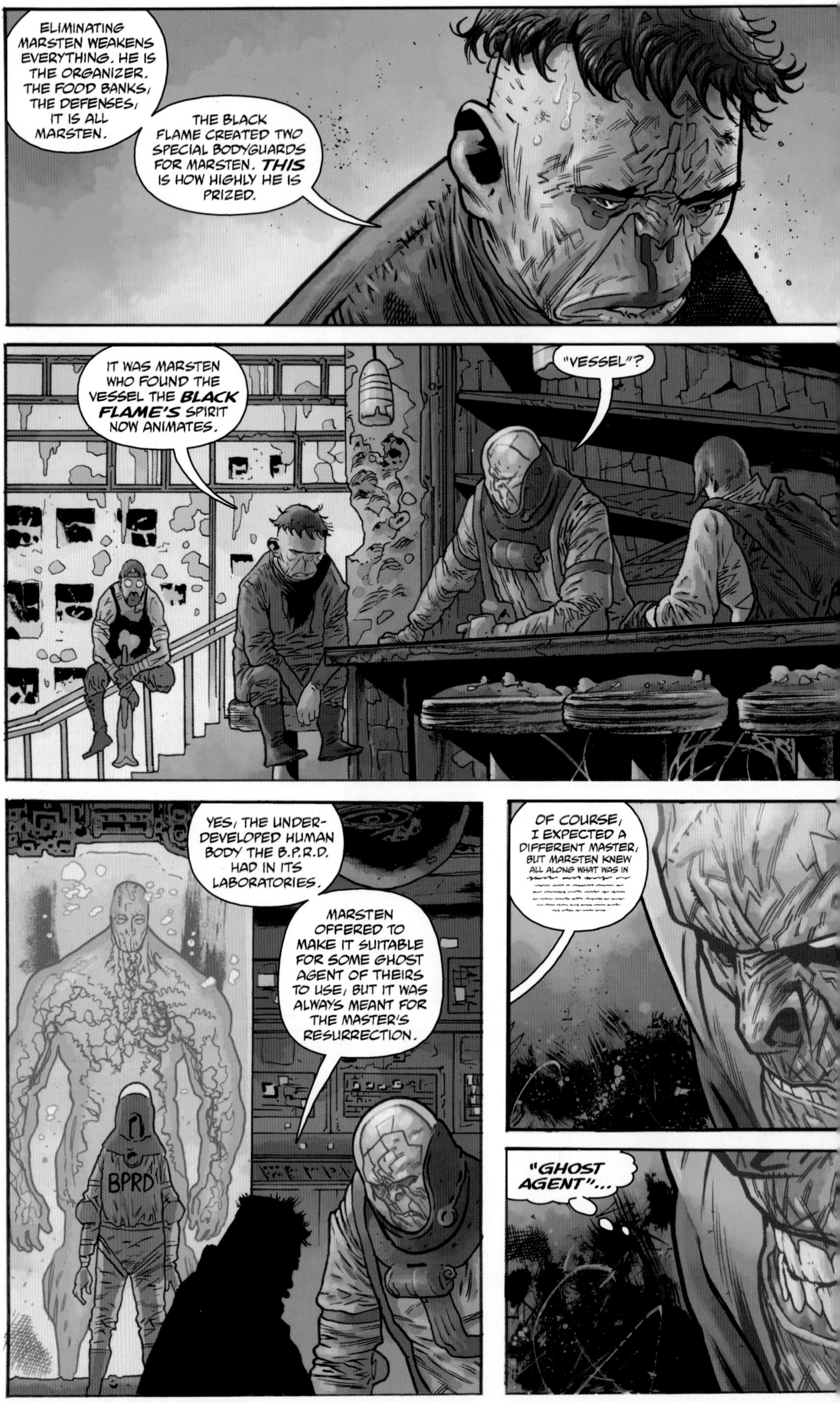
ELIMINATING MARSTEN WEAKENS EVERYTHING. HE IS THE ORGANIZER. THE FOOD BANKS, THE DEFENSES, IT IS ALL MARSTEN.
THE BLACK FLAME CREATED TWO SPECIAL BODYGUARDS FOR MARSTEN. THIS IS HOW HIGHLY HE IS PRIZED.
IT WAS MARSTEN WHO FOUND THE VESSEL THE BLACK FLAME'S SPIRIT NOW ANIMATES.
"VESSEL"?
YES, THE UNDER-DEVELOPED HUMAN BODY THE B.P.R.D. HAD IN ITS LABORATORIES.
MARSTEN OFFERED TO MAKE IT SUITABLE FOR SOME GHOST AGENT OF THEIRS TO USE, BUT IT WAS ALWAYS MEANT FOR THE MASTER'S RESURRECTION.
BPRD
OF COURSE, I EXPECTED A DIFFERENT MASTER, BUT MARSTEN KNEW ALL ALONG WHAT WAS IN
"GHOST AGENT"...

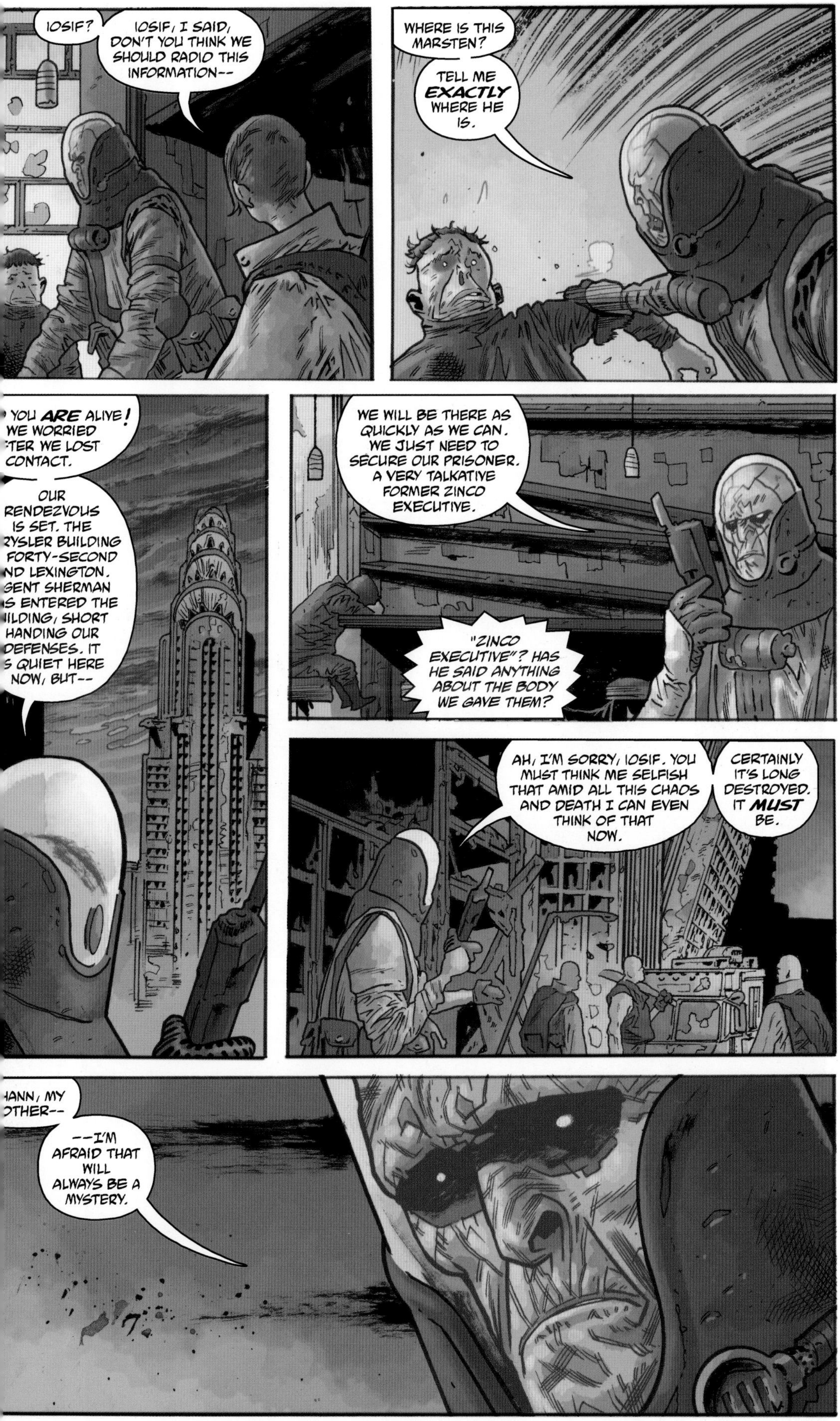
IOSIF?
IOSIF, I SAID, DON'T YOU THINK WE SHOULD RADIO THIS INFORMATION--
WHERE IS THIS MARSTEN?
TELL ME EXACTLY WHERE HE IS.
YOU ARE ALIVE! WE WORRIED TER WE LOST CONTACT.
OUR RENDEZVOUS IS SET. THE RYSLER BUILDING FORTY-SECOND ND LEXINGTON. GENT SHERMAN S ENTERED THE ILDING, SHORT HANDING OUR DEFENSES. IT S QUIET HERE NOW, BUT--
WE WILL BE THERE AS QUICKLY AS WE CAN. WE JUST NEED TO SECURE OUR PRISONER. A VERY TALKATIVE FORMER ZINCO EXECUTIVE.
"ZINCO EXECUTIVE"? HAS HE SAID ANYTHING ABOUT THE BODY WE GAVE THEM?
AH, I'M SORRY, IOSIF. YOU MUST THINK ME SELFISH THAT AMID ALL THIS CHAOS AND DEATH I CAN EVEN THINK OF THAT NOW.
CERTAINLY IT'S LONG DESTROYED. IT MUST BE.
HANN, MY OTHER--
--I'M AFRAID THAT WILL ALWAYS BE A MYSTERY.

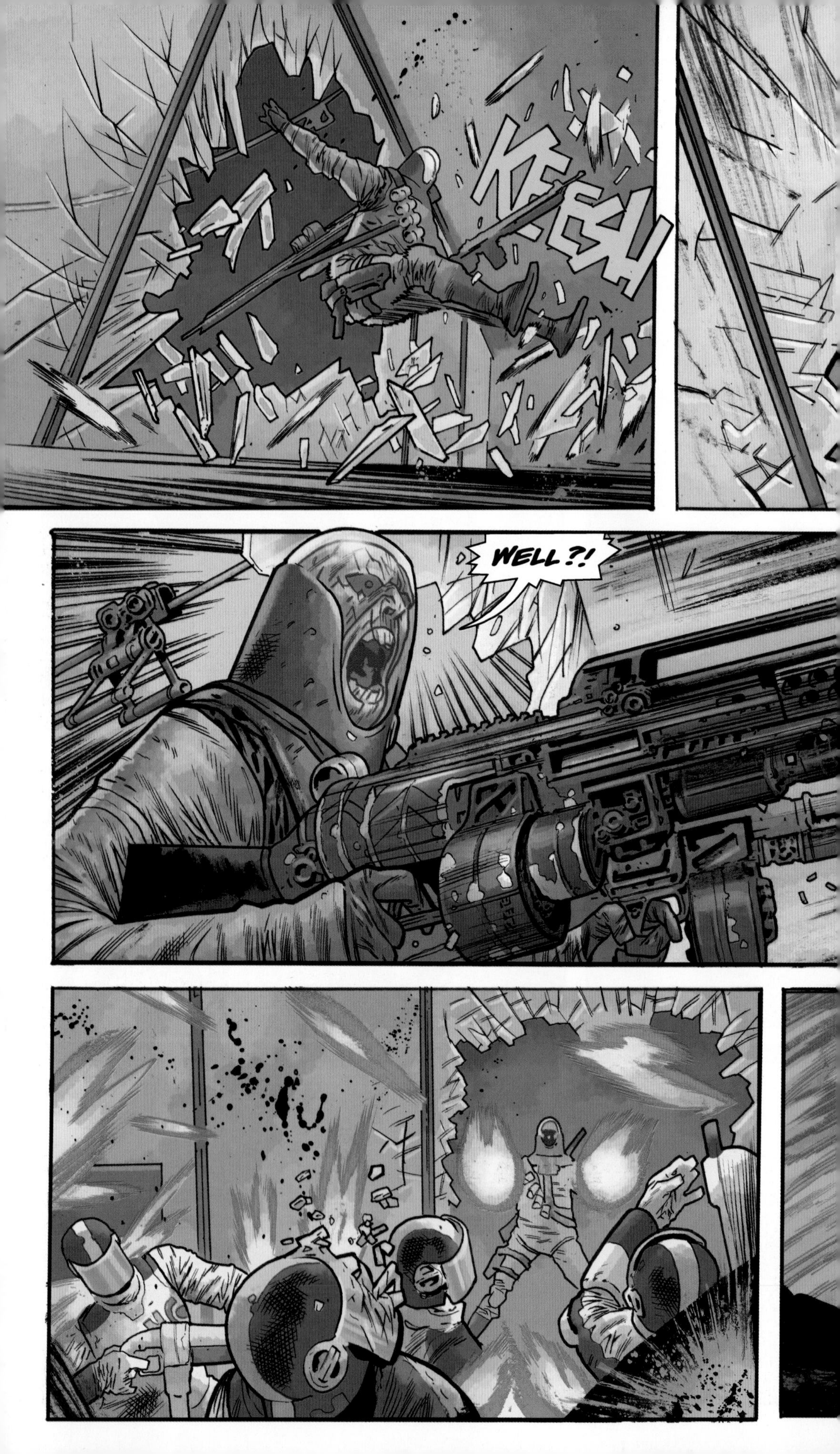
KEESH
WELL?!

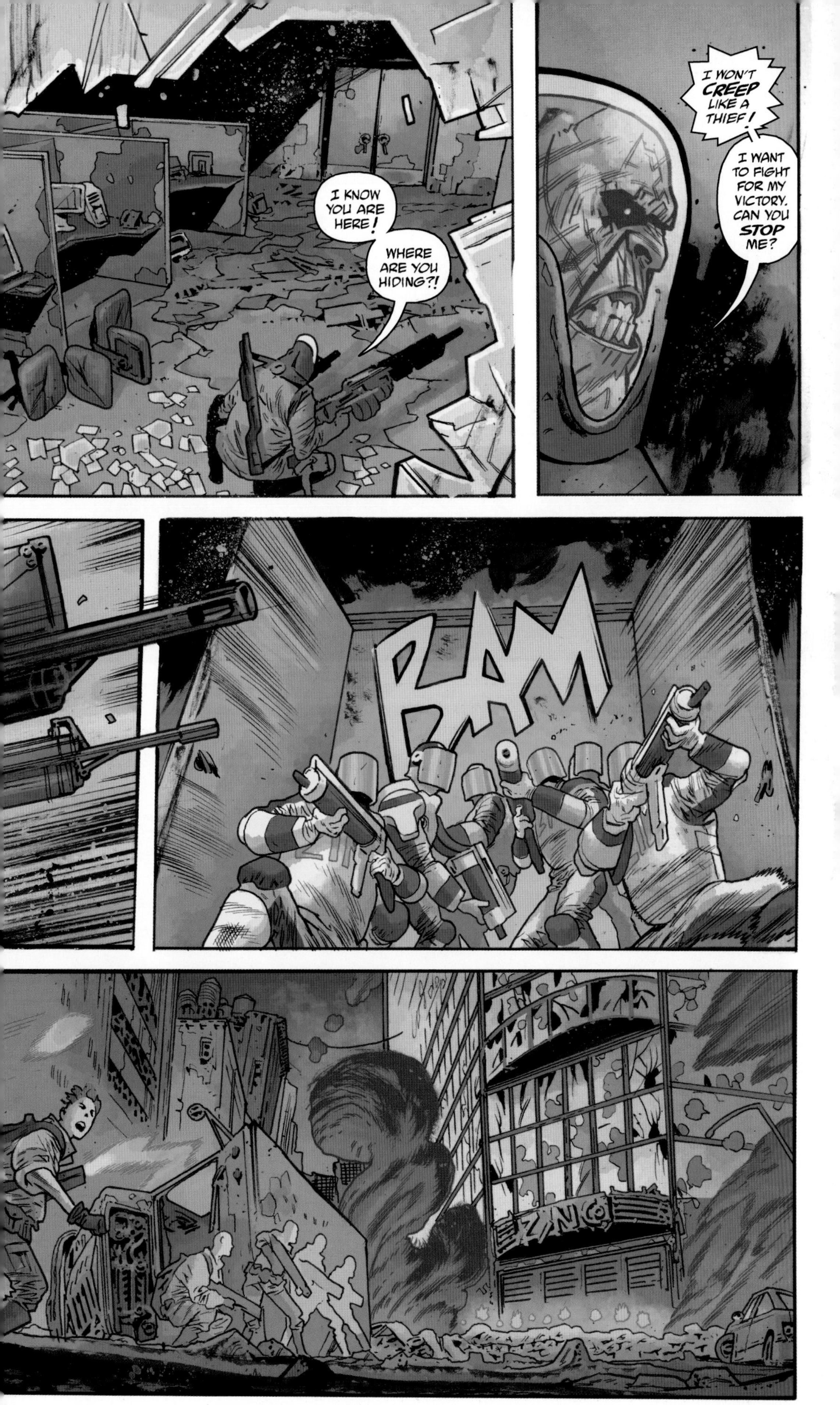
I KNOW YOU ARE HERE!
WHERE ARE YOU HIDING?!
I WON'T CREEP LIKE A THIEF!
I WANT TO FIGHT FOR MY VICTORY. CAN YOU STOP ME?
BAM
ZNC

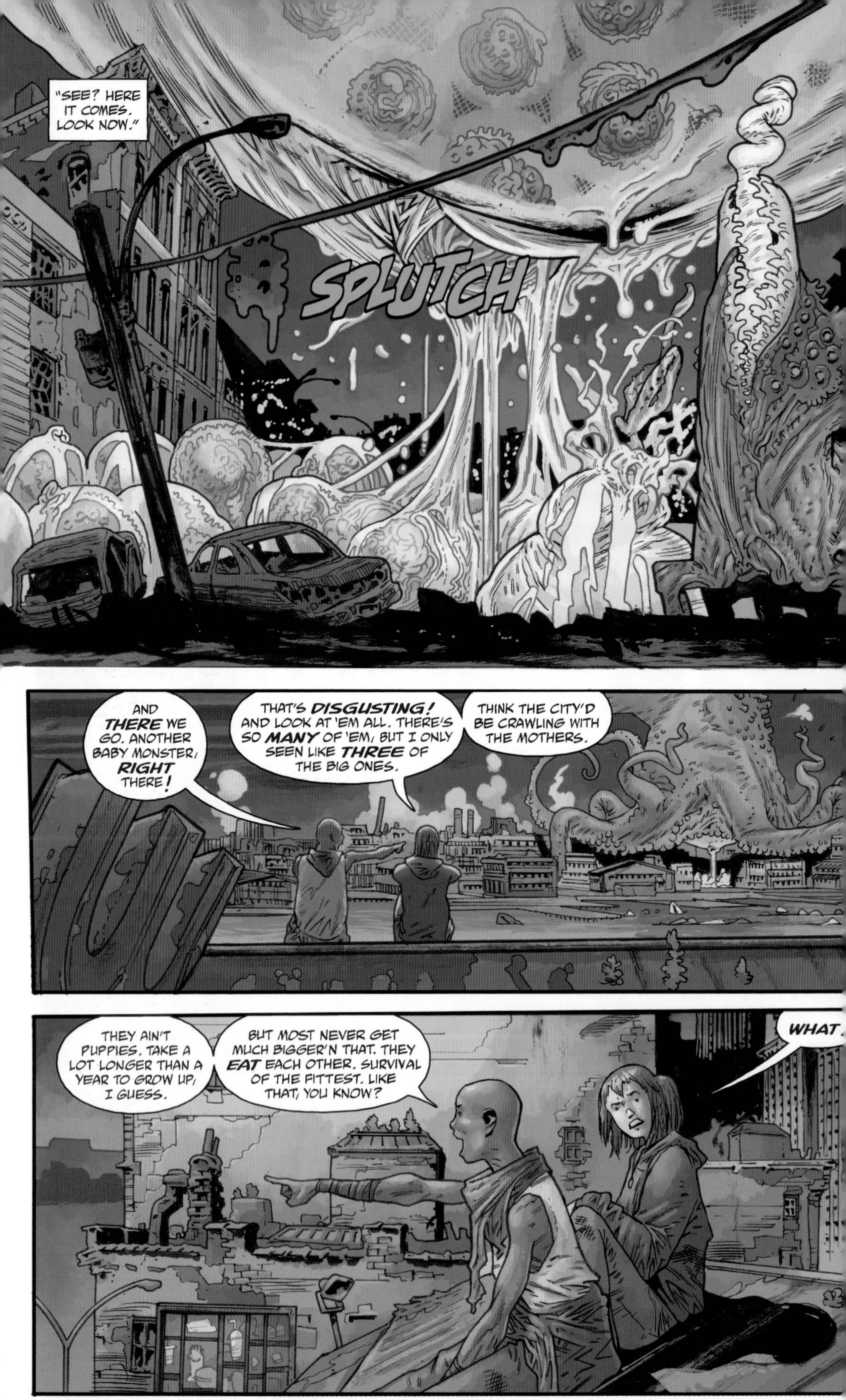

"SEE? HERE IT COMES. LOOK NOW."
SPLUTCH
AND THERE WE GO. ANOTHER BABY MONSTER, RIGHT THERE!
THAT'S DISGUSTING! AND LOOK AT 'EM ALL. THERE'S SO MANY OF 'EM, BUT I ONLY SEEN LIKE THREE OF THE BIG ONES.
THINK THE CITY'D BE CRAWLING WITH THE MOTHERS.
THEY AIN'T PUPPIES. TAKE A LOT LONGER THAN A YEAR TO GROW UP, I GUESS.
BUT MOST NEVER GET MUCH BIGGER'N THAT. THEY EAT EACH OTHER. SURVIVAL OF THE FITTEST. LIKE THAT, YOU KNOW?
WHAT.

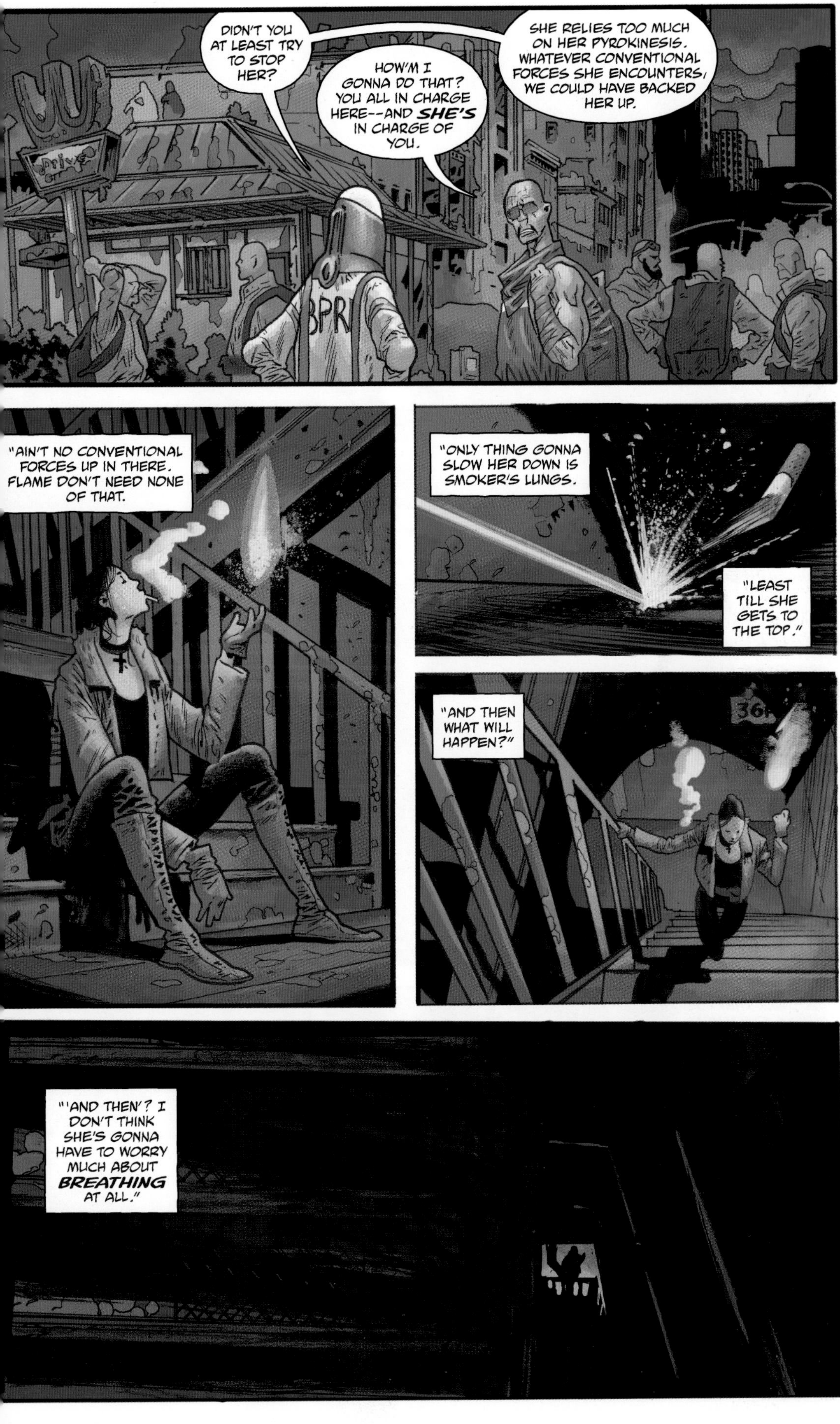
DIDN'T YOU AT LEAST TRY TO STOP HER?
HOW'M I GONNA DO THAT? YOU ALL IN CHARGE HERE--AND SHE'S IN CHARGE OF YOU.
SHE RELIES TOO MUCH ON HER PYROKINESIS. WHATEVER CONVENTIONAL FORCES SHE ENCOUNTERS, WE COULD HAVE BACKED HER UP.
BPR
"AIN'T NO CONVENTIONAL FORCES UP IN THERE. FLAME DON'T NEED NONE OF THAT.
"ONLY THING GONNA SLOW HER DOWN IS SMOKER'S LUNGS.
"LEAST TILL SHE GETS TO THE TOP."
"AND THEN WHAT WILL HAPPEN?"
"'AND THEN'? I DON'T THINK SHE'S GONNA HAVE TO WORRY MUCH ABOUT BREATHING AT ALL."

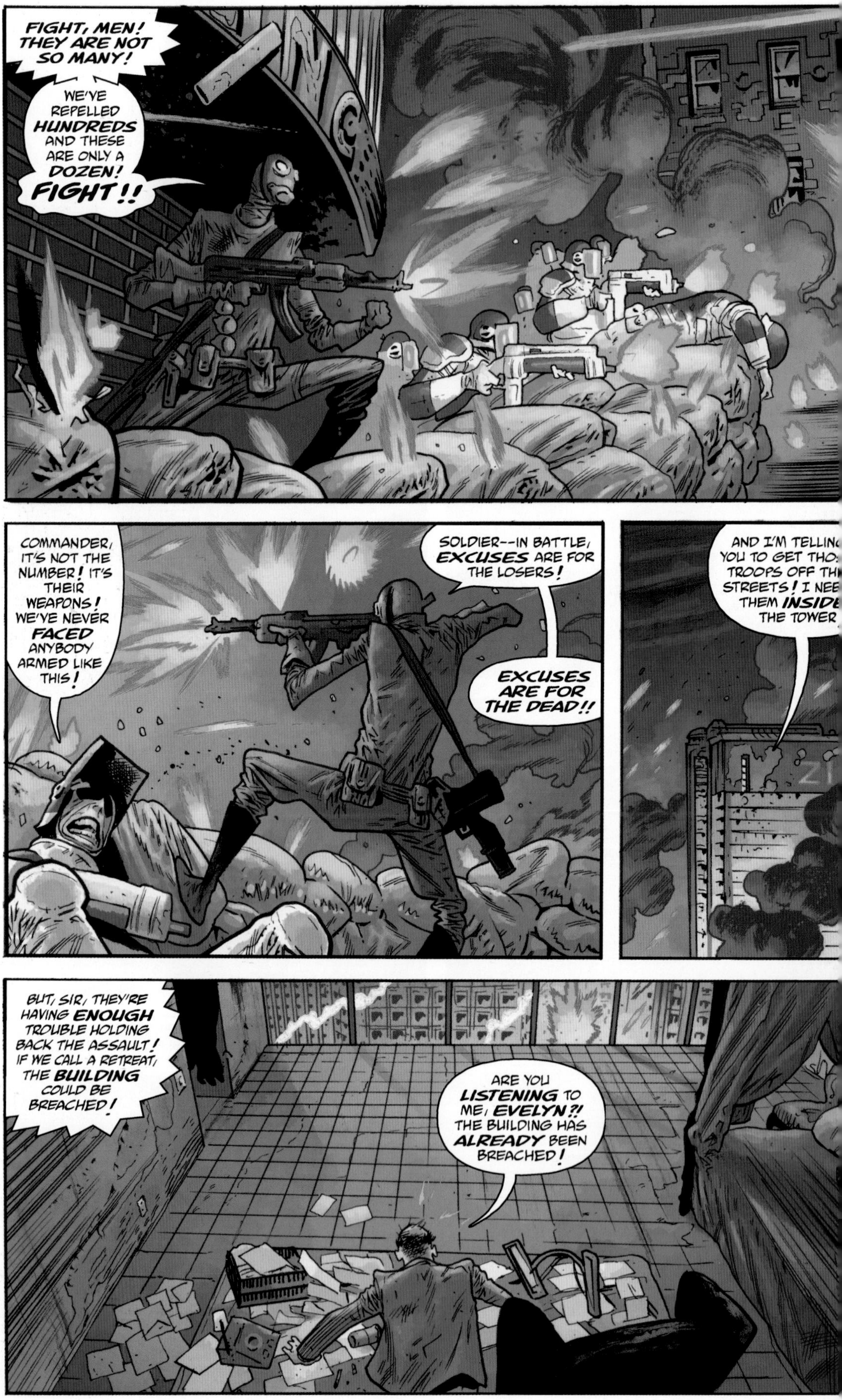
FIGHT, MEN! THEY ARE NOT SO MANY!
WE'VE REPELLED HUNDREDS AND THESE ARE ONLY A DOZEN! FIGHT!!
COMMANDER, IT'S NOT THE NUMBER! IT'S THEIR WEAPONS! WE'VE NEVER FACED ANYBODY ARMED LIKE THIS!
SOLDIER--IN BATTLE, EXCUSES ARE FOR THE LOSERS!
EXCUSES ARE FOR THE DEAD!!
AND I'M TELLING YOU TO GET THOS TROOPS OFF TH STREETS! I NEE THEM INSIDE THE TOWER
BUT, SIR, THEY'RE HAVING ENOUGH TROUBLE HOLDING BACK THE ASSAULT! IF WE CALL A RETREAT, THE BUILDING COULD BE BREACHED!
ARE YOU LISTENING TO ME, EVELYN?! THE BUILDING HAS ALREADY BEEN BREACHED!

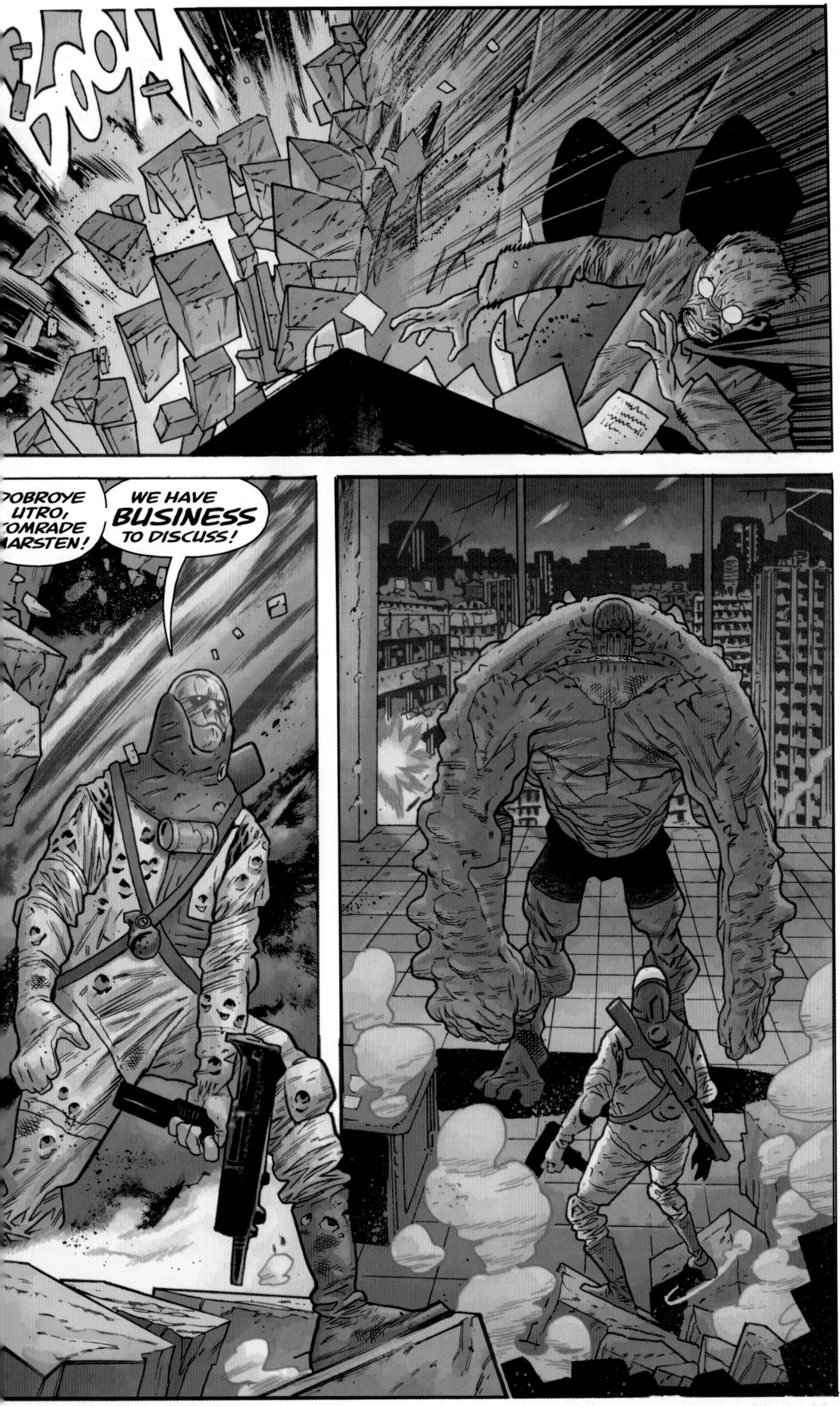
DOBROYE UTRO, COMRADE MARSTEN!
WE HAVE BUSINESS TO DISCUSS!

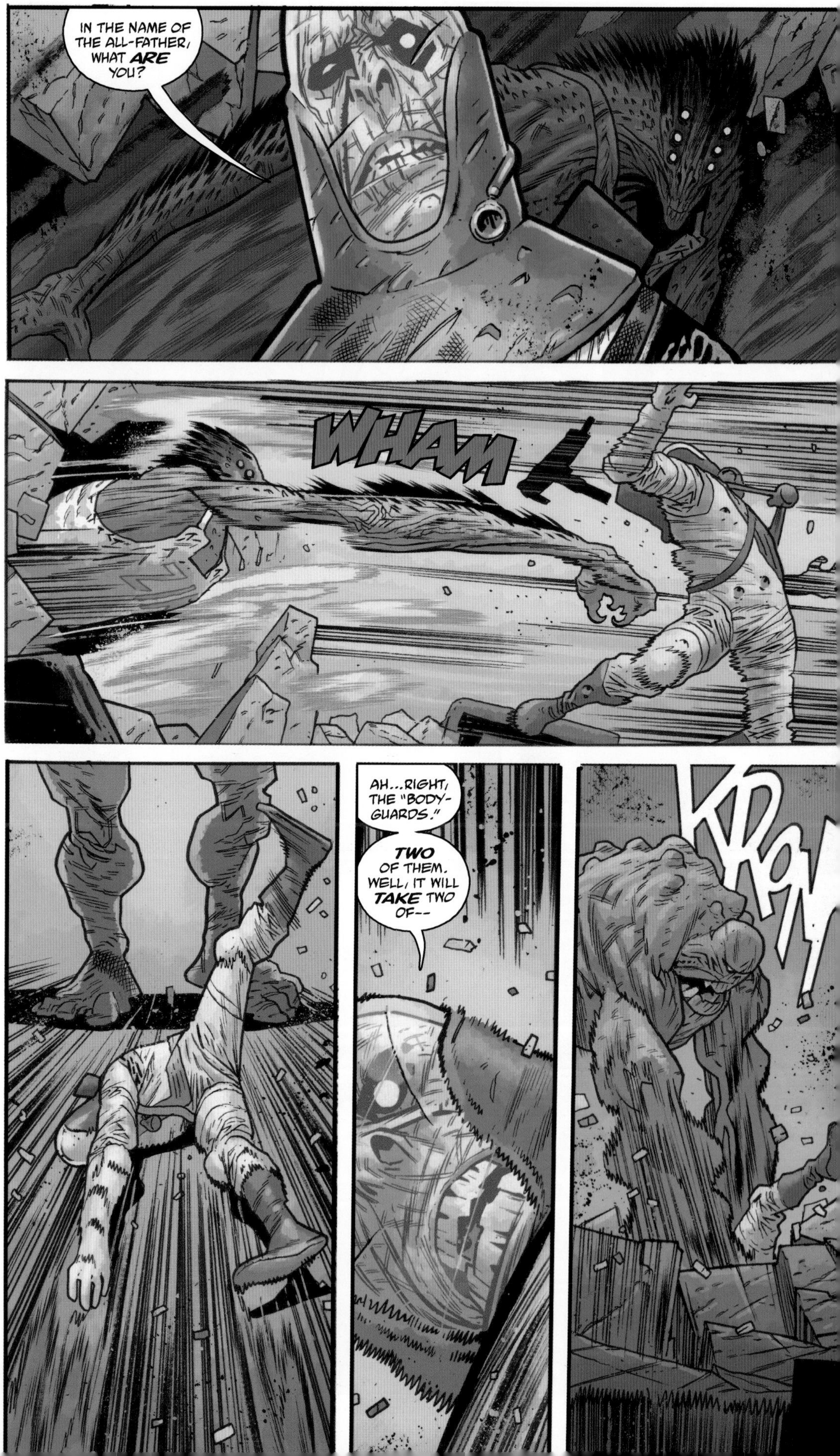
IN THE NAME OF THE ALL-FATHER, WHAT ARE YOU?
WHAM
AH...RIGHT, THE "BODY-GUARDS."
TWO OF THEM. WELL, IT WILL TAKE TWO OF--
KRON

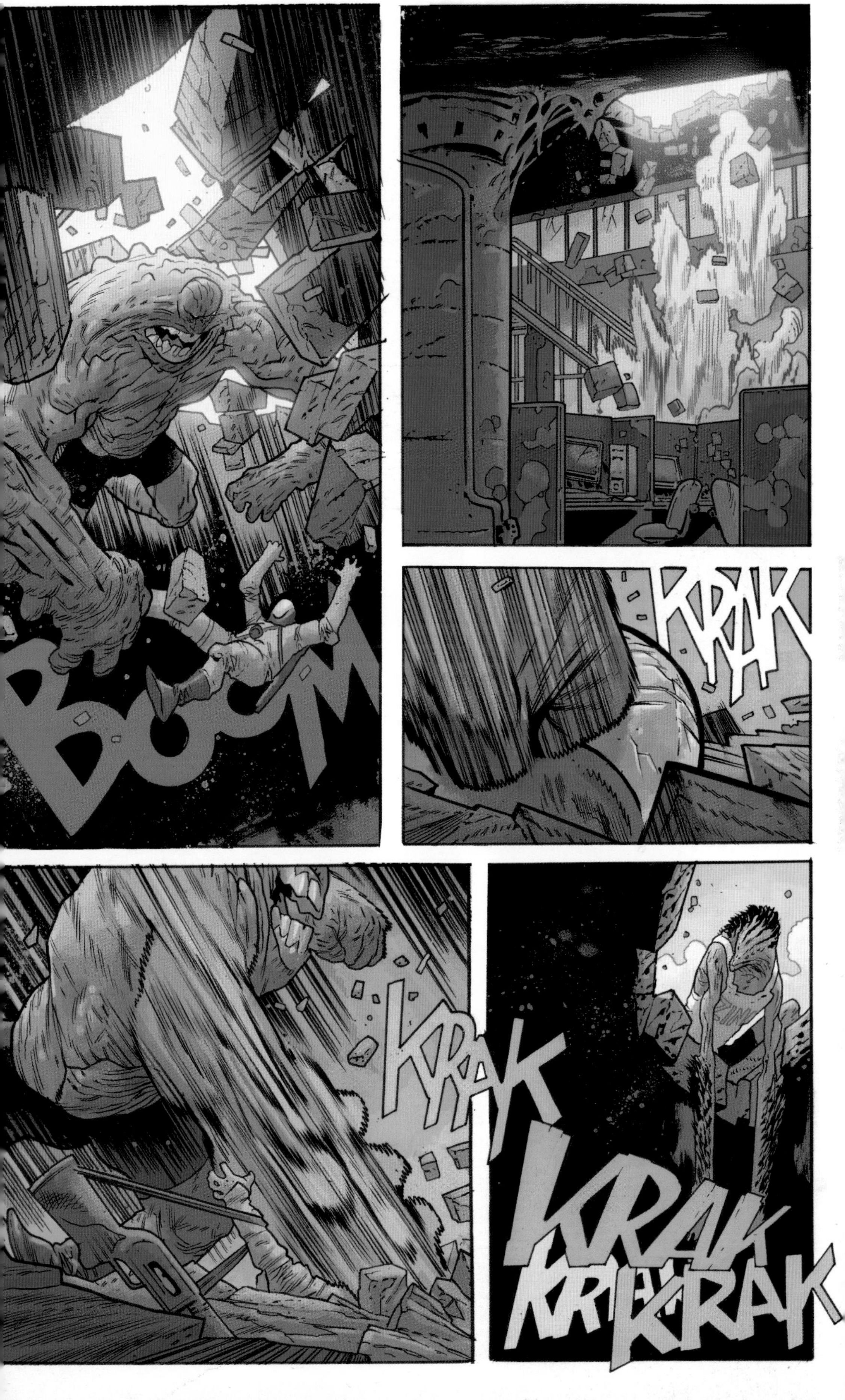
BOOM
KRAK
KRAK
KRAK
KRAK

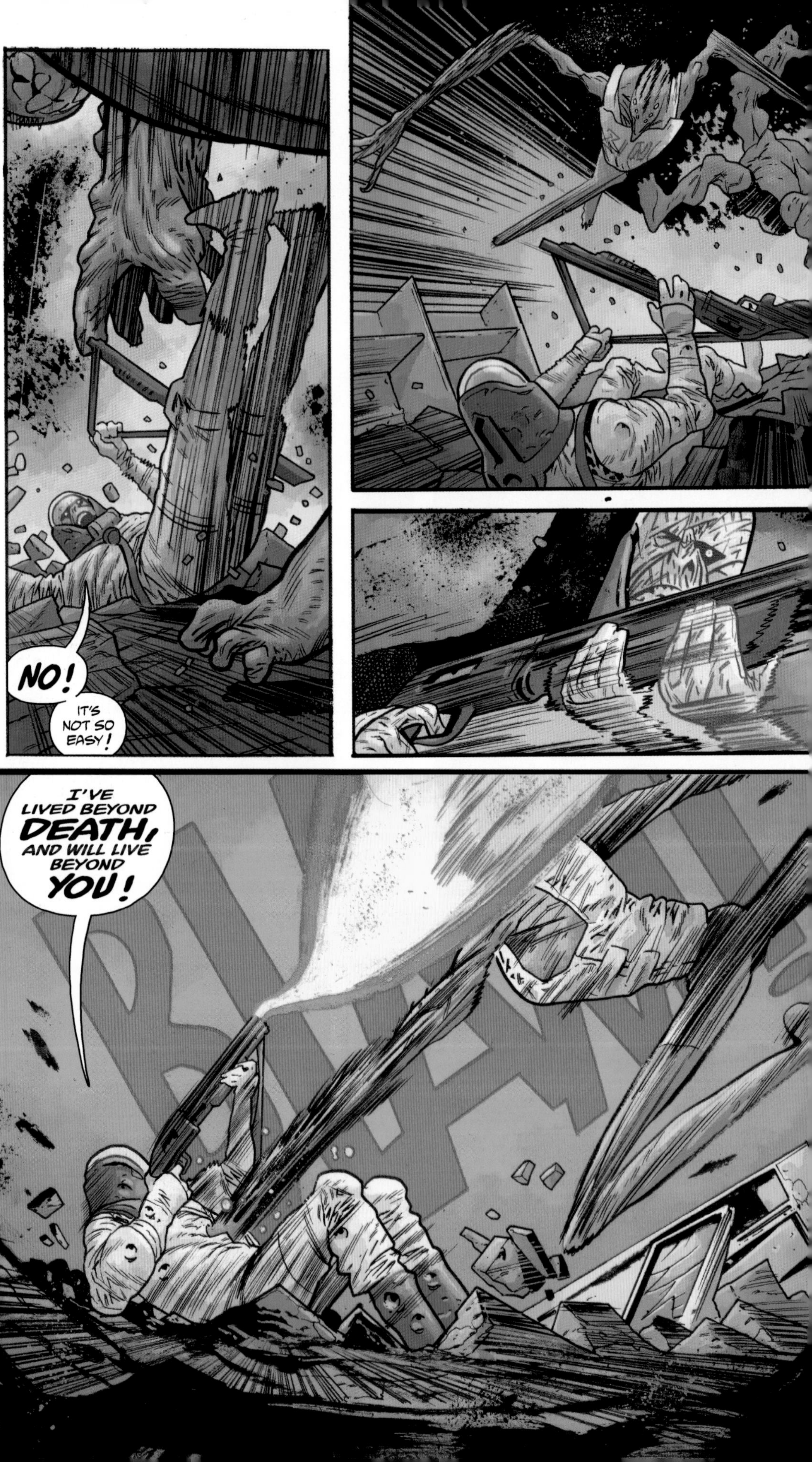
NO!
IT'S NOT SO EASY!
I'VE LIVED BEYOND DEATH, AND WILL LIVE BEYOND YOU!

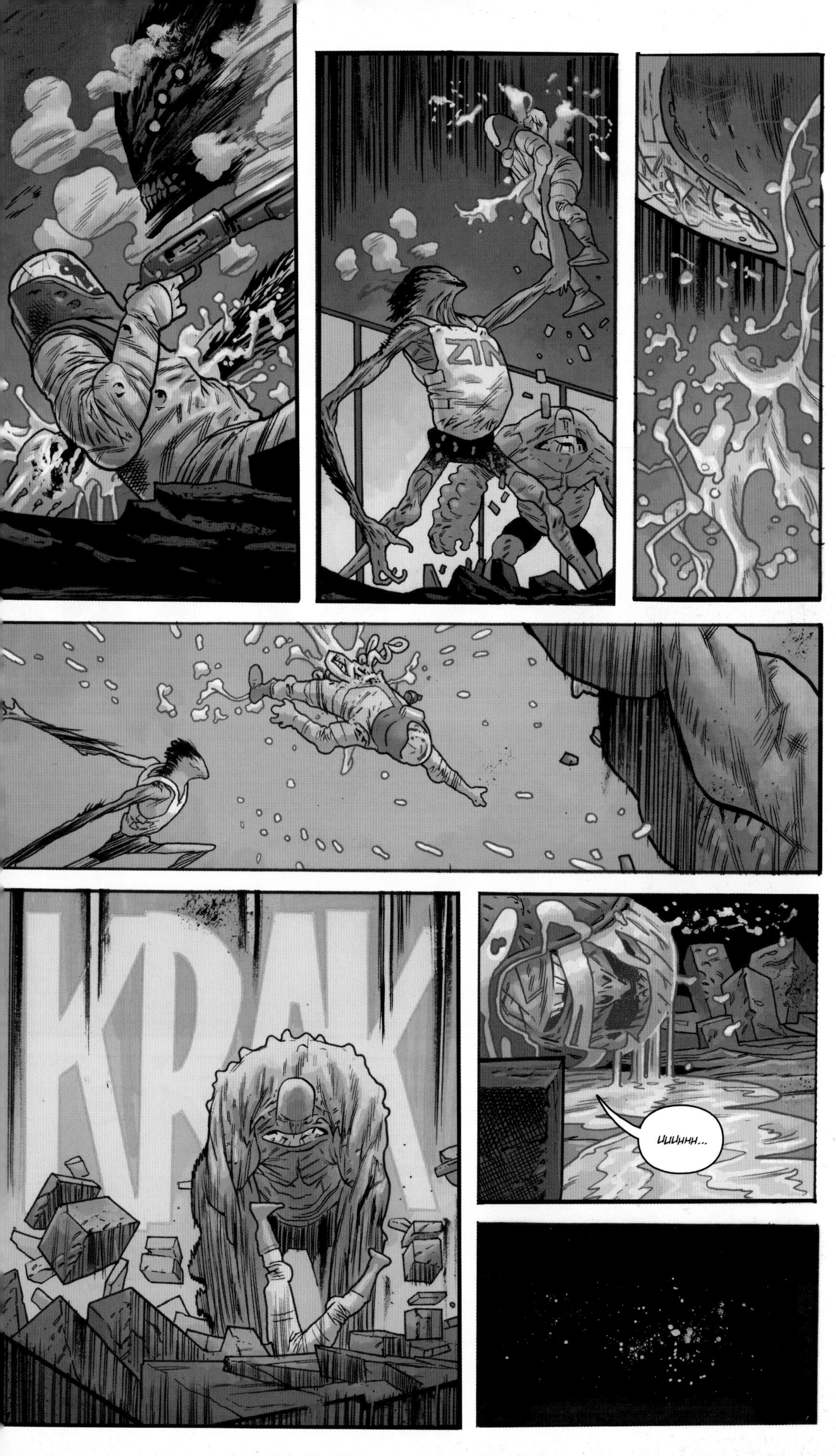
ZIN
KRAK
UUUHHH...

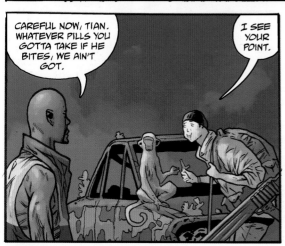

CAREFUL NOW, TIAN. WHATEVER PILLS YOU GOTTA TAKE IF HE BITES, WE AIN'T GOT.

I SEE YOUR POINT.

MONKEYS AND HYENAS IN NEW YORK. I GUESS THEY BROKE LOOSE FROM THE ZOOS AFTER THE QUAKES?

OR SOMEONE LET 'EM OUT.

THESE BOYS HUNTED 'ROUND MIDTOWN A FEW WEEKS BEFORE I CAUGHT 'EM.

I DON'T SAY THEY MAKE GOOD PETS, BUT THEY KEEP FOLKS THE HELL AWAY. EVEN ZINCO TROOPS.

'BOUT EIGHT MONTHS AGO, I SAW A TIGER WALKING RIGHT DOWN FOURTEENTH STREET BETWEEN THIRD AND FOURTH.

YOU'RE RIGHT ABOUT THAT. KEPT *ME* AWAY.

A TIGER'D KEEP *MORE* FOLKS AWAY.

HERE.

LIZ, SHE SAID TO GIVE YOU THESE.

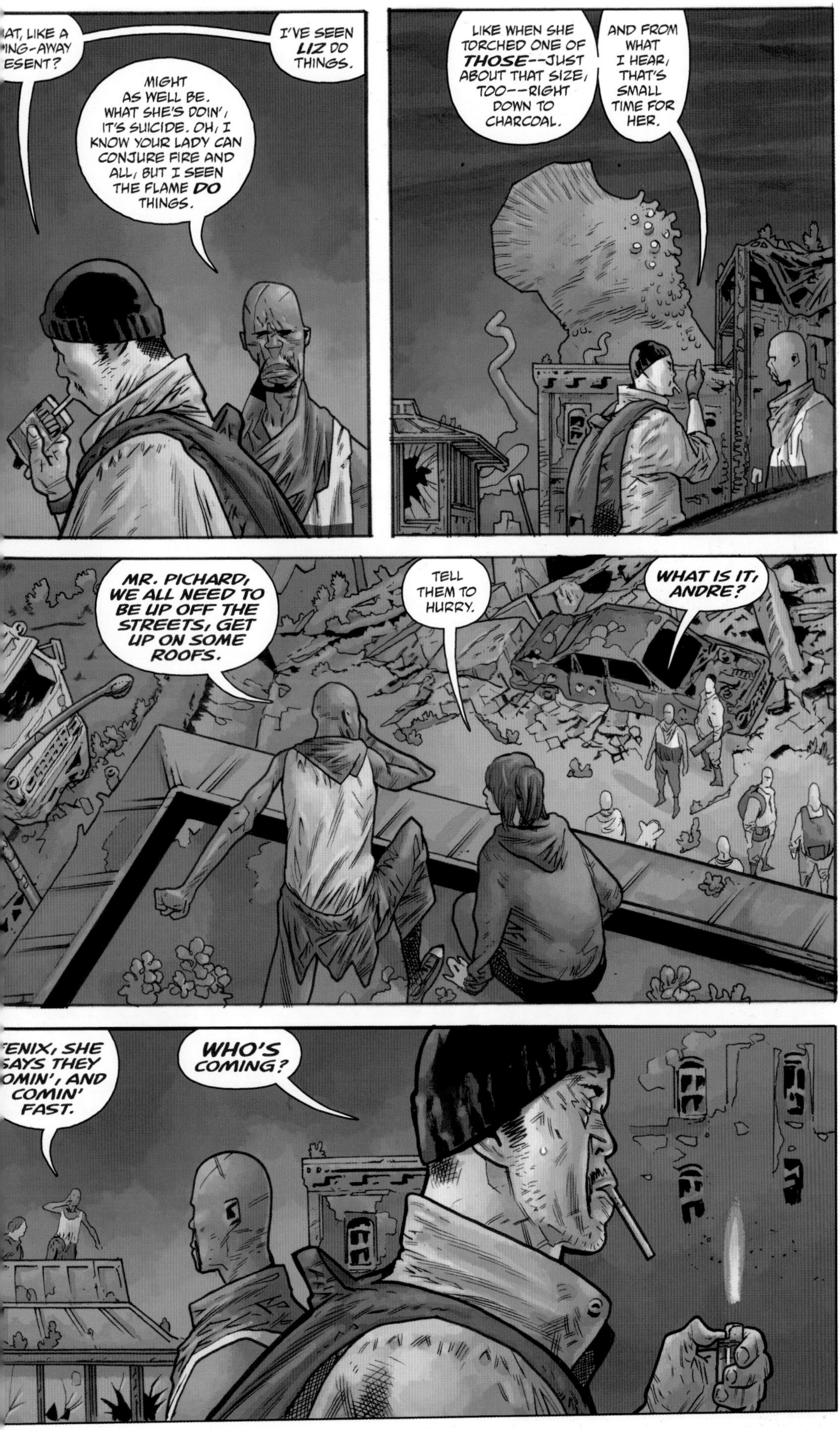

AT, LIKE A
ING-AWAY
ESENT?
I'VE SEEN LIZ DO THINGS.
MIGHT AS WELL BE. WHAT SHE'S DOIN', IT'S SUICIDE. OH, I KNOW YOUR LADY CAN CONJURE FIRE AND ALL, BUT I SEEN THE FLAME DO THINGS.
LIKE WHEN SHE TORCHED ONE OF THOSE--JUST ABOUT THAT SIZE, TOO--RIGHT DOWN TO CHARCOAL.
AND FROM WHAT I HEAR, THAT'S SMALL TIME FOR HER.
MR. PICHARD, WE ALL NEED TO BE UP OFF THE STREETS, GET UP ON SOME ROOFS.
TELL THEM TO HURRY.
WHAT IS IT, ANDRE?
ENIX, SHE
AYS THEY
OMIN', AND
COMIN'
FAST.
WHO'S COMING?

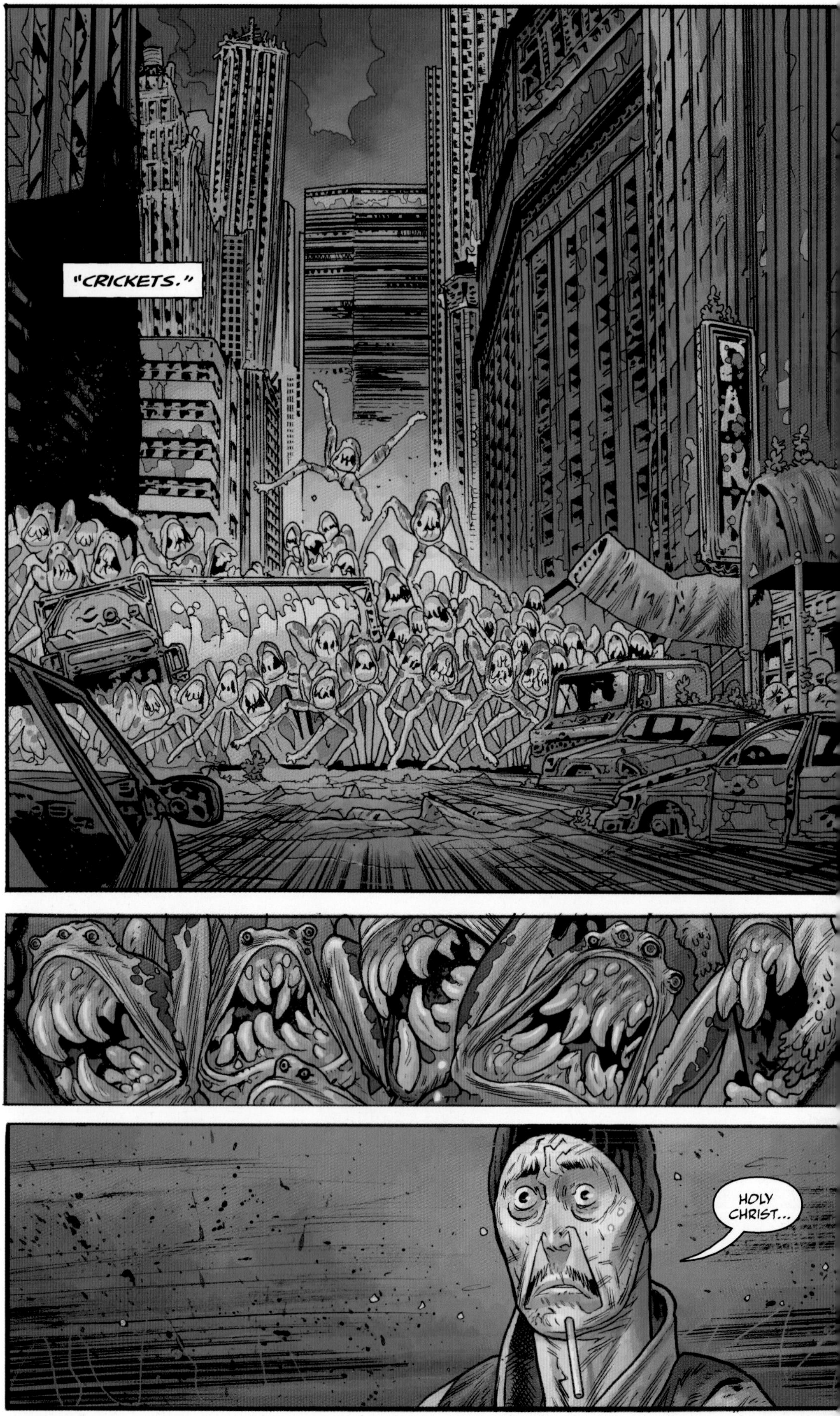
"CRICKETS."
HOLY CHRIST...

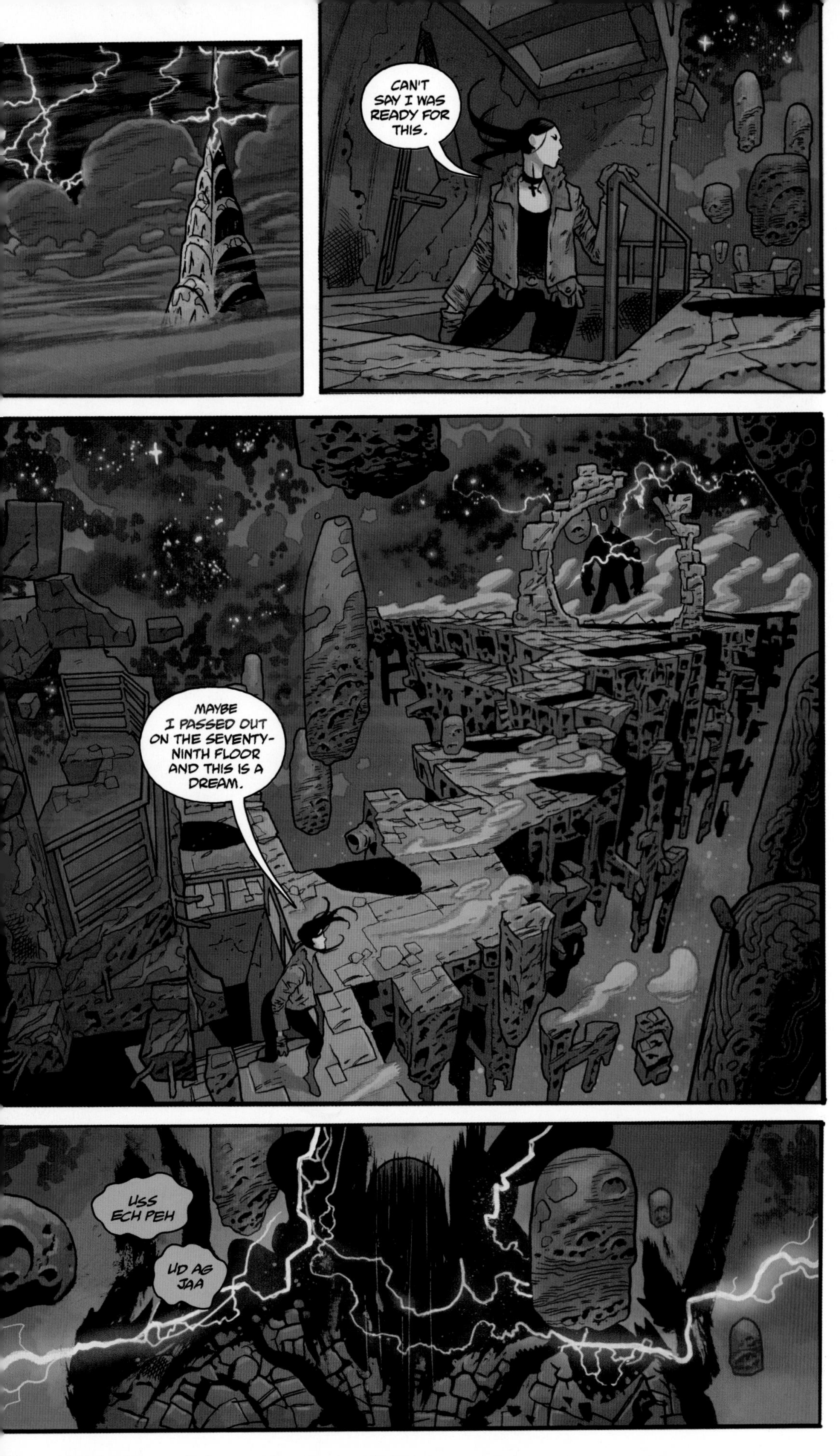
CAN'T SAY I WAS READY FOR THIS.
MAYBE I PASSED OUT ON THE SEVENTY-NINTH FLOOR AND THIS IS A DREAM.
USS ECH PEH
UD AG JAA

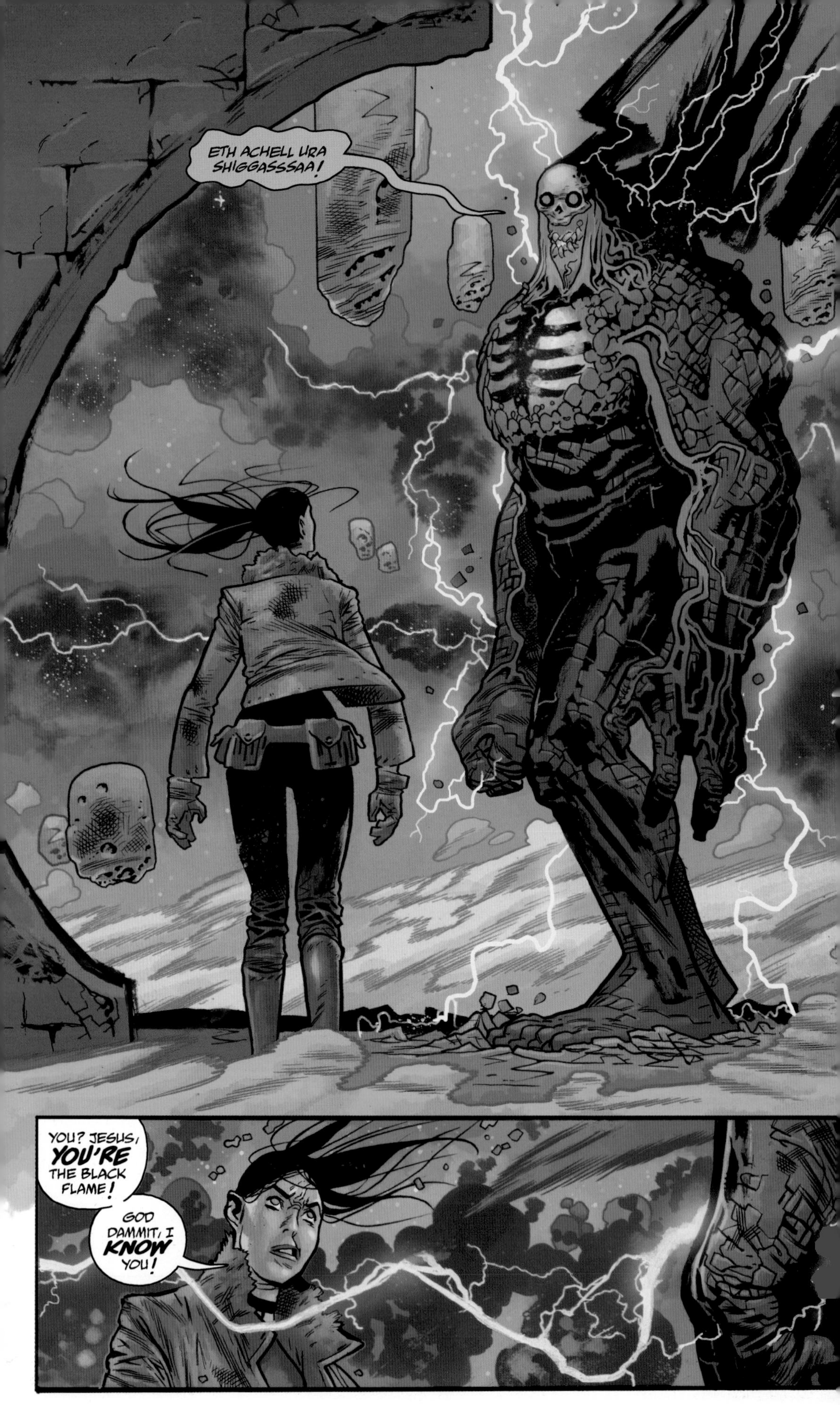
ETH ACHELL URA SHIGGASSSAA!
YOU? JESUS, YOU'RE THE BLACK FLAME!
GOD DAMMIT, I KNOW YOU!

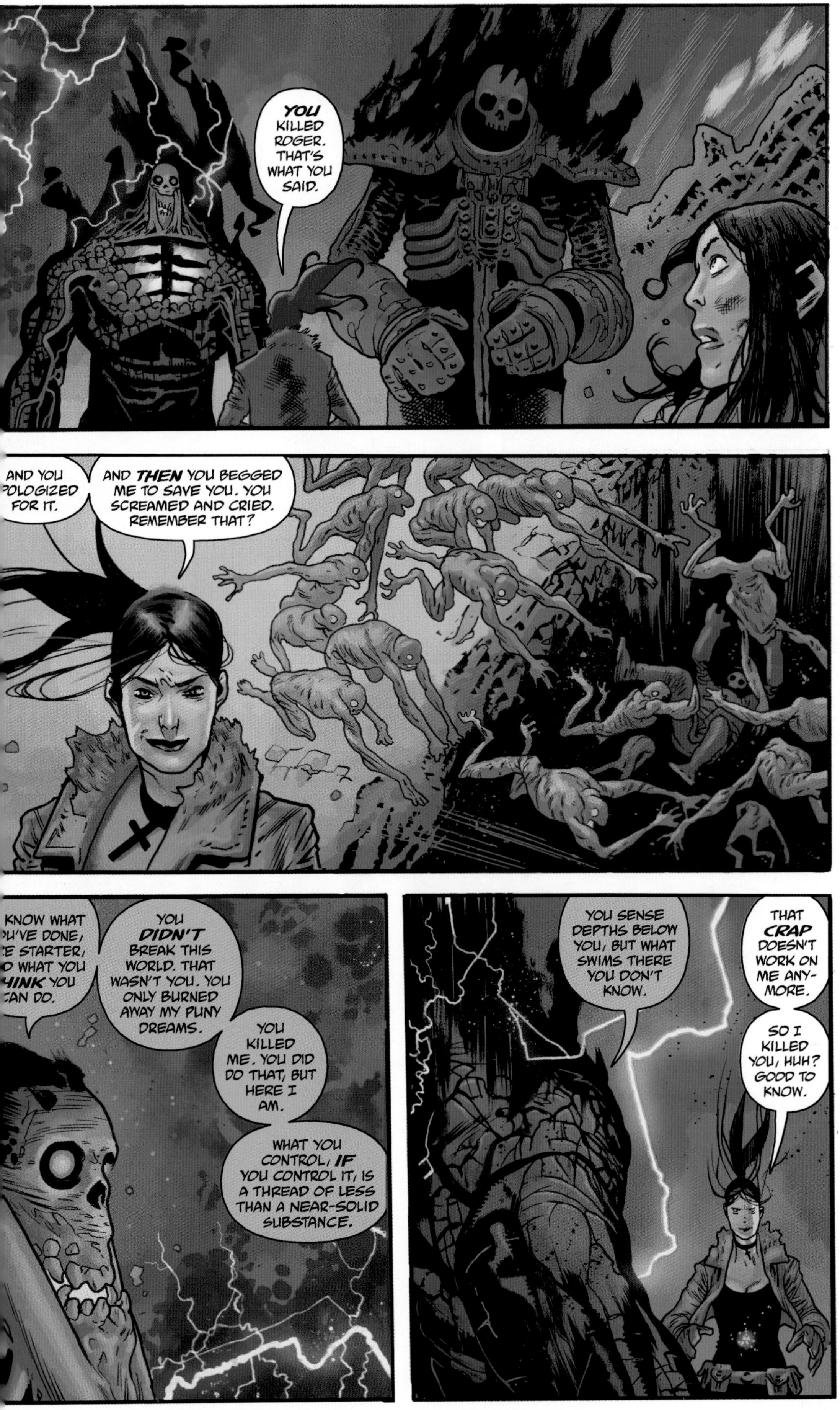
YOU KILLED ROGER. THAT'S WHAT YOU SAID.
AND YOU POLOGIZED FOR IT.
AND THEN YOU BEGGED ME TO SAVE YOU. YOU SCREAMED AND CRIED. REMEMBER THAT?
KNOW WHAT U'VE DONE, E STARTER, D WHAT YOU HINK YOU CAN DO.
YOU DIDN'T BREAK THIS WORLD. THAT WASN'T YOU. YOU ONLY BURNED AWAY MY PUNY DREAMS.
YOU KILLED ME. YOU DID DO THAT, BUT HERE I AM.
WHAT YOU CONTROL, IF YOU CONTROL IT, IS A THREAD OF LESS THAN A NEAR-SOLID SUBSTANCE.
YOU SENSE DEPTHS BELOW YOU, BUT WHAT SWIMS THERE YOU DON'T KNOW.
THAT CRAP DOESN'T WORK ON ME ANYMORE.
SO I KILLED YOU, HUH? GOOD TO KNOW.

THIS TIME I'LL GET IT **RIGHT!**

WHOOOOOSH

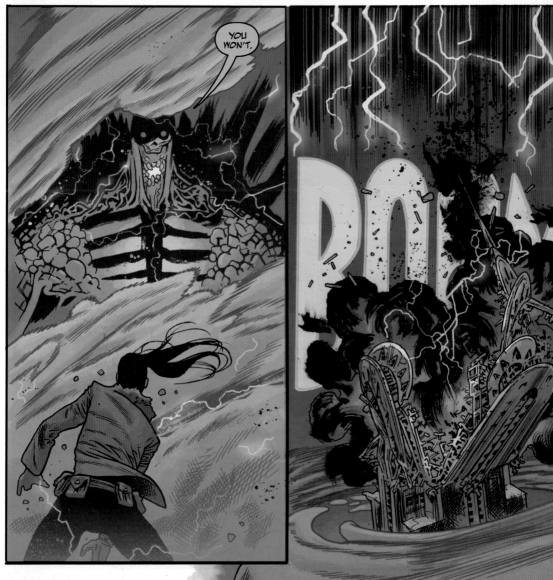

YOU WON'T.

BOA

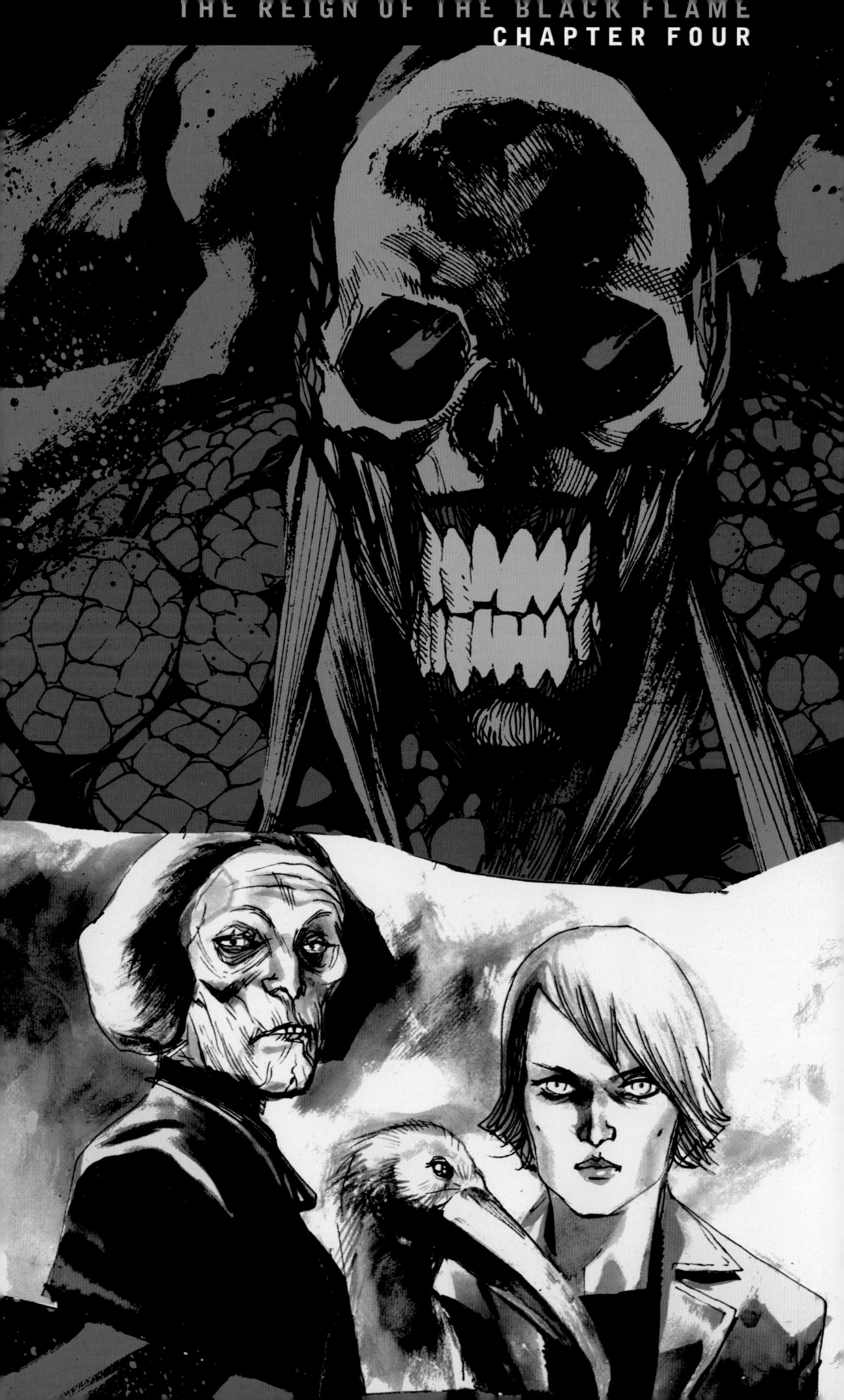
THE REIGN OF THE BLACK FLAME
CHAPTER FOUR

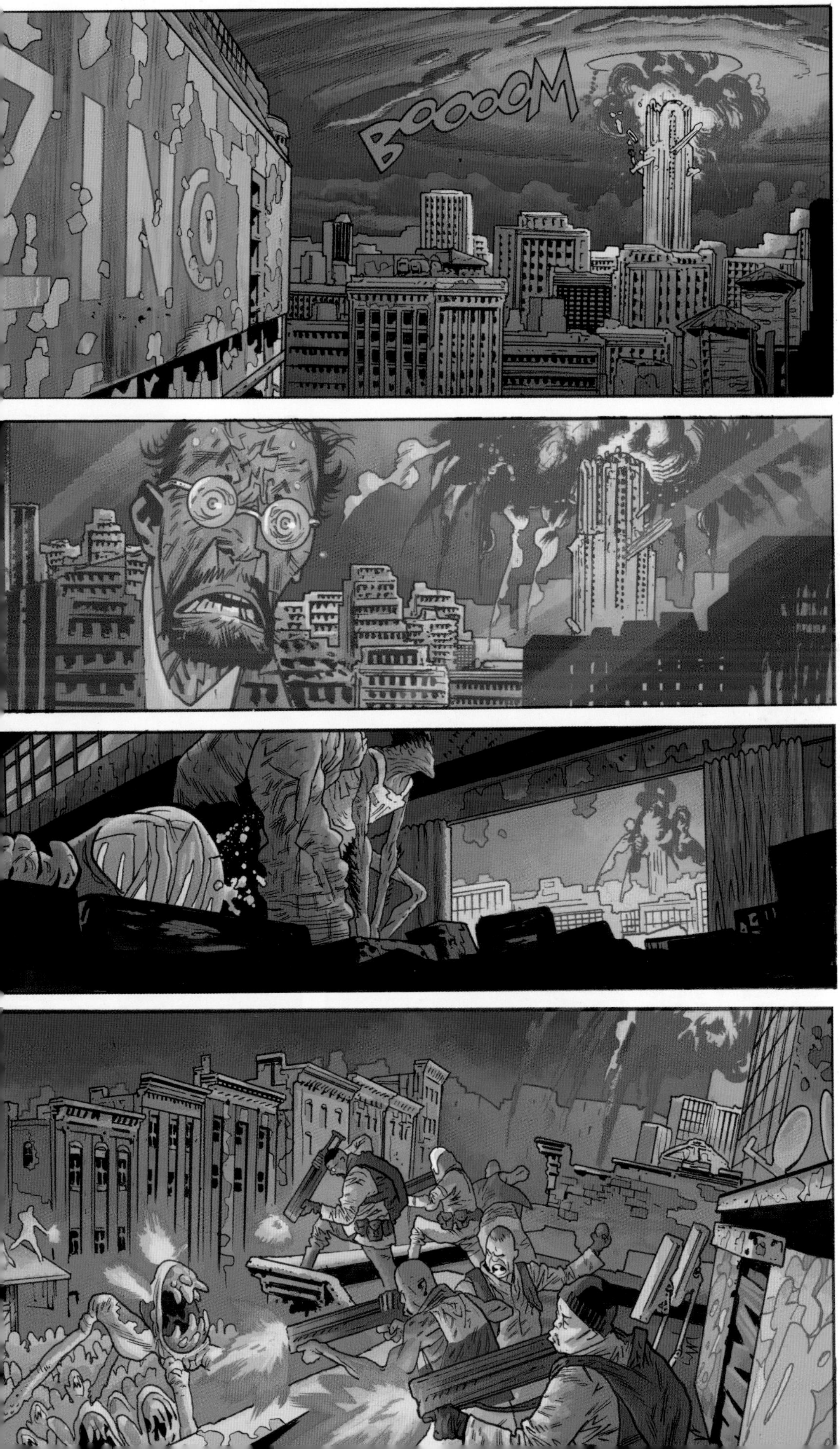
BOOOOM

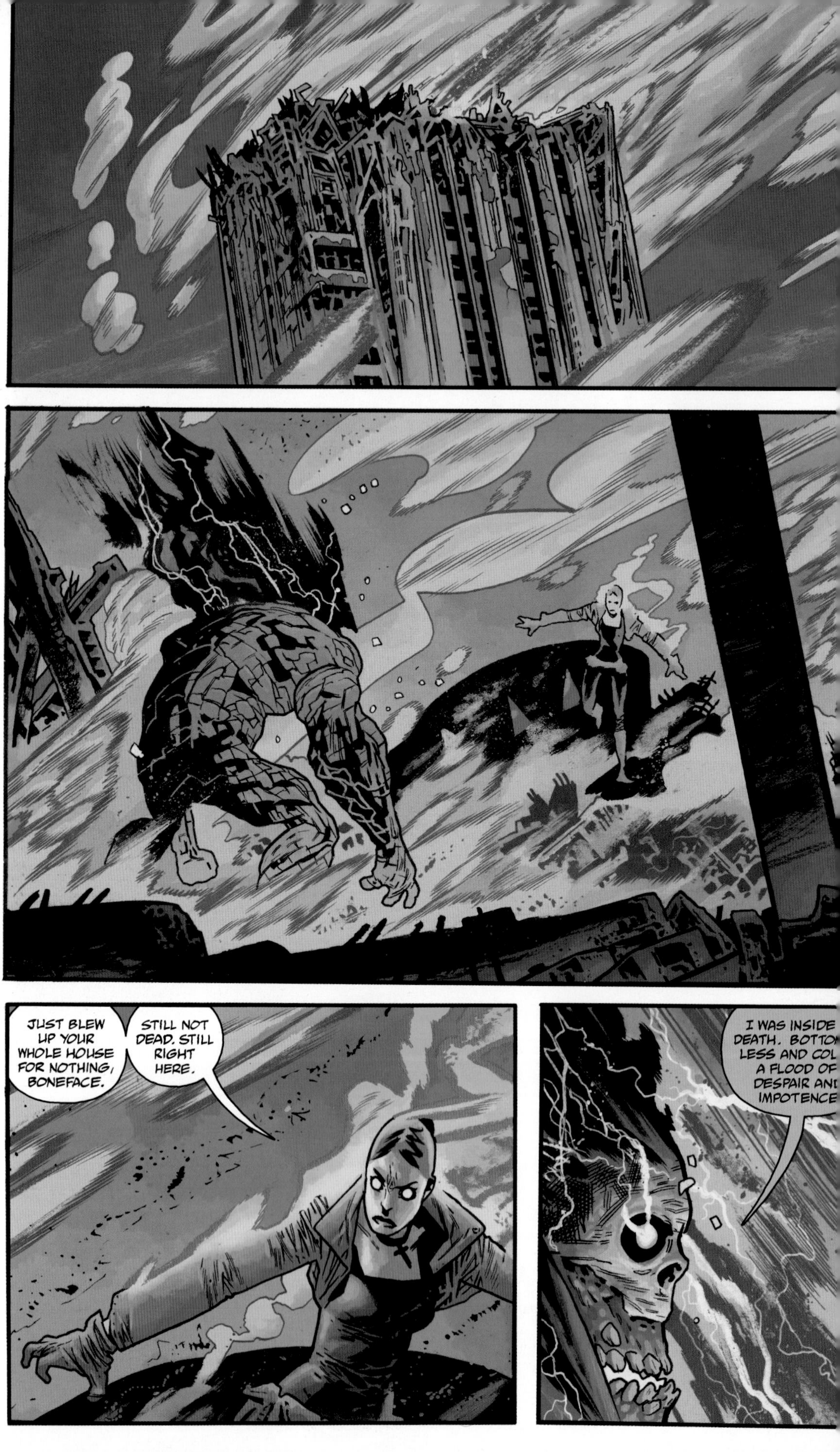
JUST BLEW UP YOUR WHOLE HOUSE FOR NOTHING, BONEFACE.
STILL NOT DEAD. STILL RIGHT HERE.
I WAS INSIDE DEATH. BOTTO LESS AND COL A FLOOD OF DESPAIR AN IMPOTENCE

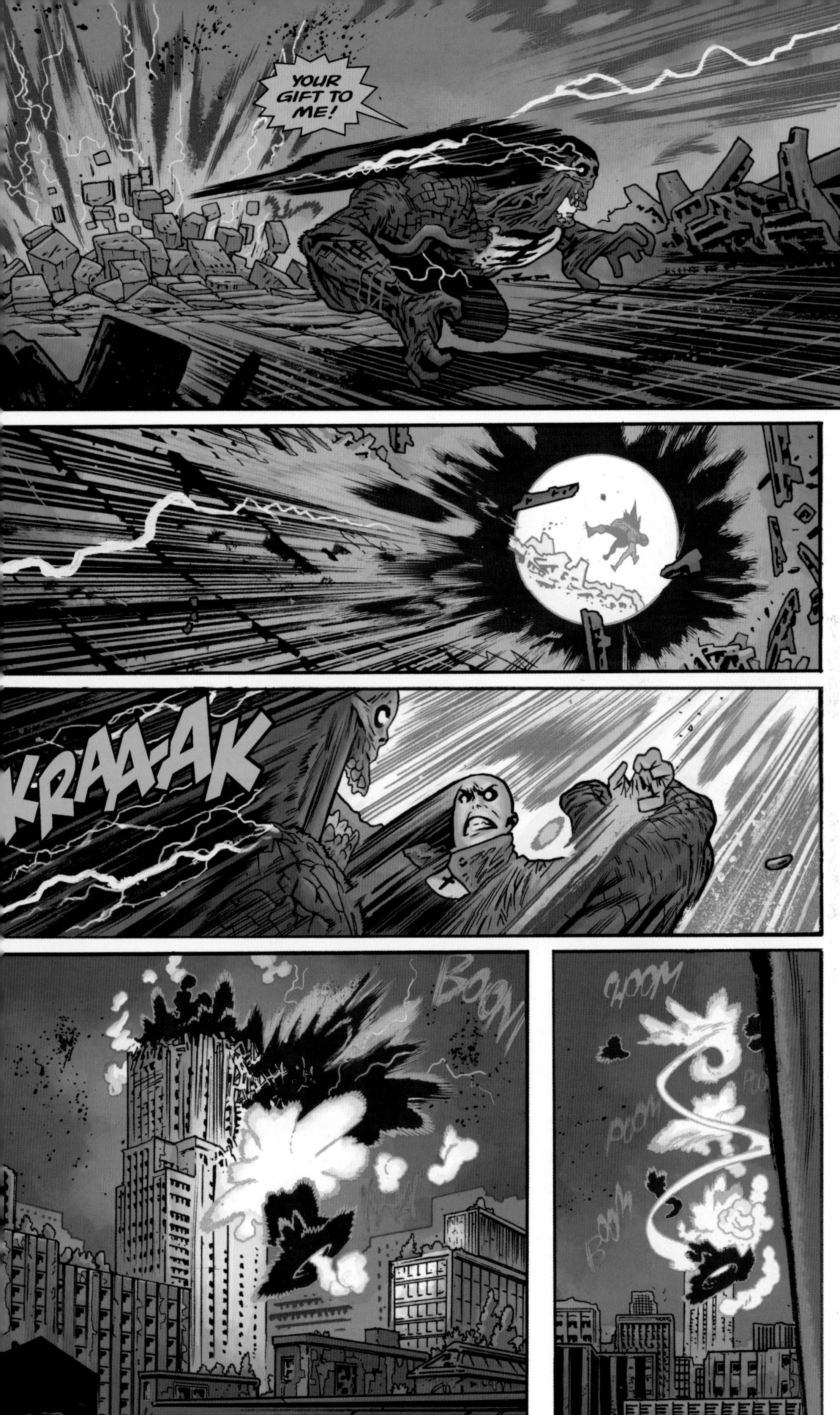
YOUR GIFT TO ME!
KRAA-AK
BOOM
POOM
BOOM

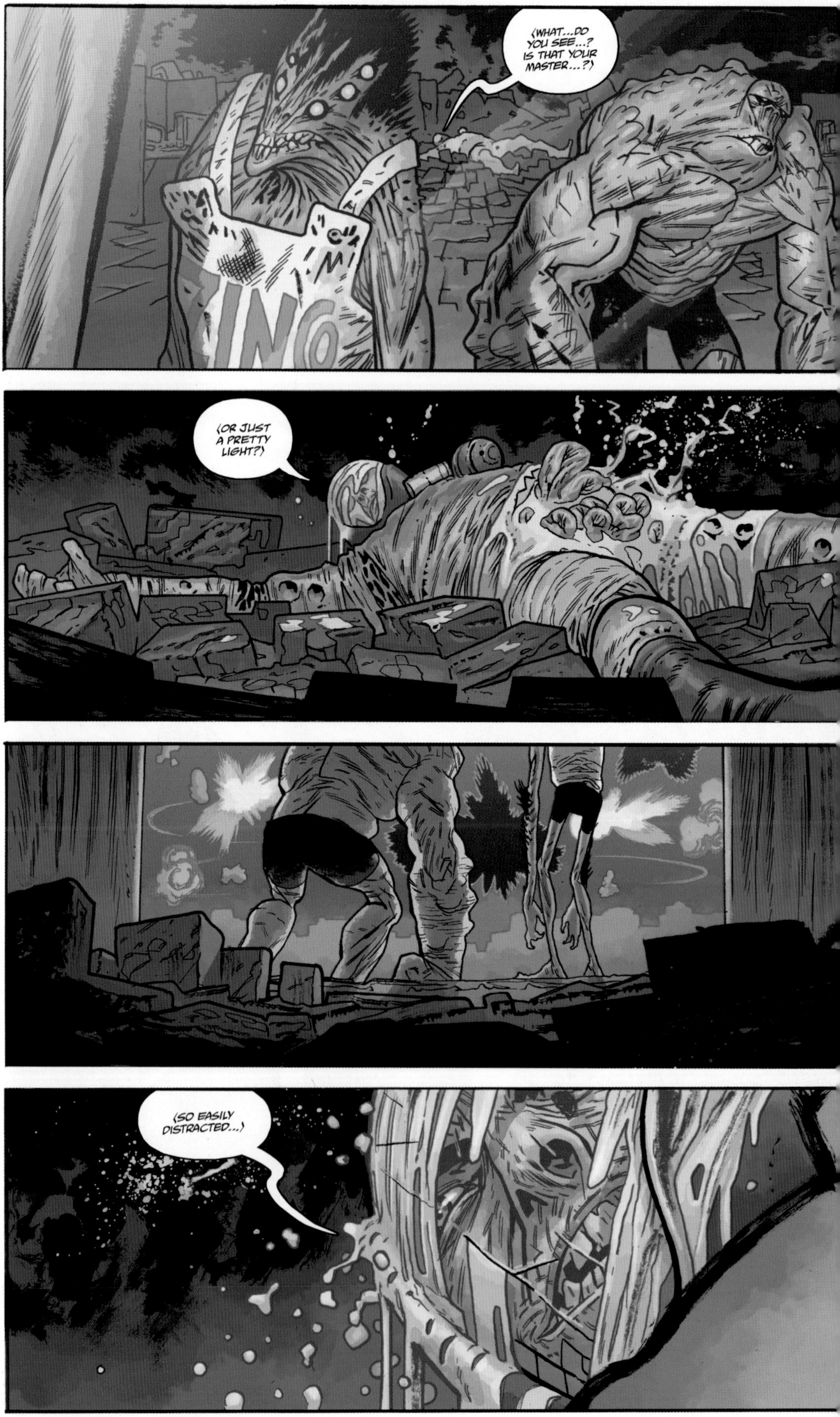
⟨WHAT...DO YOU SEE...? IS THAT YOUR MASTER...?⟩
⟨OR JUST A PRETTY LIGHT?⟩
⟨SO EASILY DISTRACTED...⟩

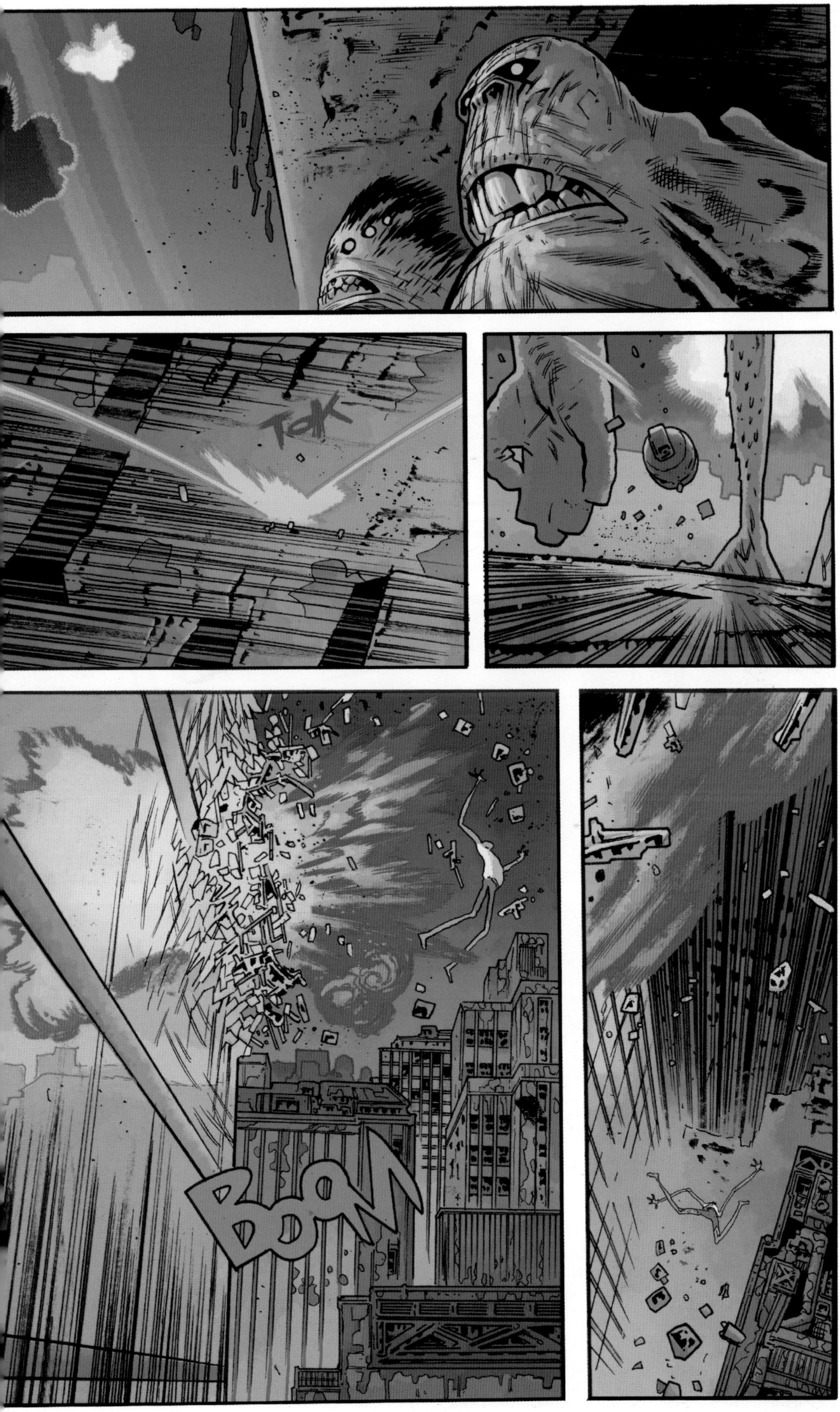
TOK
BOOM

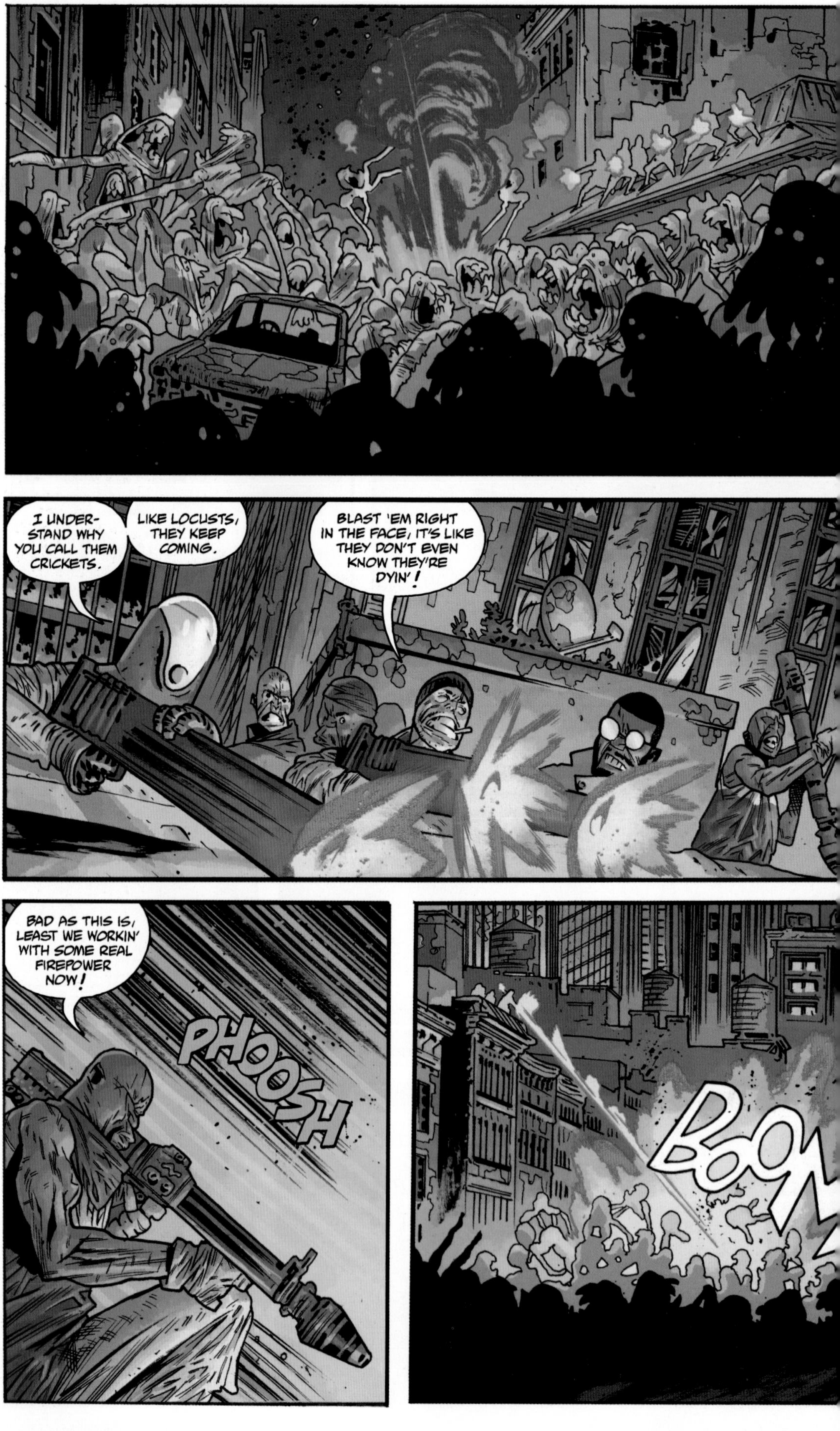

I UNDER-STAND WHY YOU CALL THEM CRICKETS.
LIKE LOCUSTS, THEY KEEP COMING.
BLAST 'EM RIGHT IN THE FACE, IT'S LIKE THEY DON'T EVEN KNOW THEY'RE DYIN'!
BAD AS THIS IS, LEAST WE WORKIN' WITH SOME REAL FIREPOWER NOW!
PHOOSH
BOOM

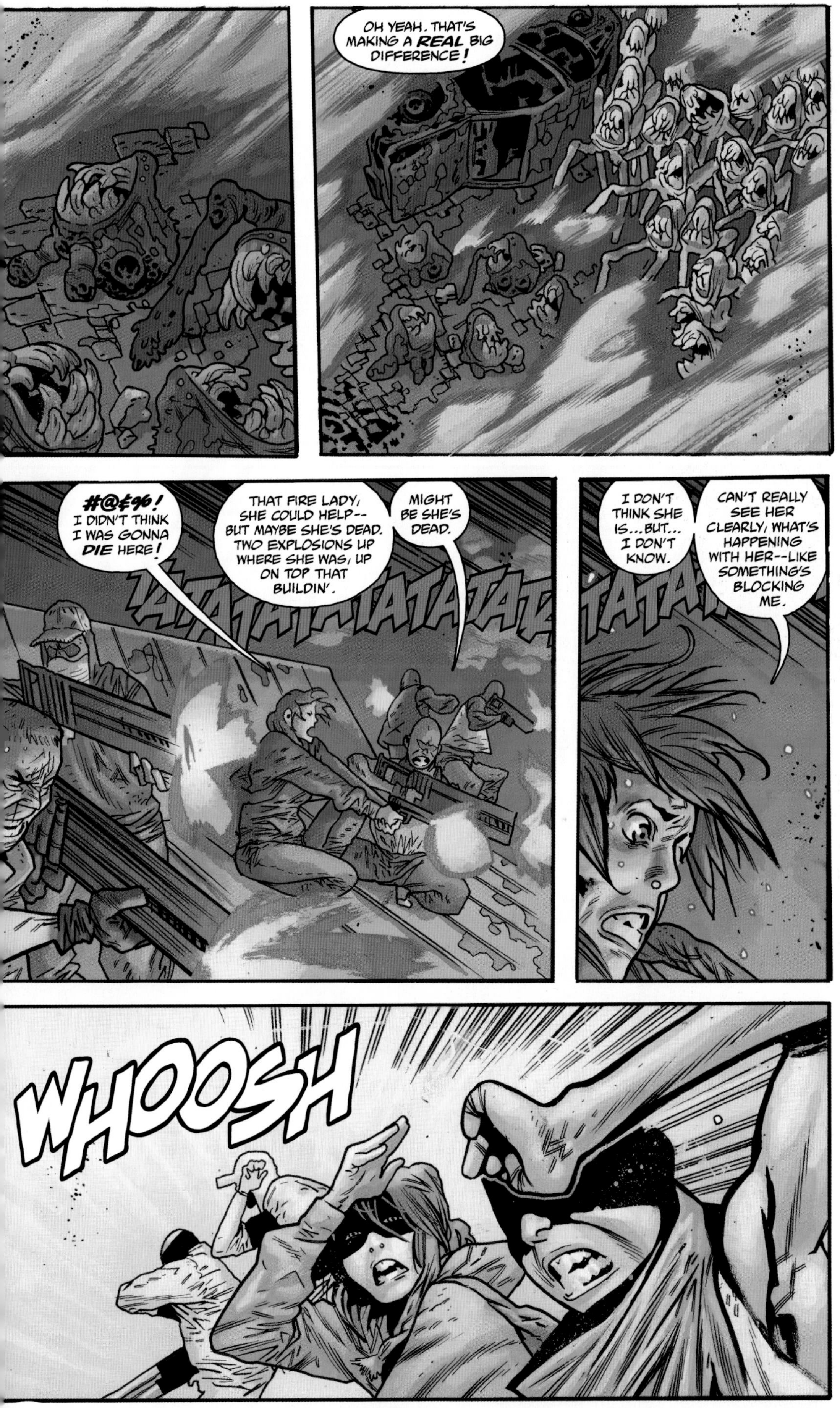
OH YEAH. THAT'S MAKING A REAL BIG DIFFERENCE!
#@¢%! I DIDN'T THINK I WAS GONNA DIE HERE!
THAT FIRE LADY, SHE COULD HELP-- BUT MAYBE SHE'S DEAD. TWO EXPLOSIONS UP WHERE SHE WAS, UP ON TOP THAT BUILDIN'.
MIGHT BE SHE'S DEAD.
TATATATATATATATA
I DON'T THINK SHE IS...BUT... I DON'T KNOW.
CAN'T REALLY SEE HER CLEARLY, WHAT'S HAPPENING WITH HER--LIKE SOMETHING'S BLOCKING ME.
TATAT
WHOOSH

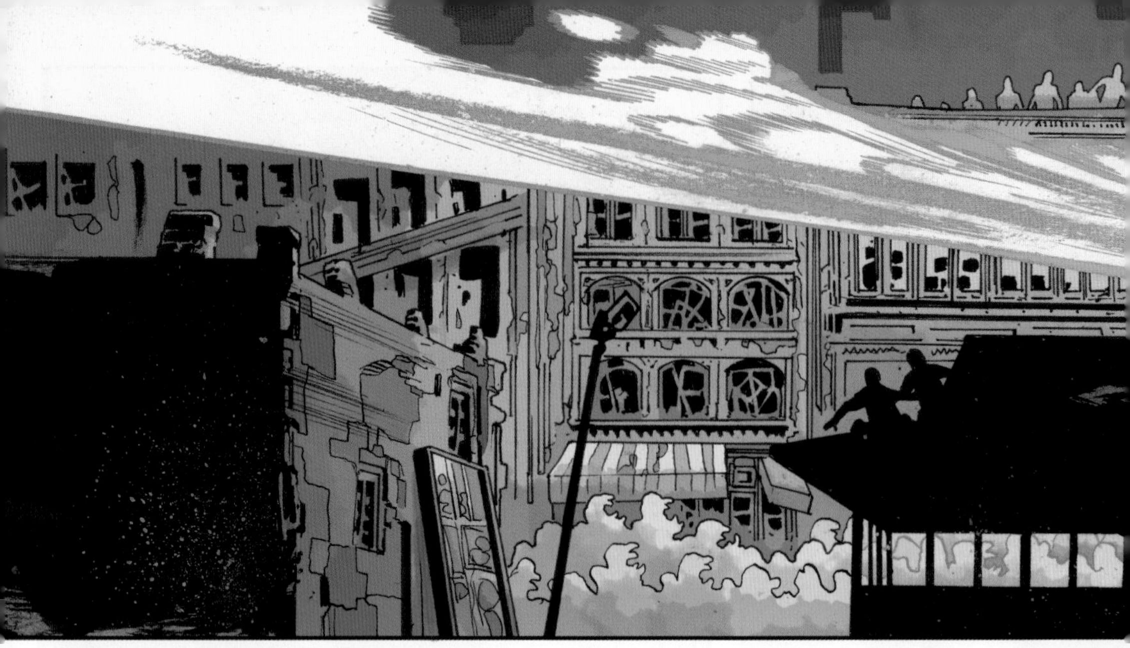

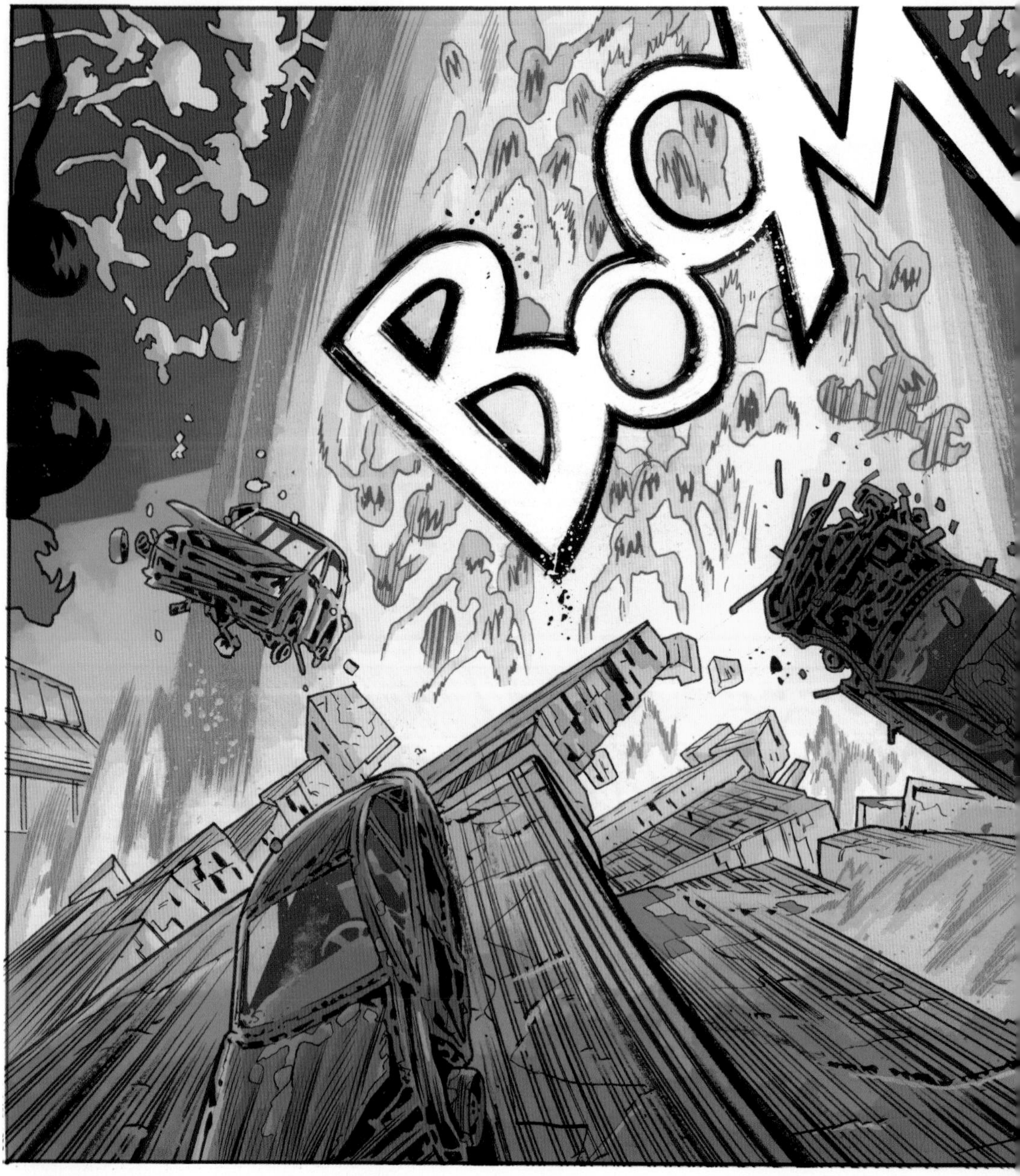
BOOM

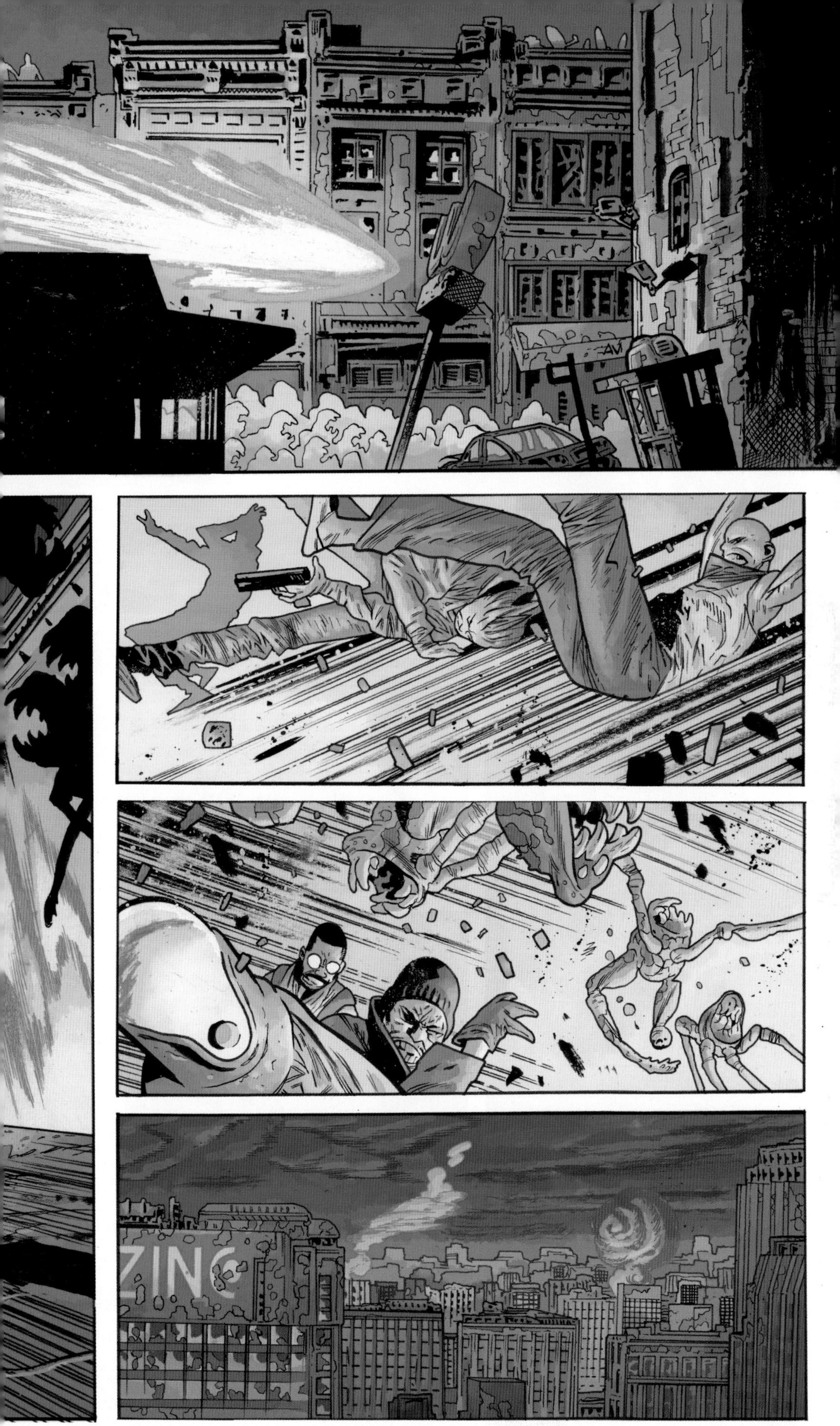
ZINC

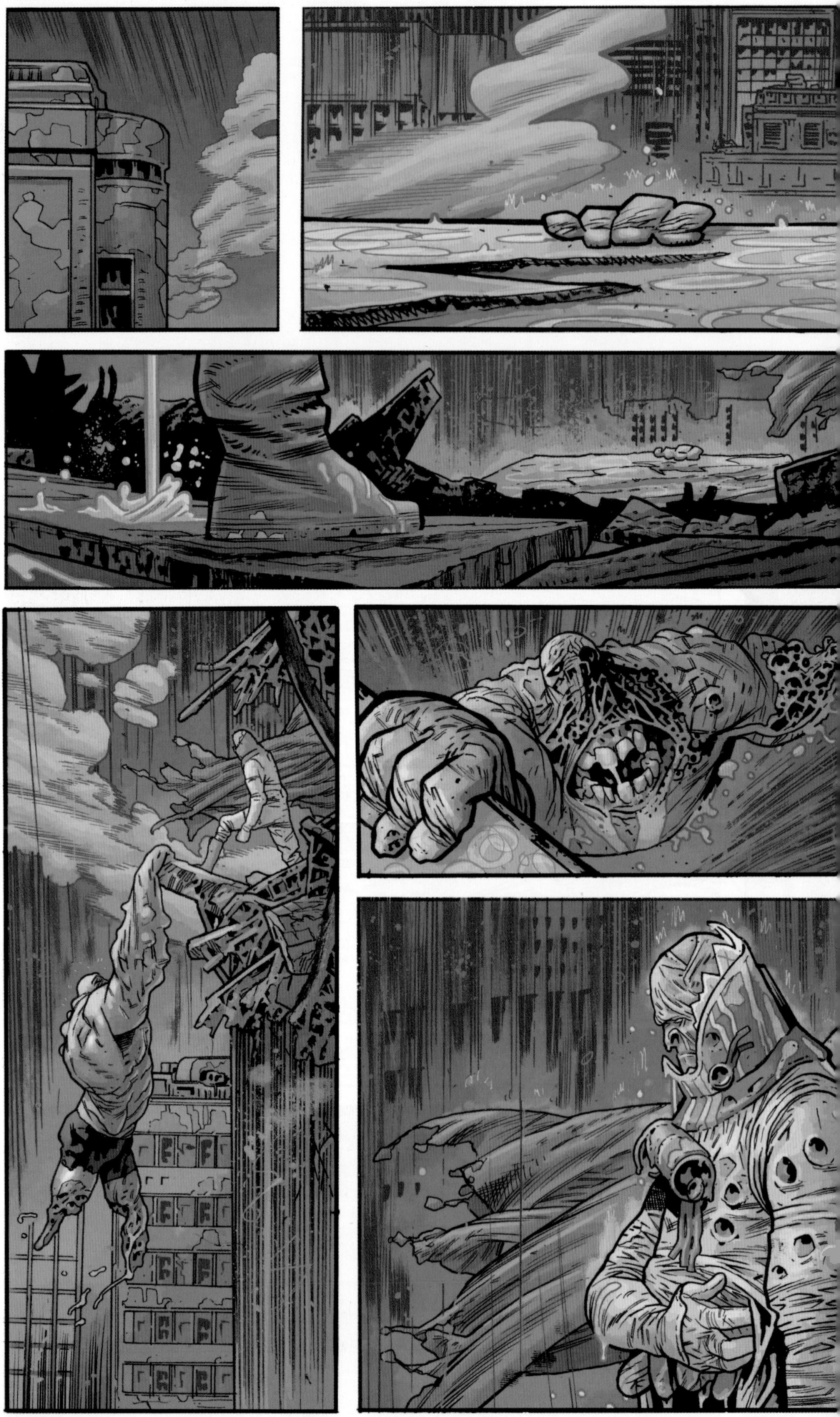

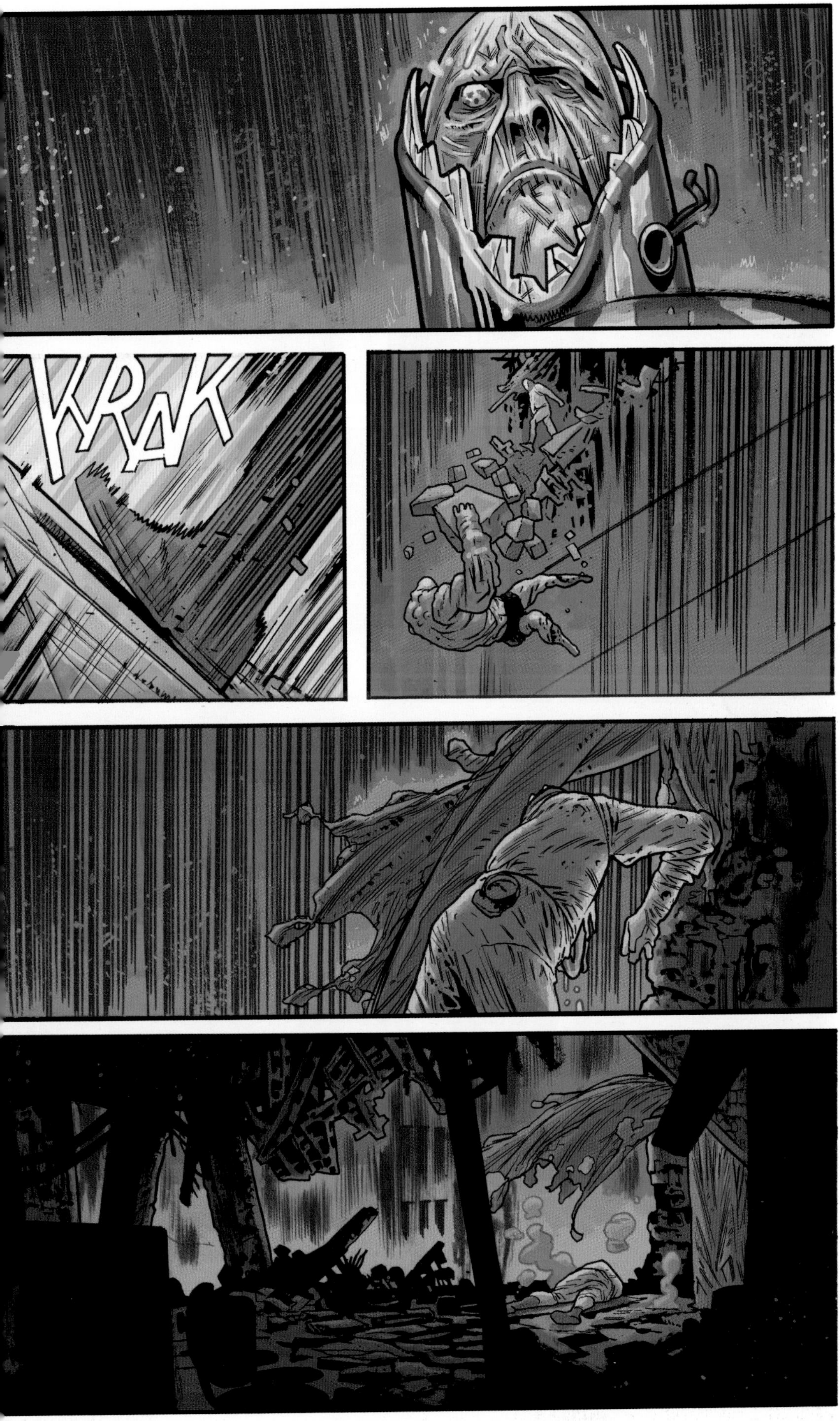
KRAK

"YOU WERE HAPPY, FIRESTARTER."

I SAW YOU SMILE WHEN YOU FOUND OUT THAT YOU'D KILLED ME ONCE.

WHEN YOU DID THAT, DO YOU KNOW WHERE YOU SENT ME?

EVERY DISCIPLE OF THE OGDRU JAHAD WANTS TO BE WHERE I'VE BEEN.

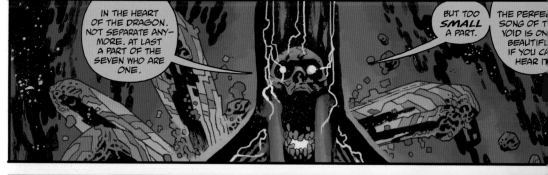

IN THE HEART OF THE DRAGON. NOT SEPARATE ANY—MORE. AT LAST A PART OF THE SEVEN WHO ARE ONE.

BUT TOO *SMALL* A PART.

THE PERFE SONG OF T VOID IS ON BEAUTIFL IF YOU C HEAR IT

MIGHTY MUSIC–– BUT NOT MINE.

THE THROBBING OF LIFE, ALL LIFE, IS WHAT'S PRECIOUS.

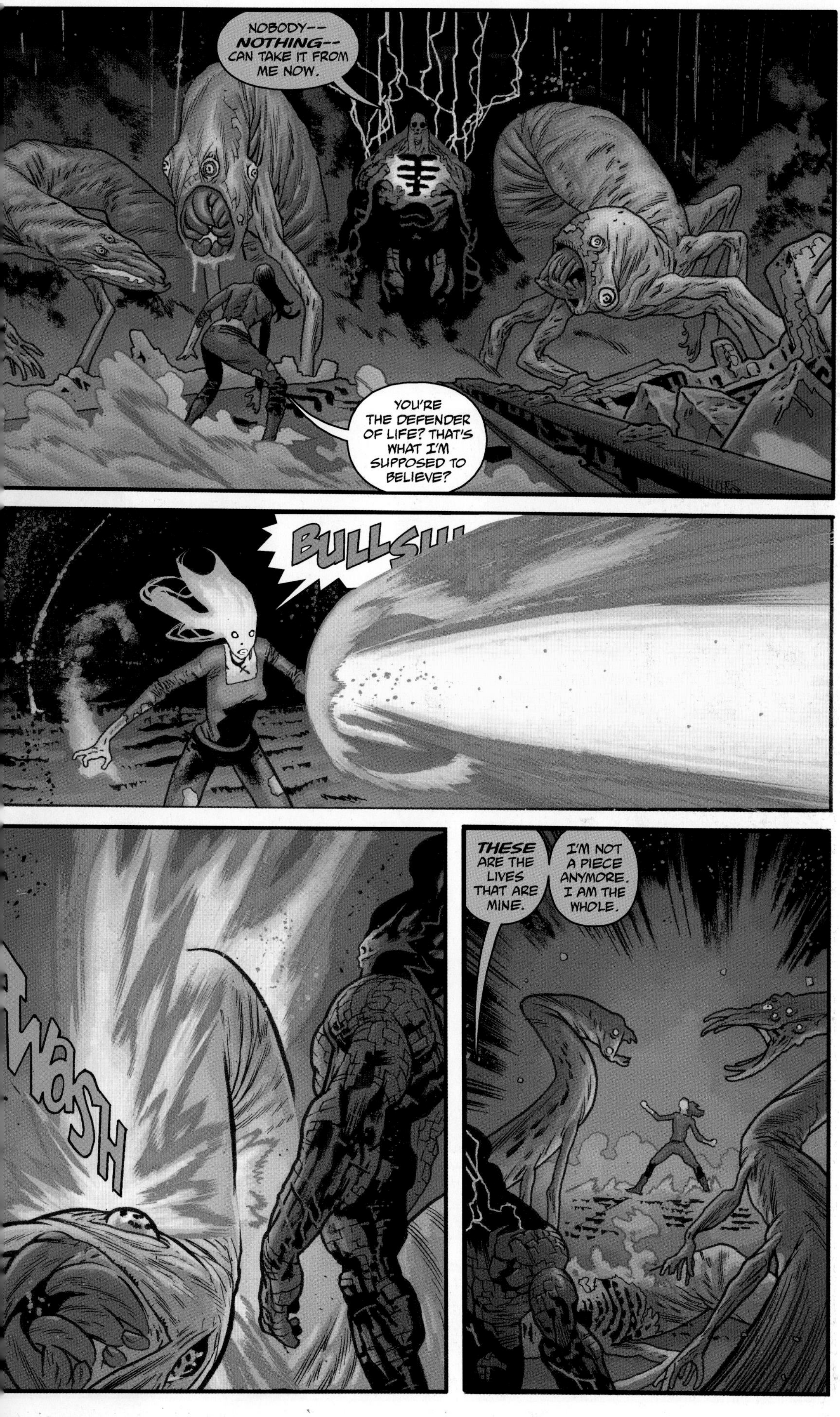
NOBODY-- NOTHING-- CAN TAKE IT FROM ME NOW.
YOU'RE THE DEFENDER OF LIFE? THAT'S WHAT I'M SUPPOSED TO BELIEVE?
BULLSH
WASH
THESE ARE THE LIVES THAT ARE MINE.
I'M NOT A PIECE ANYMORE. I AM THE WHOLE.

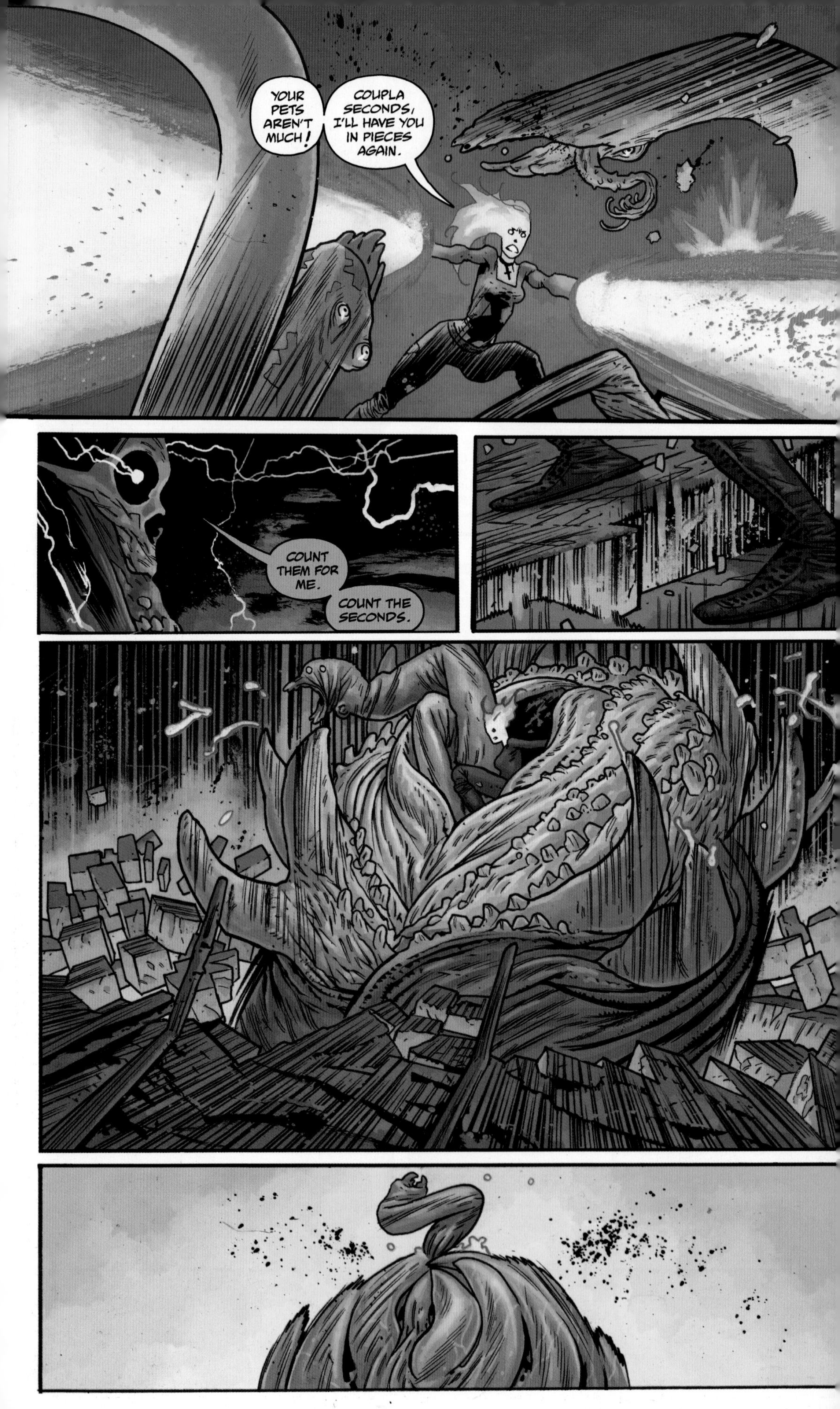
YOUR PETS AREN'T MUCH!
COUPLA SECONDS, I'LL HAVE YOU IN PIECES AGAIN.
COUNT THEM FOR ME.
COUNT THE SECONDS.

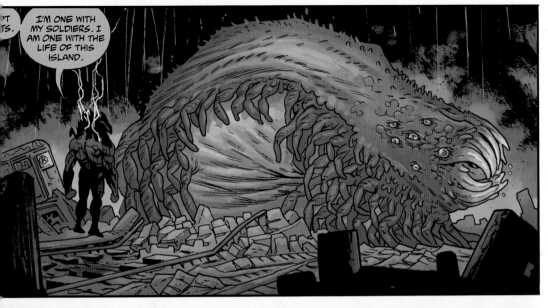

I'M ONE WITH MY SOLDIERS. I AM ONE WITH THE LIFE OF THIS ISLAND.

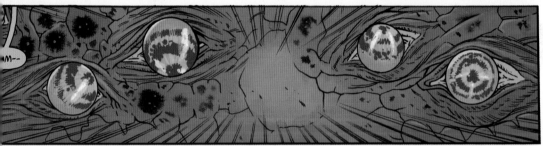

SPLORCH!

FWOOSH!

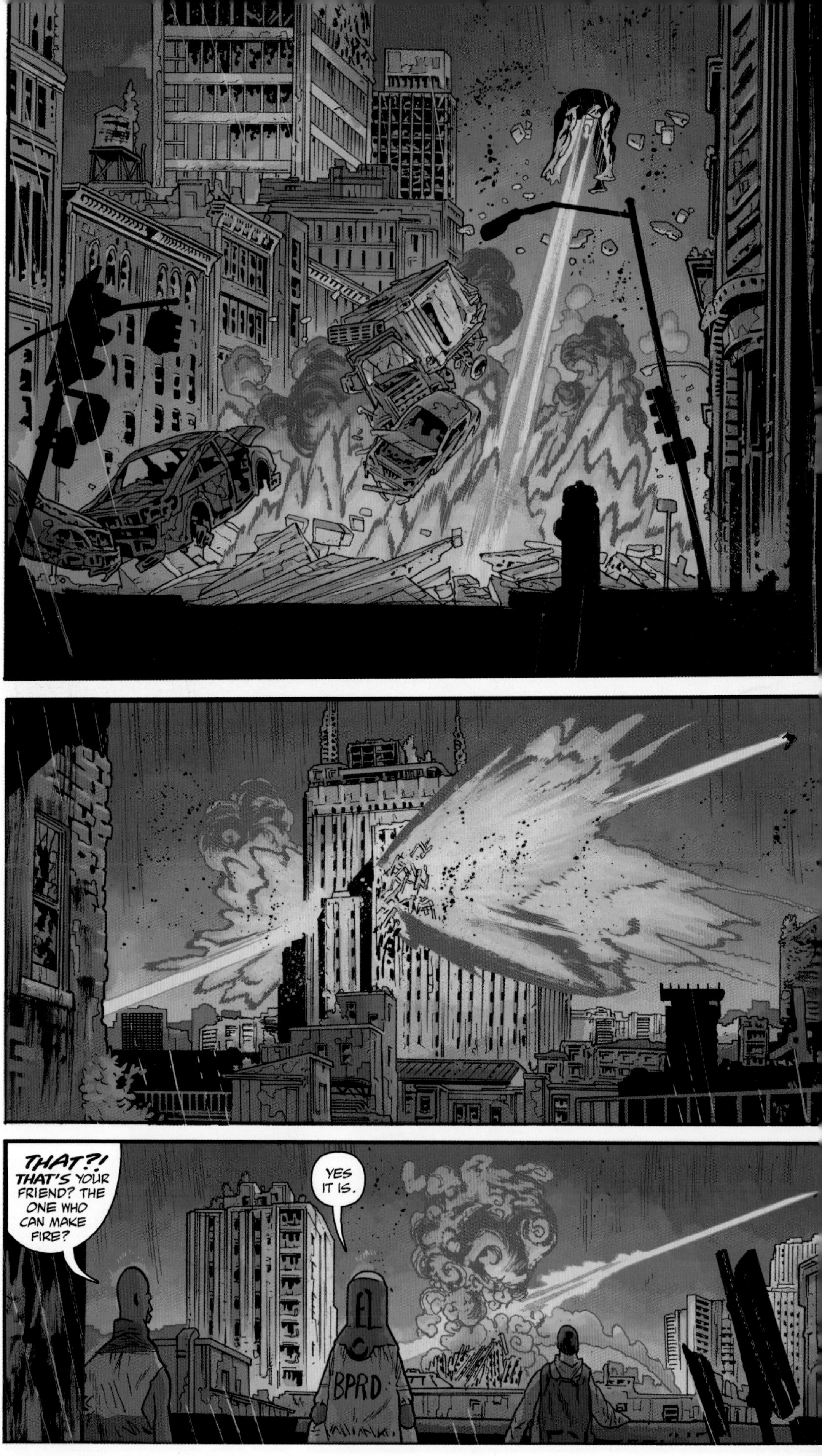
THAT?! THAT'S YOUR FRIEND? THE ONE WHO CAN MAKE FIRE?
YES IT IS.
BPRD

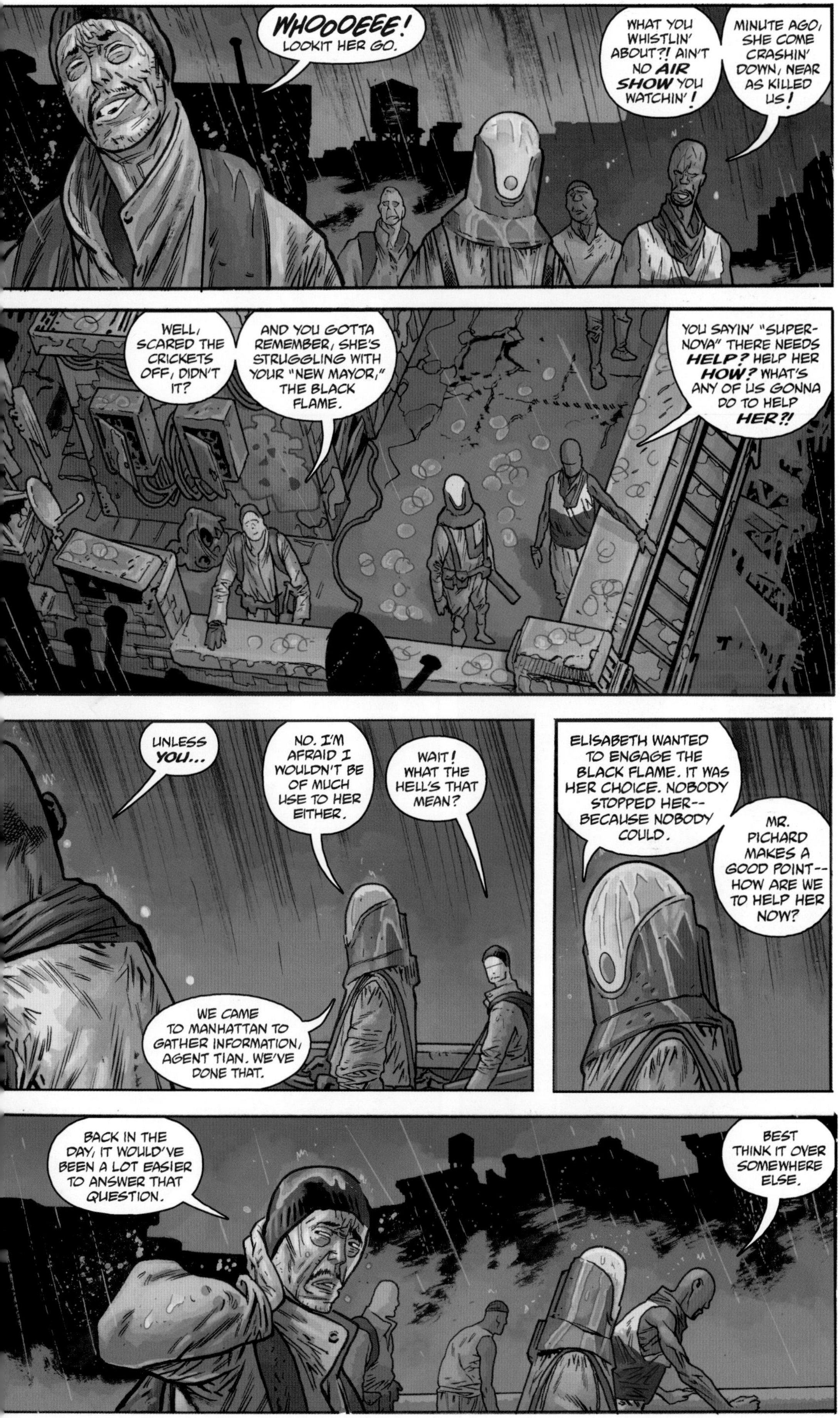
WHOOOEEE! LOOKIT HER GO.
WHAT YOU WHISTLIN' ABOUT?! AIN'T NO AIR SHOW YOU WATCHIN'!
MINUTE AGO, SHE COME CRASHIN' DOWN, NEAR AS KILLED US!
WELL, SCARED THE CRICKETS OFF, DIDN'T IT?
AND YOU GOTTA REMEMBER, SHE'S STRUGGLING WITH YOUR "NEW MAYOR," THE BLACK FLAME.
YOU SAYIN' "SUPER-NOVA" THERE NEEDS HELP? HELP HER HOW? WHAT'S ANY OF US GONNA DO TO HELP HER?!
UNLESS YOU...
NO. I'M AFRAID I WOULDN'T BE OF MUCH USE TO HER EITHER.
WAIT! WHAT THE HELL'S THAT MEAN?
WE CAME TO MANHATTAN TO GATHER INFORMATION, AGENT TIAN. WE'VE DONE THAT.
ELISABETH WANTED TO ENGAGE THE BLACK FLAME. IT WAS HER CHOICE. NOBODY STOPPED HER-- BECAUSE NOBODY COULD.
MR. PICHARD MAKES A GOOD POINT-- HOW ARE WE TO HELP HER NOW?
BACK IN THE DAY, IT WOULD'VE BEEN A LOT EASIER TO ANSWER THAT QUESTION.
BEST THINK IT OVER SOMEWHERE ELSE.

BEFORE WE'RE *ALL* BEYOND HELP.

--AND WE'LL NOTIFY TEAM INDIGO TO MOVE AHEAD TO TOMORROW'S EXIT RENDEZVOUS LOCATION BY THE BRIDGE. ELISABETH ALREADY KNOWS IT. SHE'LL MEET US THERE TOMORROW IF SHE IS ABLE.

WHAT IF SHE'S NOT?

FENIX, DIDN'T YOU POINT OUT TO ME EARLIER THAT THIS IS A FACT-FINDING--

CRAD!

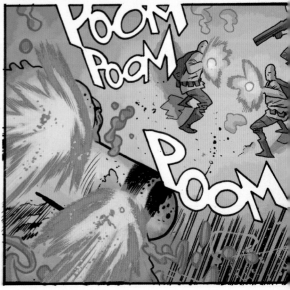

POOM POOM

POOM

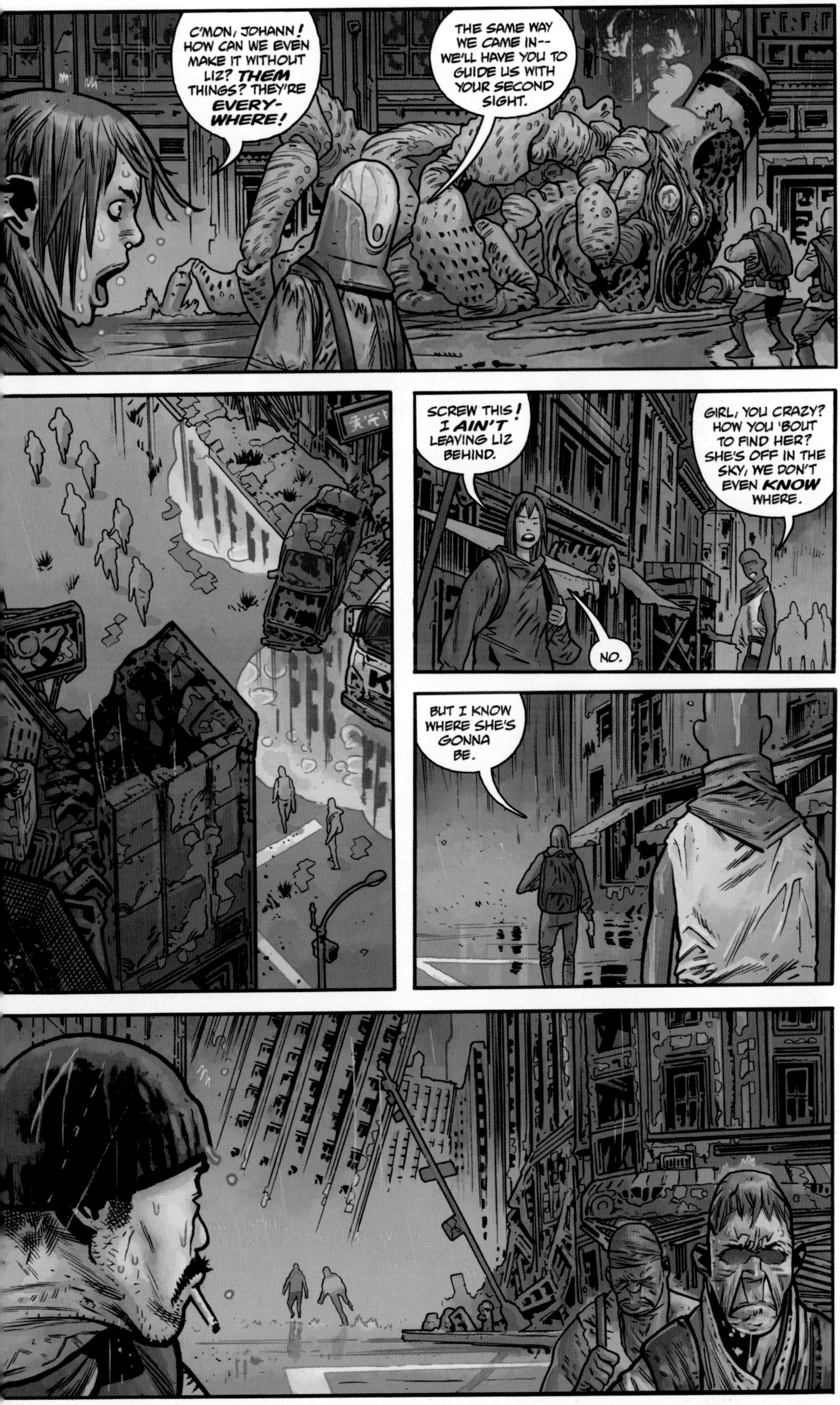
C'MON, JOHANN! HOW CAN WE EVEN MAKE IT WITHOUT LIZ? THEM THINGS? THEY'RE EVERY-WHERE!
THE SAME WAY WE CAME IN-- WE'LL HAVE YOU TO GUIDE US WITH YOUR SECOND SIGHT.
SCREW THIS! I AIN'T LEAVING LIZ BEHIND.
NO.
GIRL, YOU CRAZY? HOW YOU 'BOUT TO FIND HER? SHE'S OFF IN THE SKY, WE DON'T EVEN KNOW WHERE.
BUT I KNOW WHERE SHE'S GONNA BE.

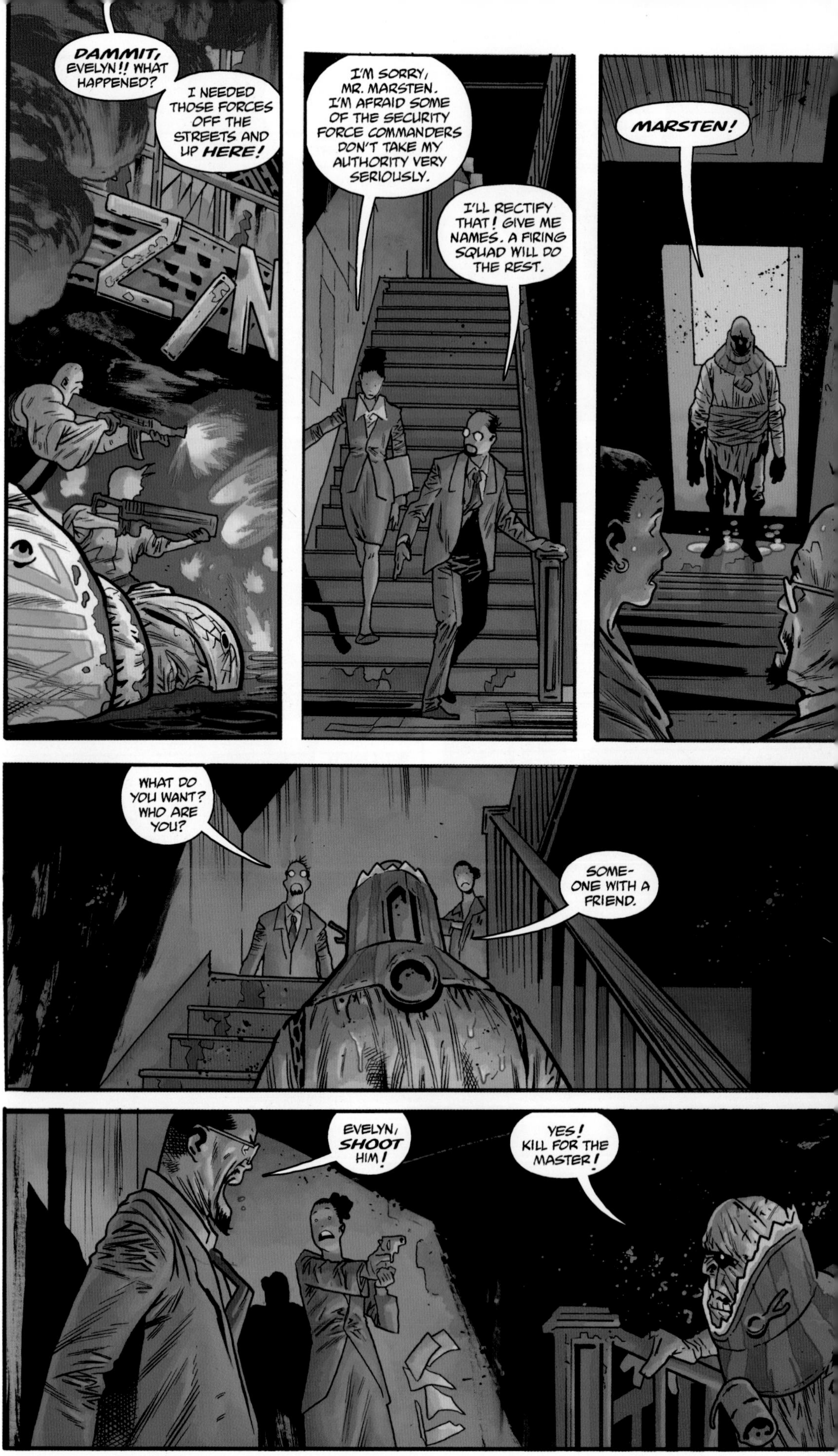
DAMMIT, EVELYN!! WHAT HAPPENED?
I NEEDED THOSE FORCES OFF THE STREETS AND UP HERE!
I'M SORRY, MR. MARSTEN. I'M AFRAID SOME OF THE SECURITY FORCE COMMANDERS DON'T TAKE MY AUTHORITY VERY SERIOUSLY.
I'LL RECTIFY THAT! GIVE ME NAMES. A FIRING SQUAD WILL DO THE REST.
MARSTEN!
WHAT DO YOU WANT? WHO ARE YOU?
SOME-ONE WITH A FRIEND.
EVELYN, SHOOT HIM!
YES! KILL FOR THE MASTER!

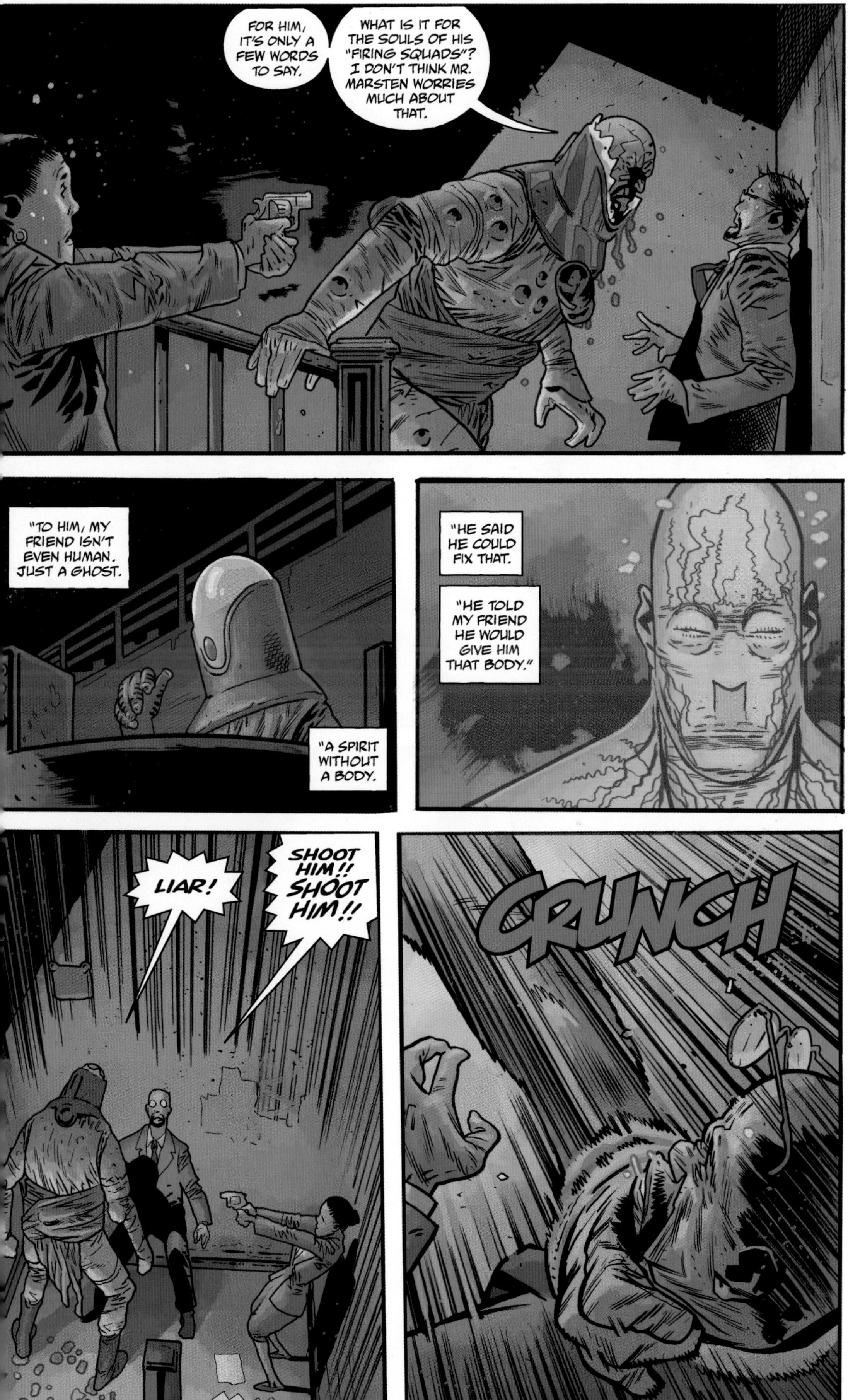
FOR HIM, IT'S ONLY A FEW WORDS TO SAY.
WHAT IS IT FOR THE SOULS OF HIS "FIRING SQUADS"? I DON'T THINK MR. MARSTEN WORRIES MUCH ABOUT THAT.
"TO HIM, MY FRIEND ISN'T EVEN HUMAN. JUST A GHOST.
"A SPIRIT WITHOUT A BODY.
"HE SAID HE COULD FIX THAT.
"HE TOLD MY FRIEND HE WOULD GIVE HIM THAT BODY."
LIAR!
SHOOT HIM!! SHOOT HIM!!
CRUNCH

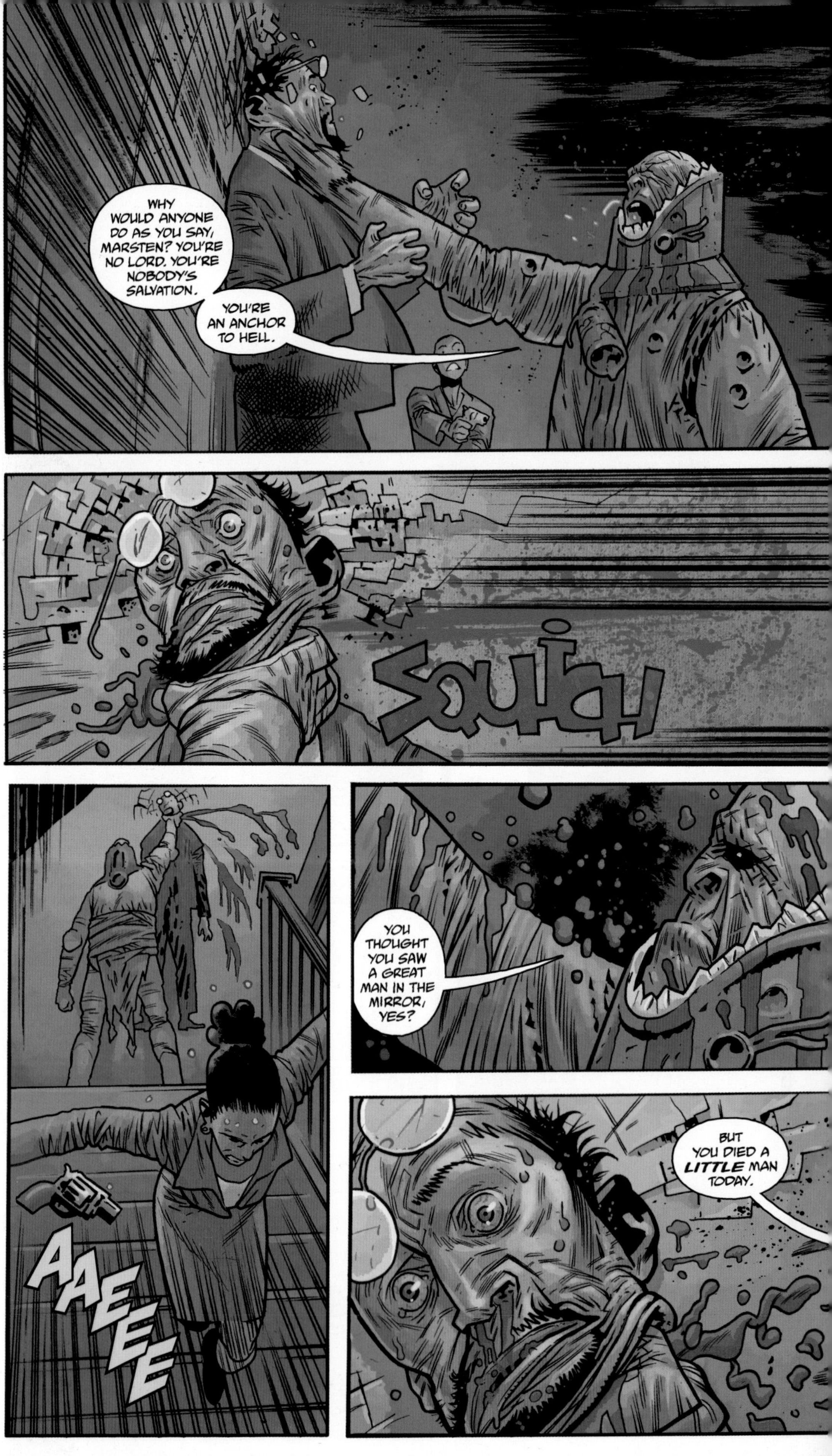

WHY WOULD ANYONE DO AS YOU SAY, MARSTEN? YOU'RE NO LORD. YOU'RE NOBODY'S SALVATION.
YOU'RE AN ANCHOR TO HELL.
SQUTCH
YOU THOUGHT YOU SAW A GREAT MAN IN THE MIRROR, YES?
AAEEEE
BUT YOU DIED A LITTLE MAN TODAY.

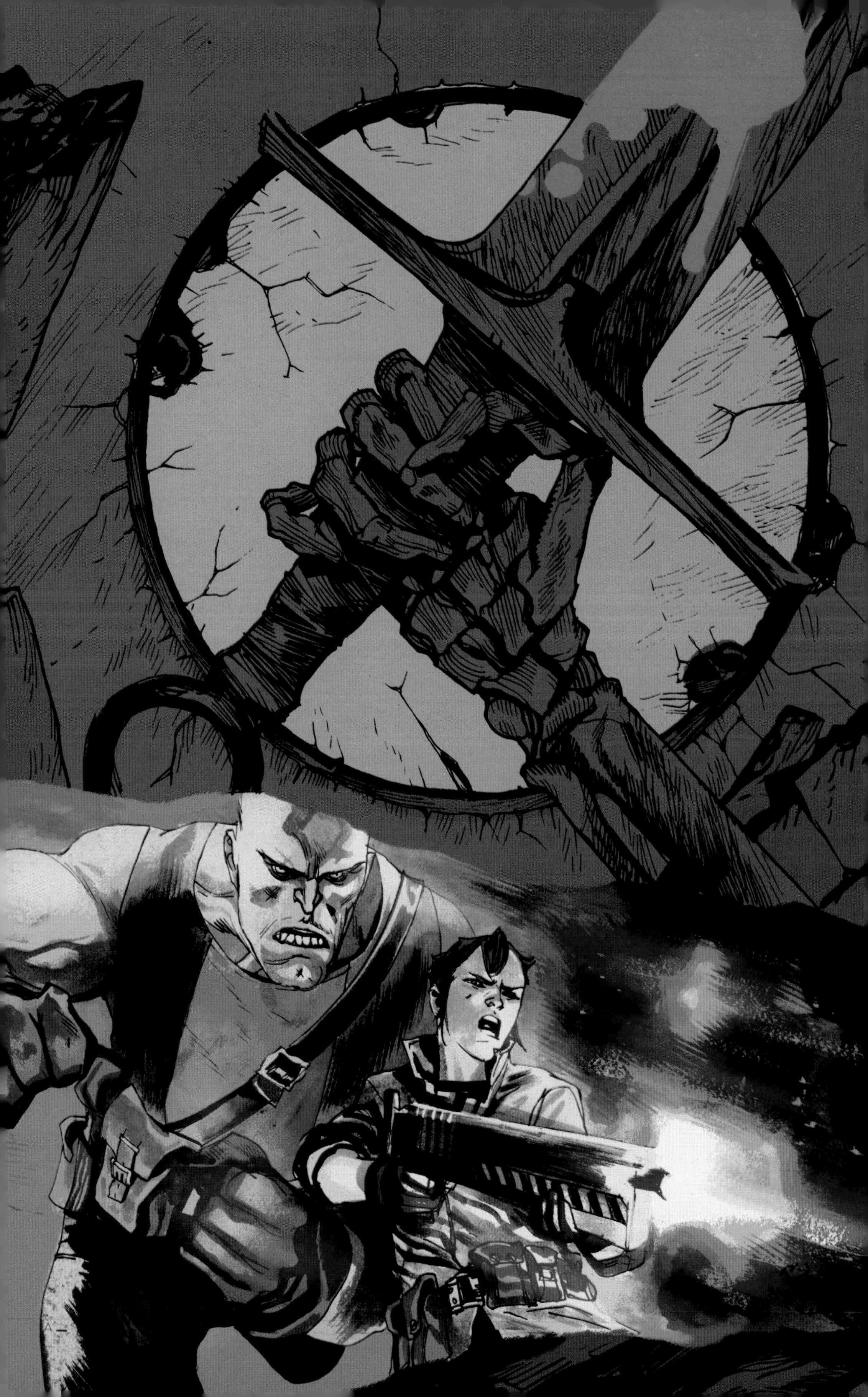

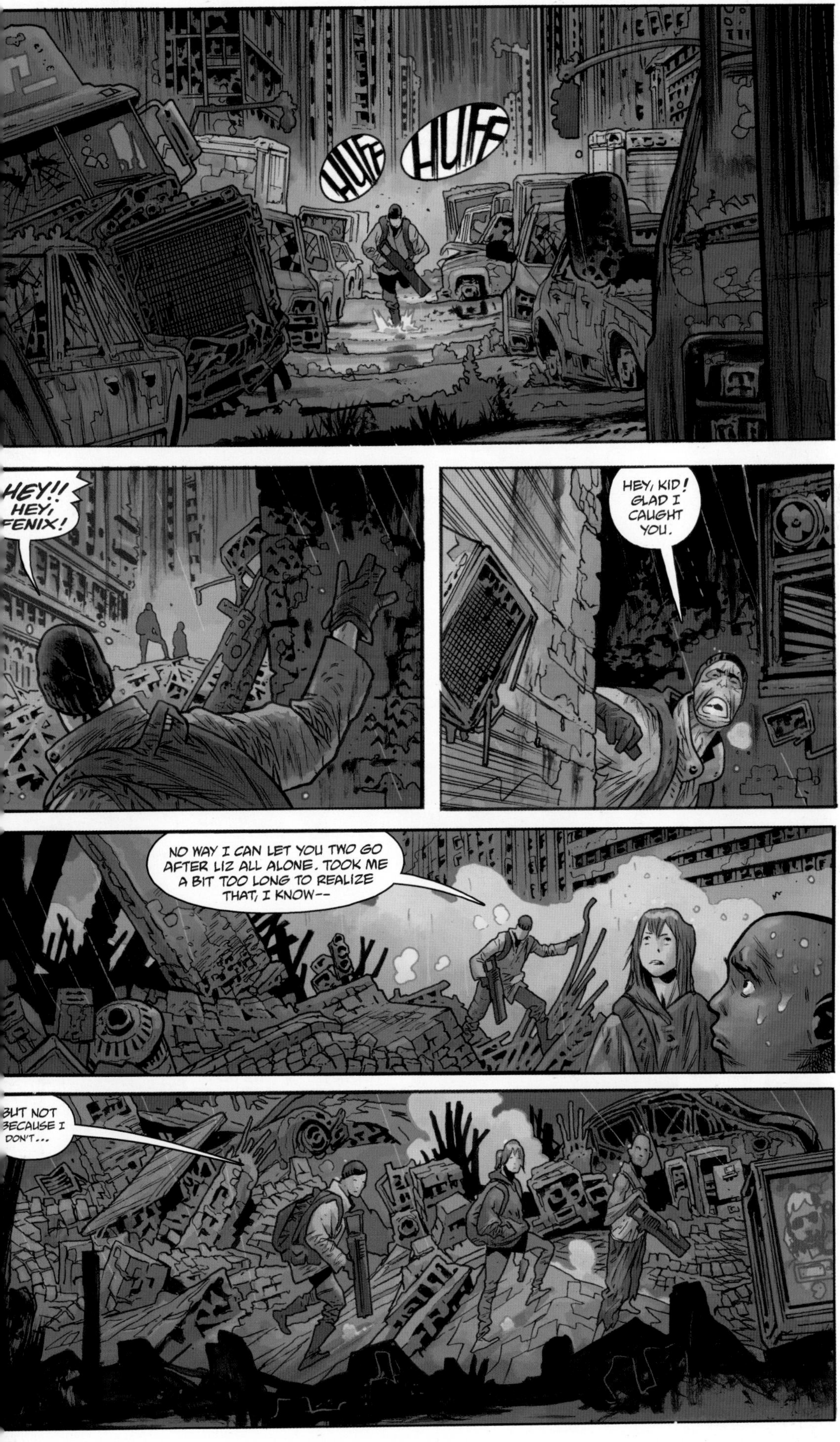
HUFF
HUFF
HEY!! HEY, FENIX!
HEY, KID! GLAD I CAUGHT YOU.
NO WAY I CAN LET YOU TWO GO AFTER LIZ ALL ALONE. TOOK ME A BIT TOO LONG TO REALIZE THAT, I KNOW--
BUT NOT BECAUSE I DON'T...

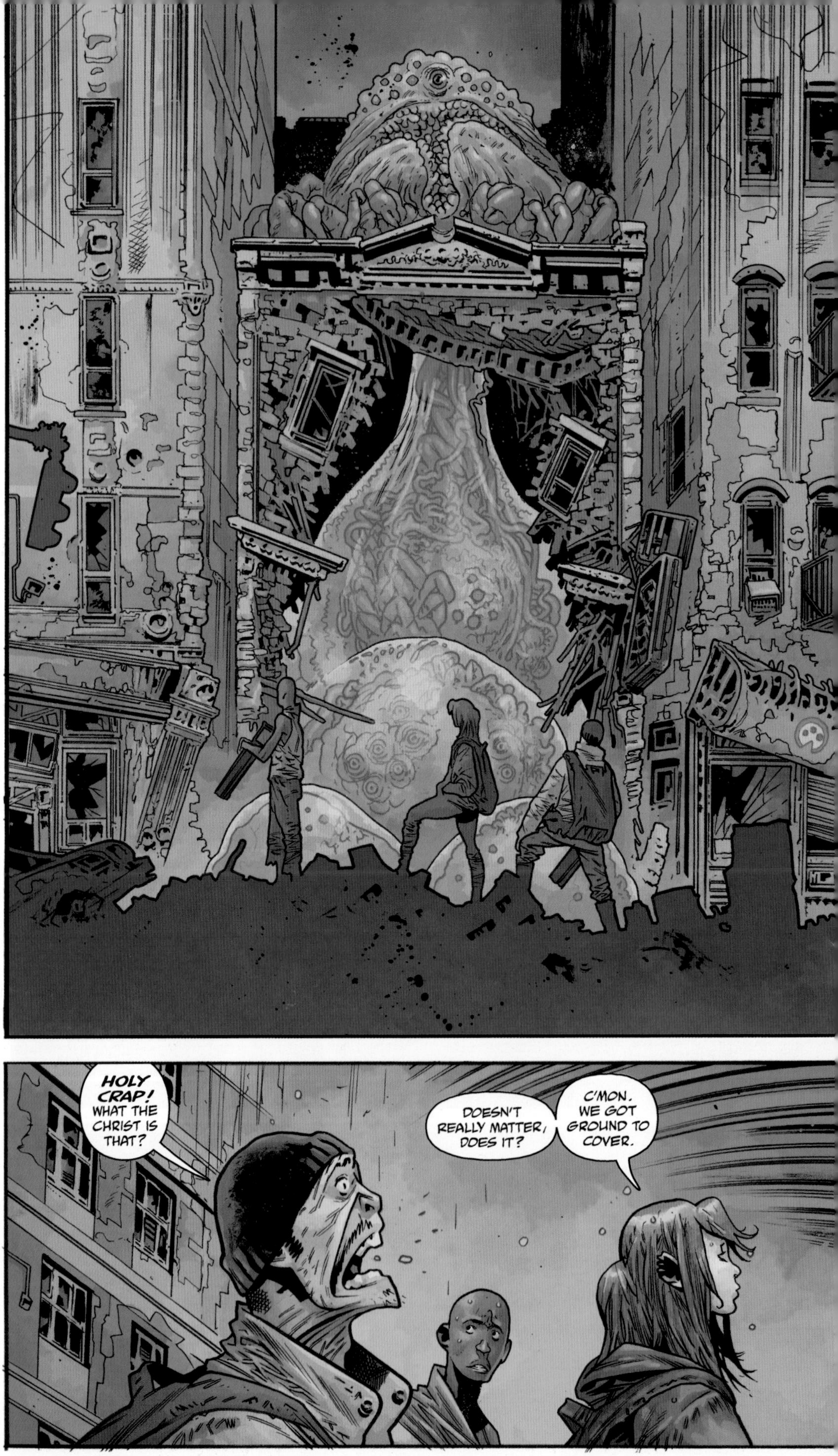

HOLY CRAP! WHAT THE CHRIST IS THAT?
DOESN'T REALLY MATTER, DOES IT?
C'MON. WE GOT GROUND TO COVER.

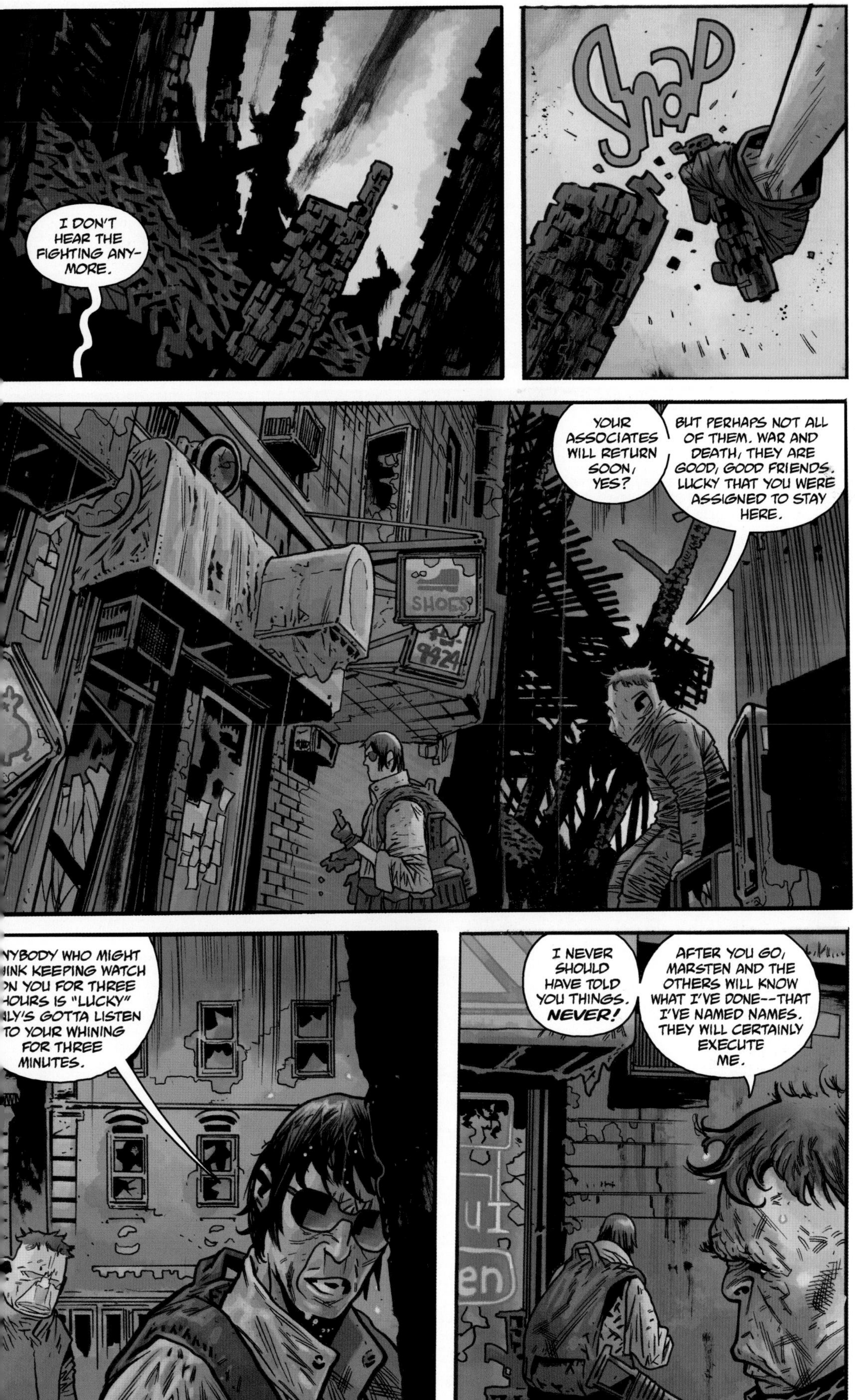
I DON'T HEAR THE FIGHTING ANY-MORE.
SNAP
YOUR ASSOCIATES WILL RETURN SOON, YES?
BUT PERHAPS NOT ALL OF THEM. WAR AND DEATH, THEY ARE GOOD, GOOD FRIENDS. LUCKY THAT YOU WERE ASSIGNED TO STAY HERE.
SHOES
NYBODY WHO MIGHT HINK KEEPING WATCH ON YOU FOR THREE HOURS IS "LUCKY" NLY'S GOTTA LISTEN TO YOUR WHINING FOR THREE MINUTES.
I NEVER SHOULD HAVE TOLD YOU THINGS. ***NEVER!***
AFTER YOU GO, MARSTEN AND THE OTHERS WILL KNOW WHAT I'VE DONE--THAT I'VE NAMED NAMES. THEY WILL CERTAINLY EXECUTE ME.

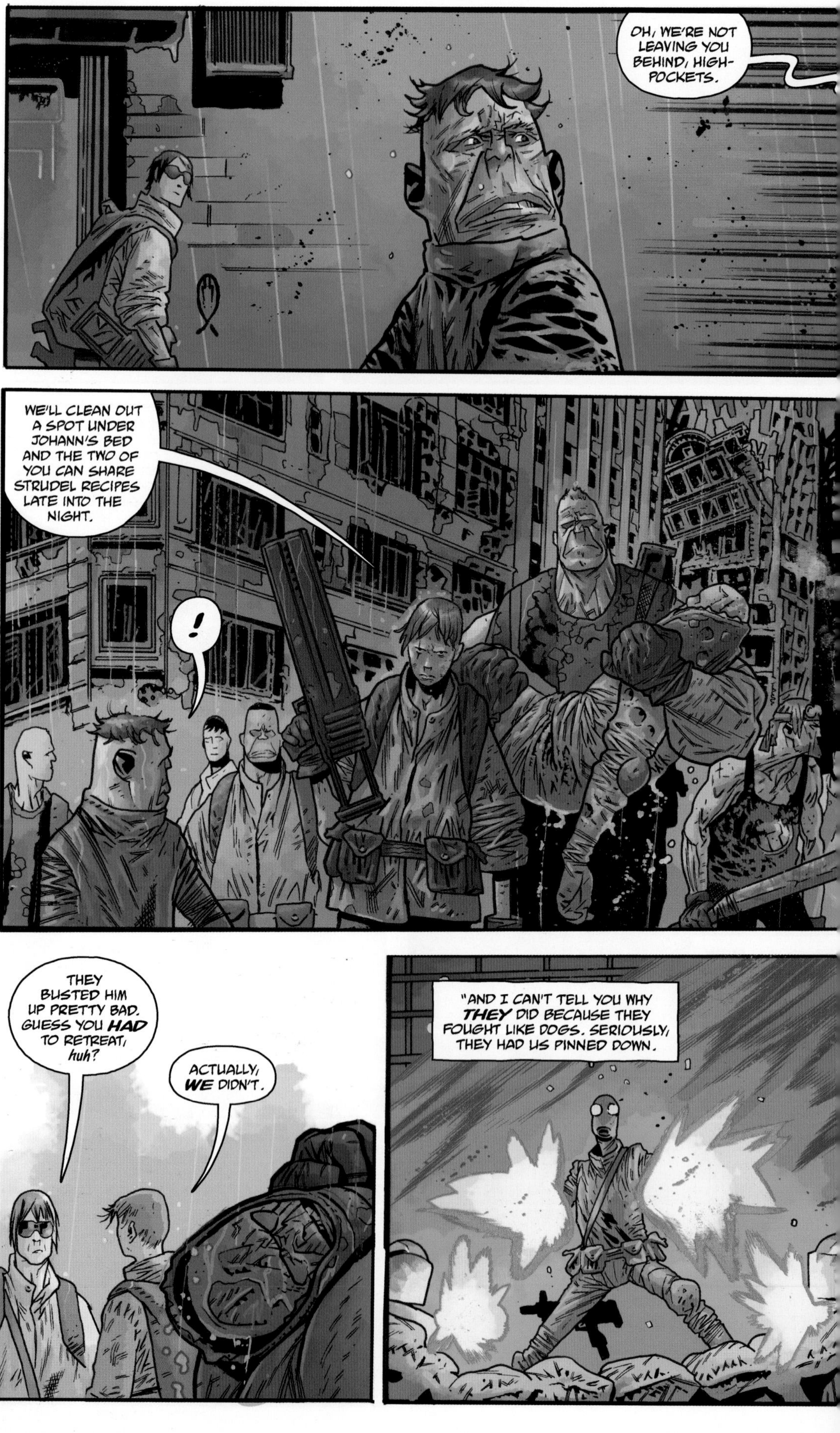
OH, WE'RE NOT LEAVING YOU BEHIND, HIGH-POCKETS.
WE'LL CLEAN OUT A SPOT UNDER JOHANN'S BED AND THE TWO OF YOU CAN SHARE STRUDEL RECIPES LATE INTO THE NIGHT.
!
THEY BUSTED HIM UP PRETTY BAD. GUESS YOU HAD TO RETREAT, huh?
ACTUALLY, WE DIDN'T.
"AND I CAN'T TELL YOU WHY THEY DID BECAUSE THEY FOUGHT LIKE DOGS. SERIOUSLY, THEY HAD US PINNED DOWN.

"AND THEN SUDDENLY THEY WERE GONE--LIKE THEY WERE CALLED OFF.

ZINC

"THAT'S WHEN IOSIF--"

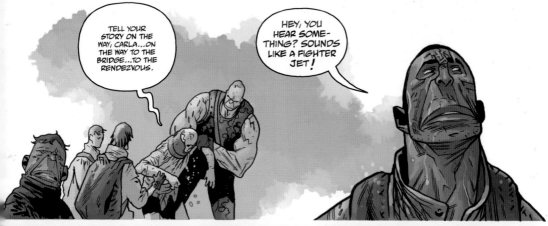

TELL YOUR STORY ON THE WAY, CARLA...ON THE WAY TO THE BRIDGE...TO THE RENDEZVOUS.

HEY, YOU HEAR SOMETHING? SOUNDS LIKE A FIGHTER JET!

I DON'T THINK SO.

NO. GUESS NOT.

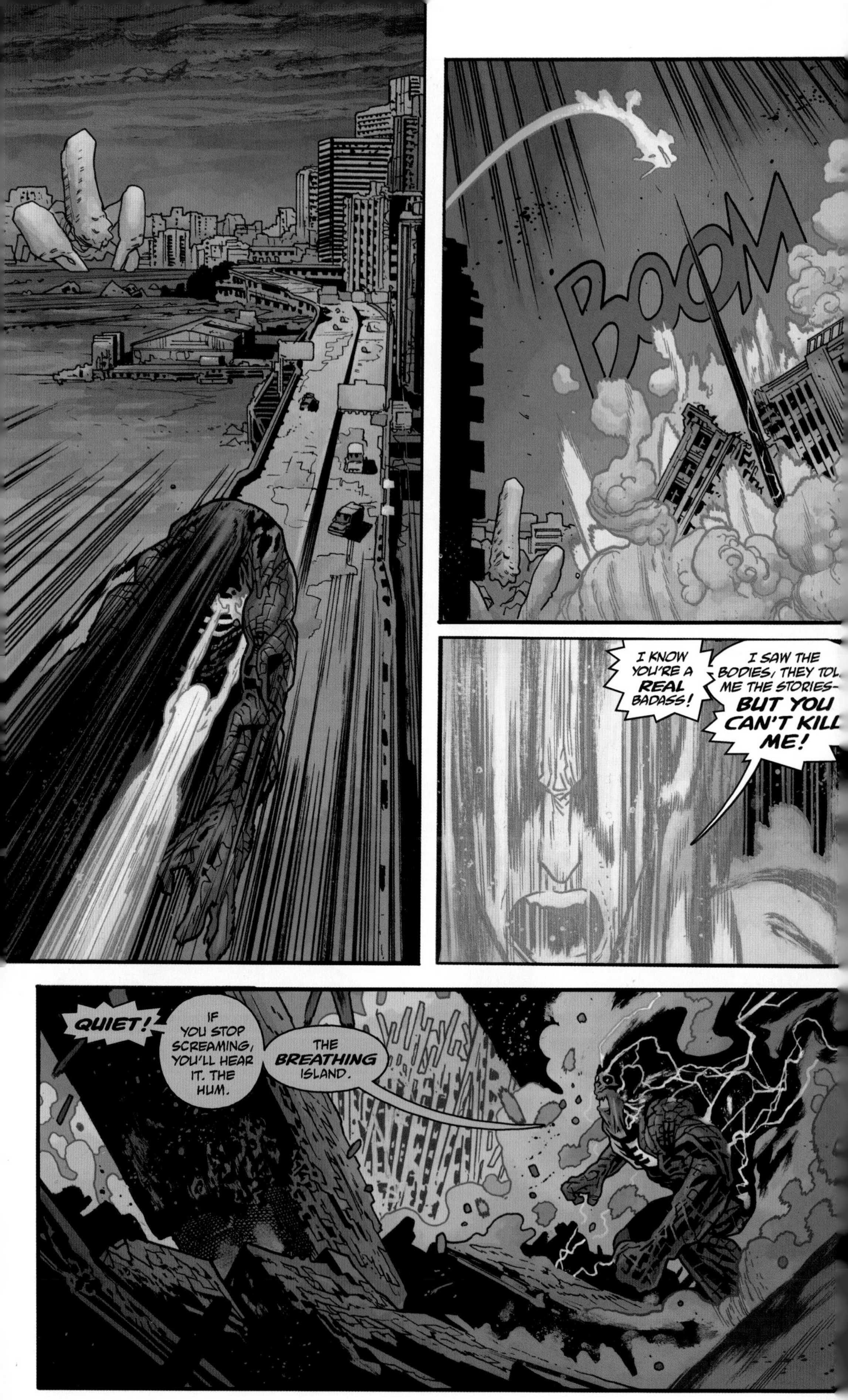
BOOM
I KNOW YOU'RE A REAL BADASS!
I SAW THE BODIES, THEY TOL ME THE STORIES- BUT YOU CAN'T KILL ME!
QUIET!
IF YOU STOP SCREAMING, YOU'LL HEAR IT. THE HUM.
THE BREATHING ISLAND.

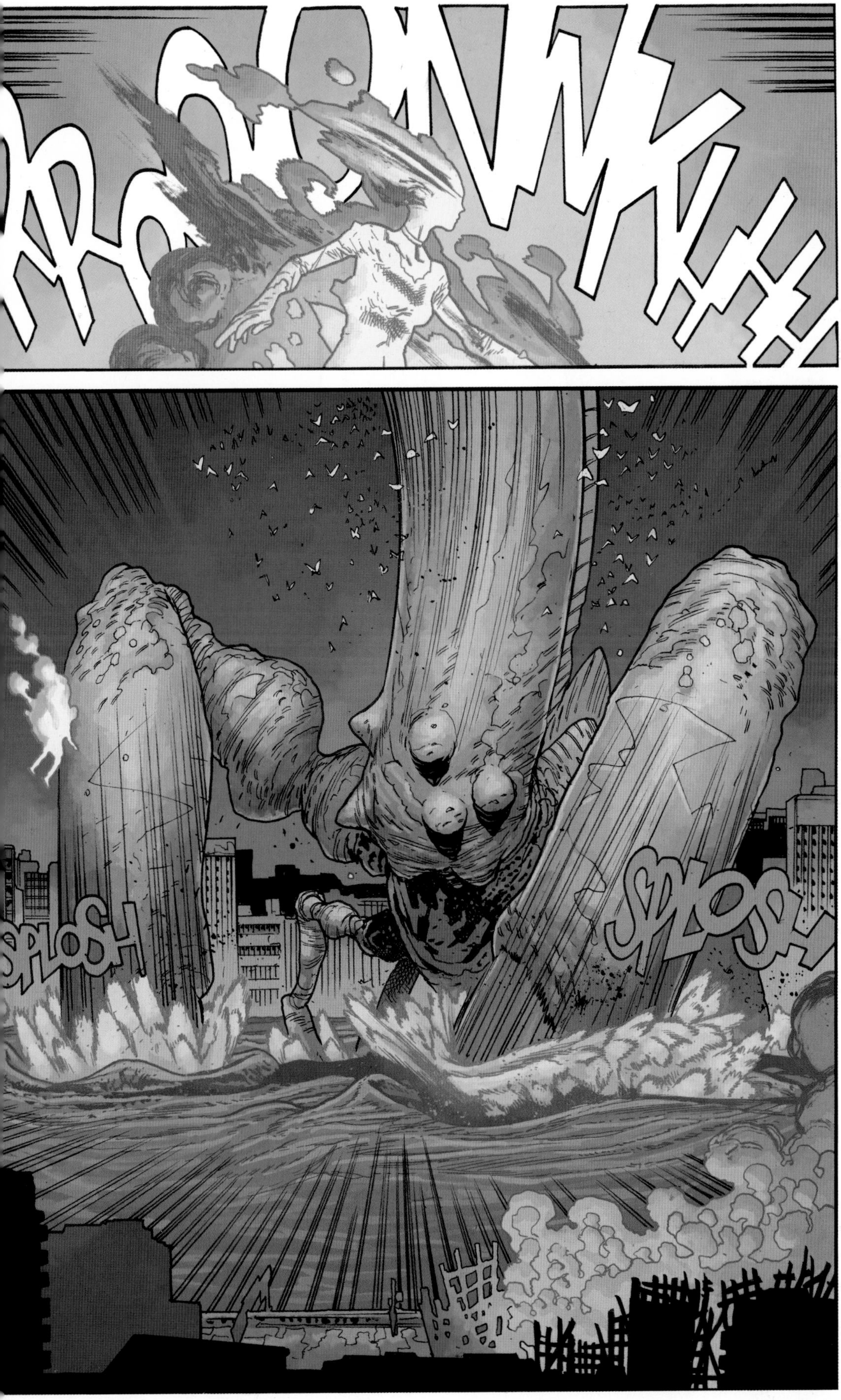
SPLOSH
SPLOSH

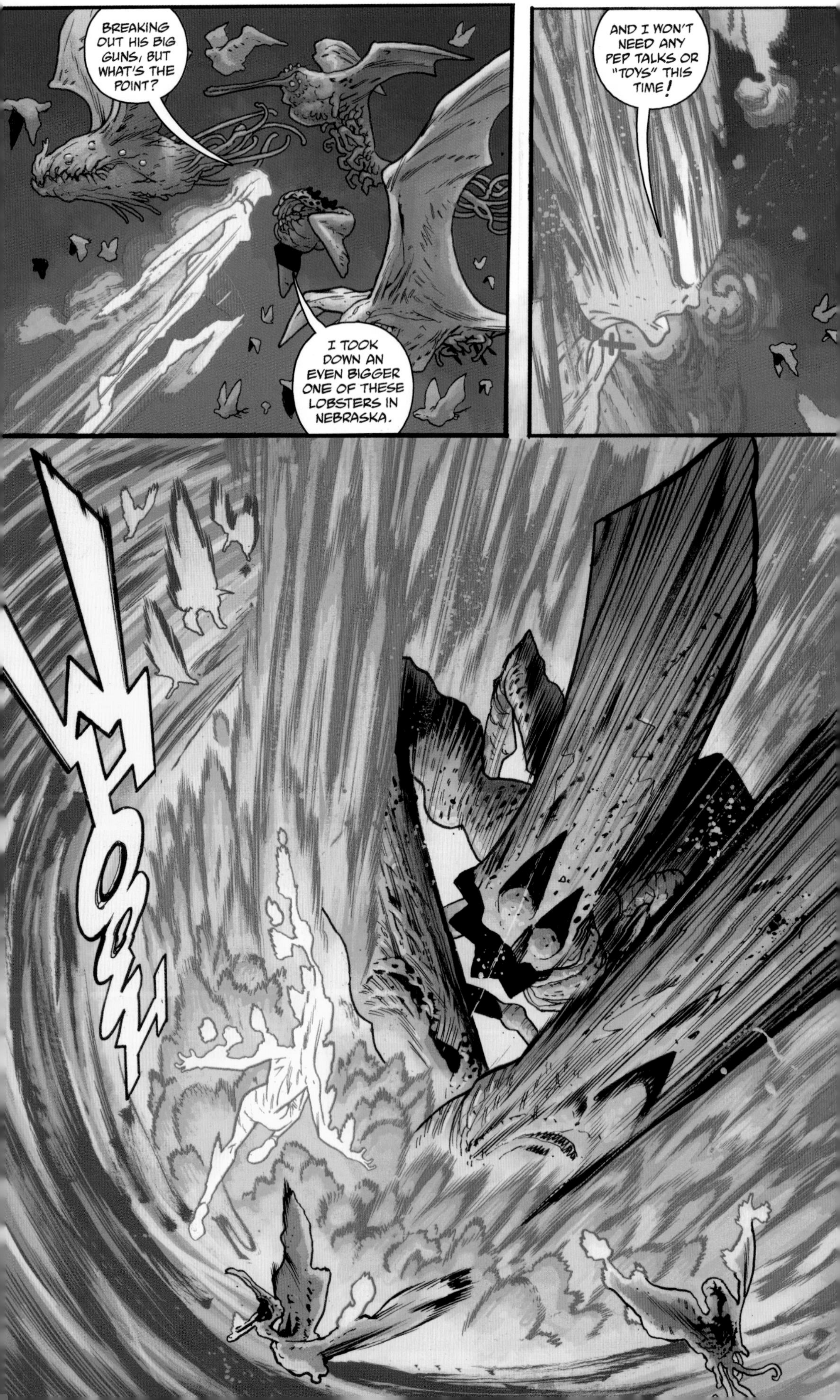
BREAKING OUT HIS BIG GUNS, BUT WHAT'S THE POINT?
I TOOK DOWN AN EVEN BIGGER ONE OF THESE LOBSTERS IN NEBRASKA.
AND I WON'T NEED ANY PEP TALKS OR "TOYS" THIS TIME!
WHOOM

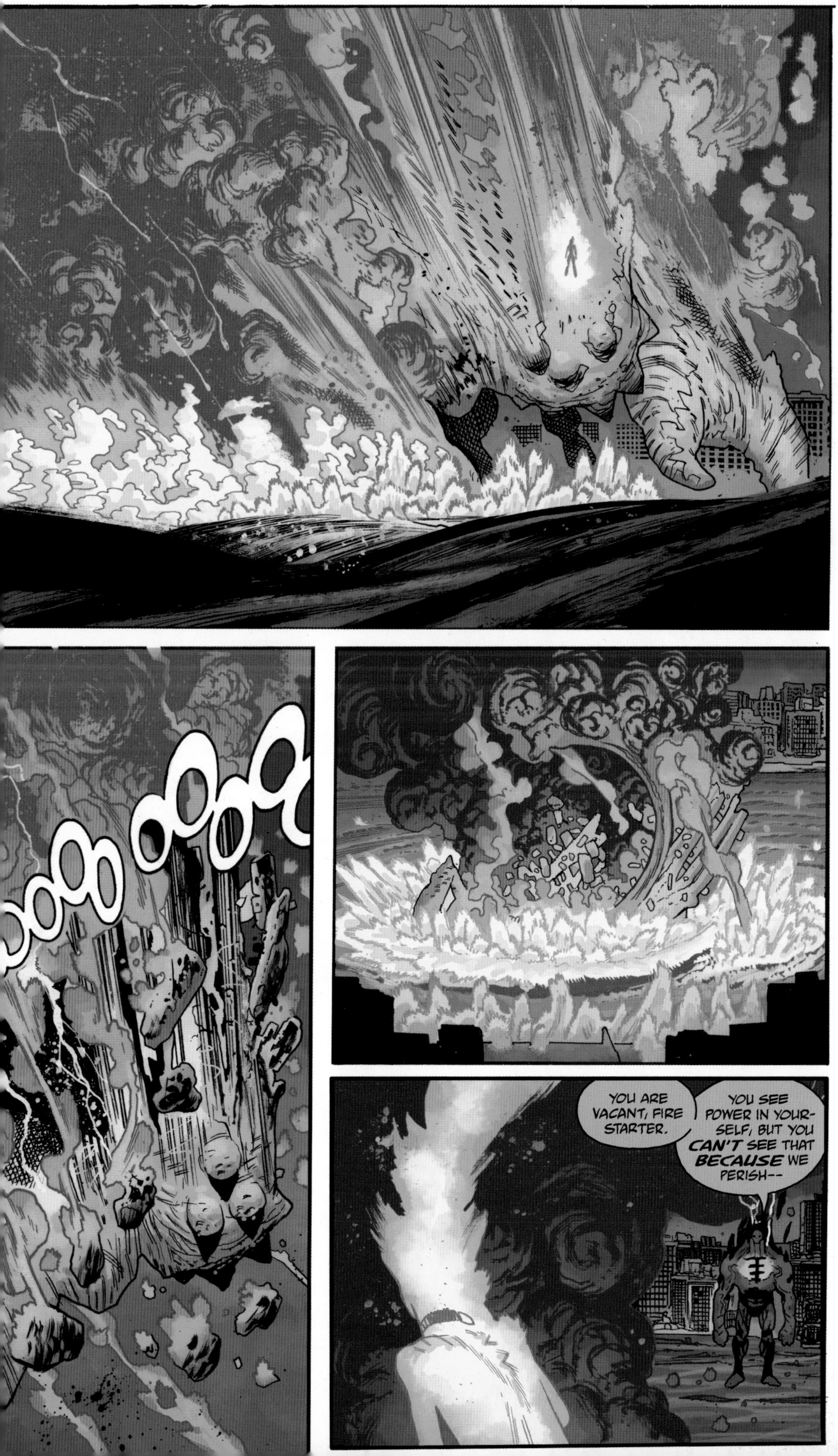
OOOOOOOOO
YOU ARE VACANT, FIRE STARTER.
YOU SEE POWER IN YOURSELF, BUT YOU **CAN'T** SEE THAT **BECAUSE** WE PERISH--

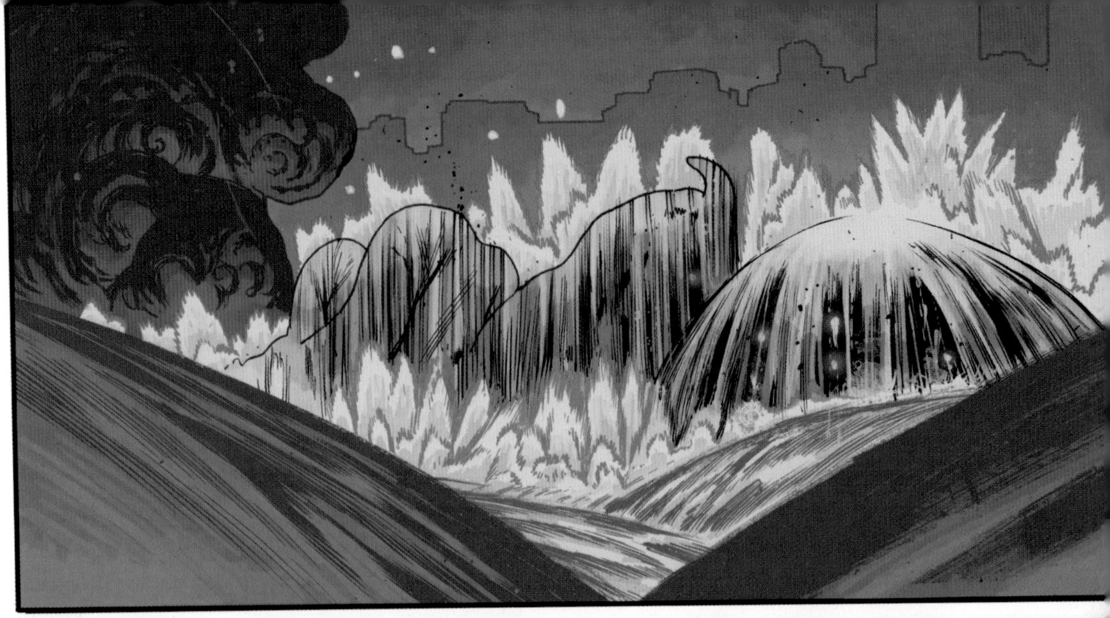

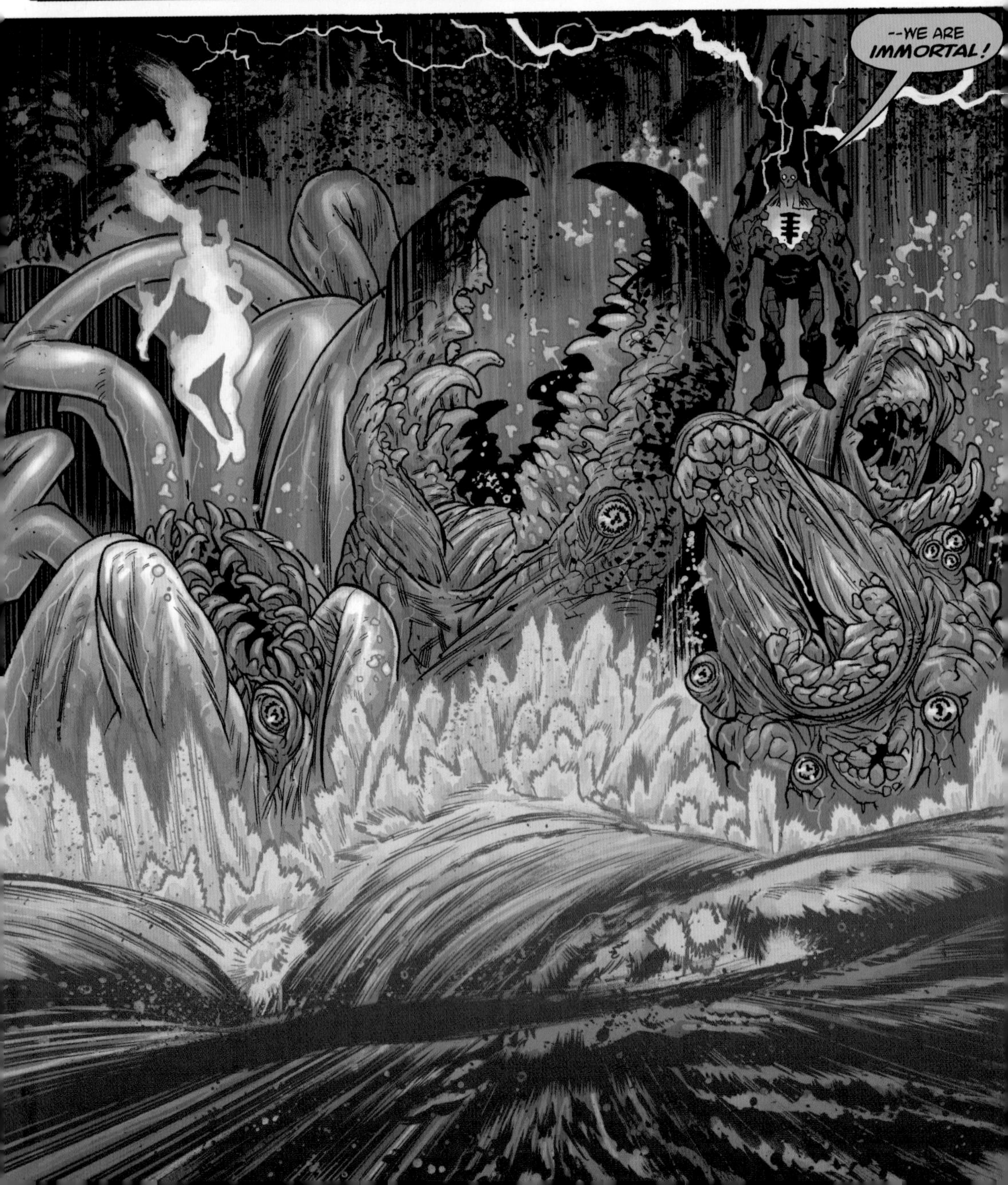
--WE ARE IMMORTAL!

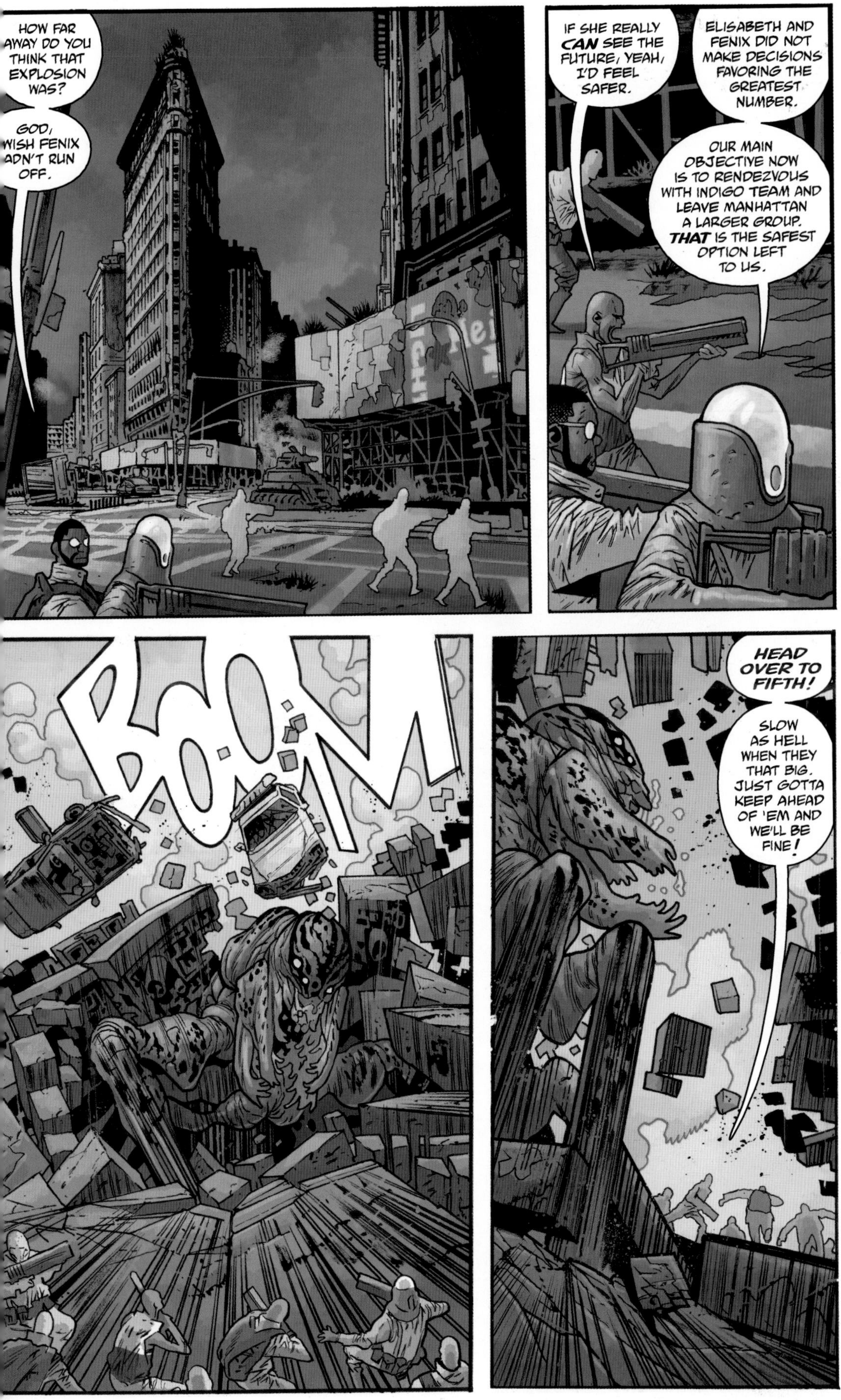
HOW FAR AWAY DO YOU THINK THAT EXPLOSION WAS?
GOD, WISH FENIX ADN'T RUN OFF.
IF SHE REALLY CAN SEE THE FUTURE, YEAH, I'D FEEL SAFER.
ELISABETH AND FENIX DID NOT MAKE DECISIONS FAVORING THE GREATEST NUMBER.
OUR MAIN OBJECTIVE NOW IS TO RENDEZVOUS WITH INDIGO TEAM AND LEAVE MANHATTAN A LARGER GROUP. THAT IS THE SAFEST OPTION LEFT TO US.
BOOOM!
HEAD OVER TO FIFTH!
SLOW AS HELL WHEN THEY THAT BIG. JUST GOTTA KEEP AHEAD OF 'EM AND WE'LL BE FINE!

GOD DAMN! THEY *ALL* OUT TODAY!

BAM RATATAT RATATAT BLAM BLAM BLAM RATITOOM RATATAT

HELL WITH THAT LITTLE TEENAGER! IT'S YOUR *FIRE LADY* I'M MISSIN' RIGHT NOW!

IT'S NOT POSSIBLE TO FIGHT WITH WHAT YOU WANT.

"SO FIGHT WITH WHAT YOU HAVE."

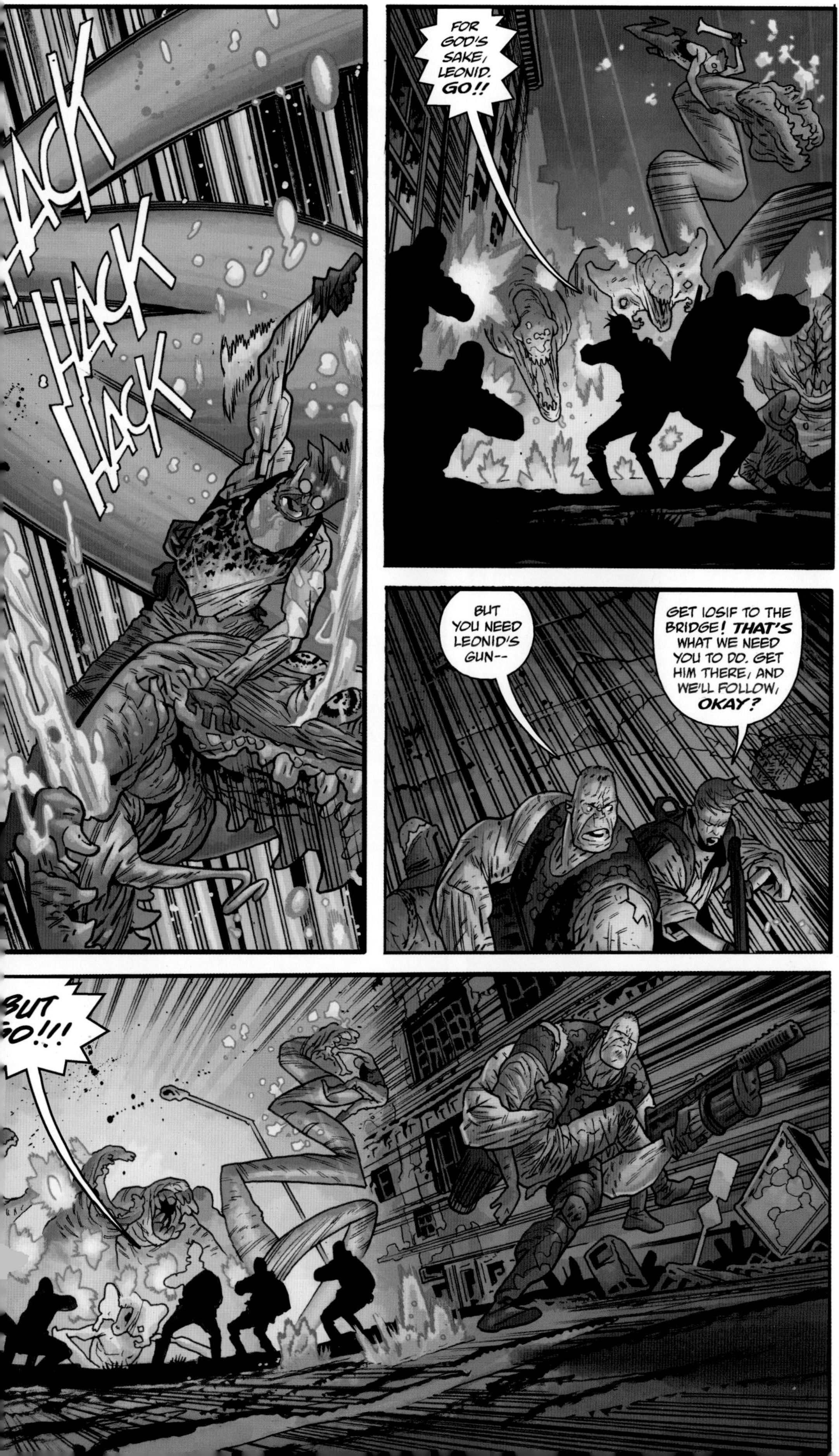

HACK HACK HACK
FOR GOD'S SAKE, LEONID. GO!!
BUT YOU NEED LEONID'S GUN--
GET IOSIF TO THE BRIDGE! THAT'S WHAT WE NEED YOU TO DO. GET HIM THERE, AND WE'LL FOLLOW, OKAY?
BUT GO!!!

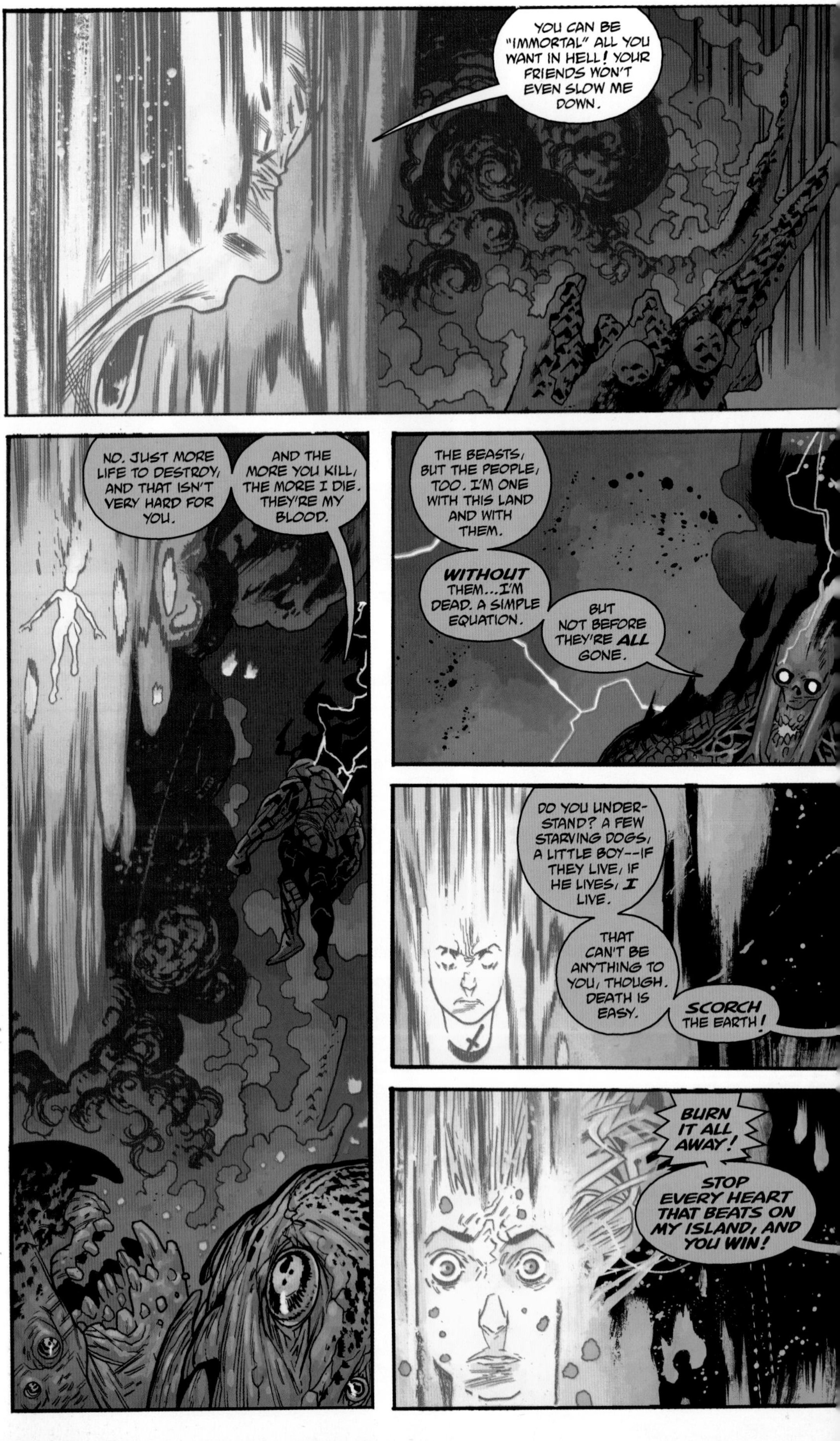
YOU CAN BE "IMMORTAL" ALL YOU WANT IN HELL! YOUR FRIENDS WON'T EVEN SLOW ME DOWN.
NO. JUST MORE LIFE TO DESTROY, AND THAT ISN'T VERY HARD FOR YOU.
AND THE MORE YOU KILL, THE MORE I DIE. THEY'RE MY BLOOD.
THE BEASTS, BUT THE PEOPLE, TOO. I'M ONE WITH THIS LAND AND WITH THEM.
WITHOUT THEM... I'M DEAD. A SIMPLE EQUATION.
BUT NOT BEFORE THEY'RE ALL GONE.
DO YOU UNDER-STAND? A FEW STARVING DOGS, A LITTLE BOY--IF THEY LIVE, IF HE LIVES, I LIVE.
THAT CAN'T BE ANYTHING TO YOU, THOUGH. DEATH IS EASY.
SCORCH THE EARTH!
BURN IT ALL AWAY!
STOP EVERY HEART THAT BEATS ON MY ISLAND, AND YOU WIN!

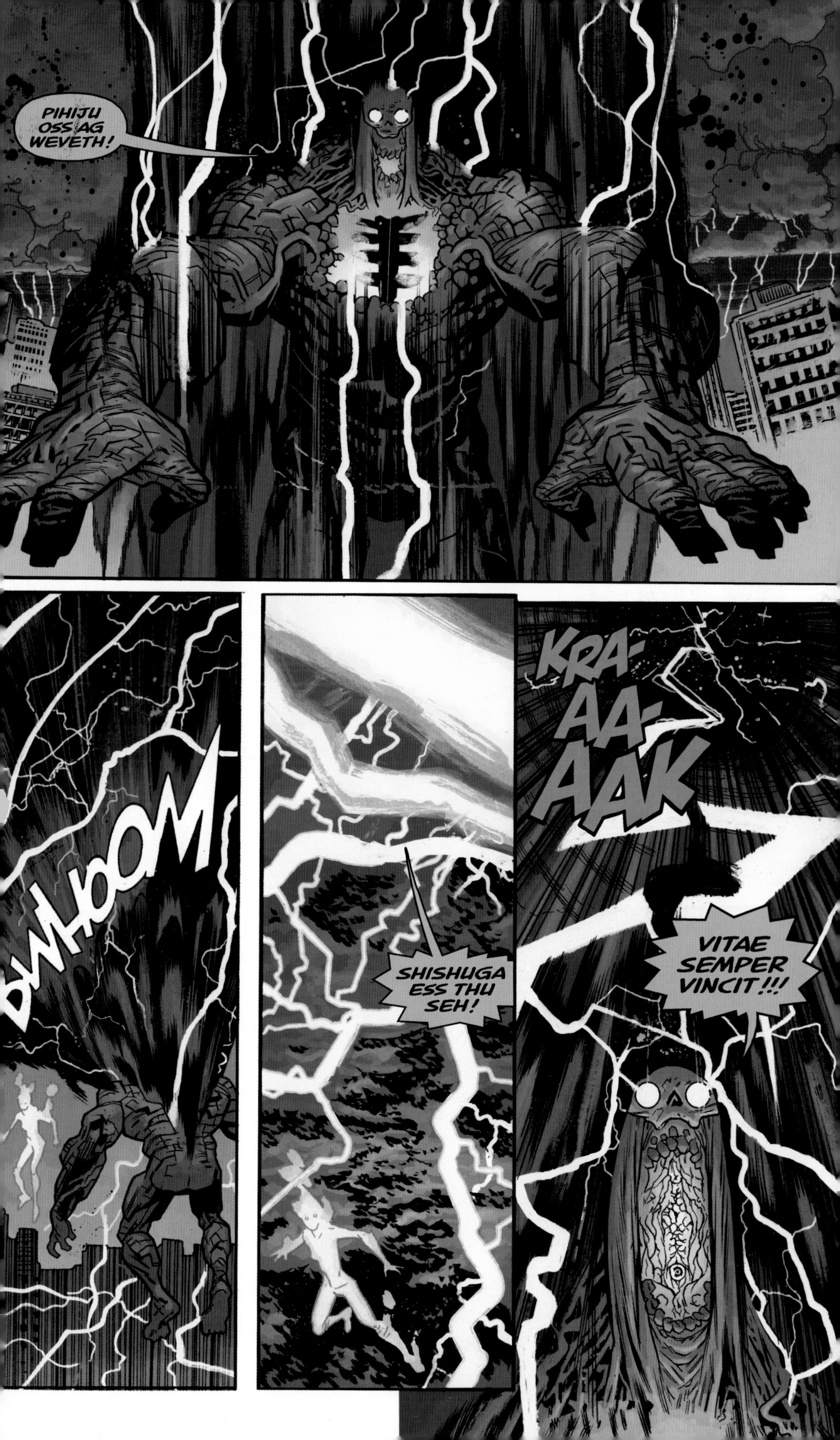
PIHIJU OSS AG WEVETH!
BWHOOM
SHISHUGA ESS THU SEH!
KRA-AA-AAK
VITAE SEMPER VINCIT!!!

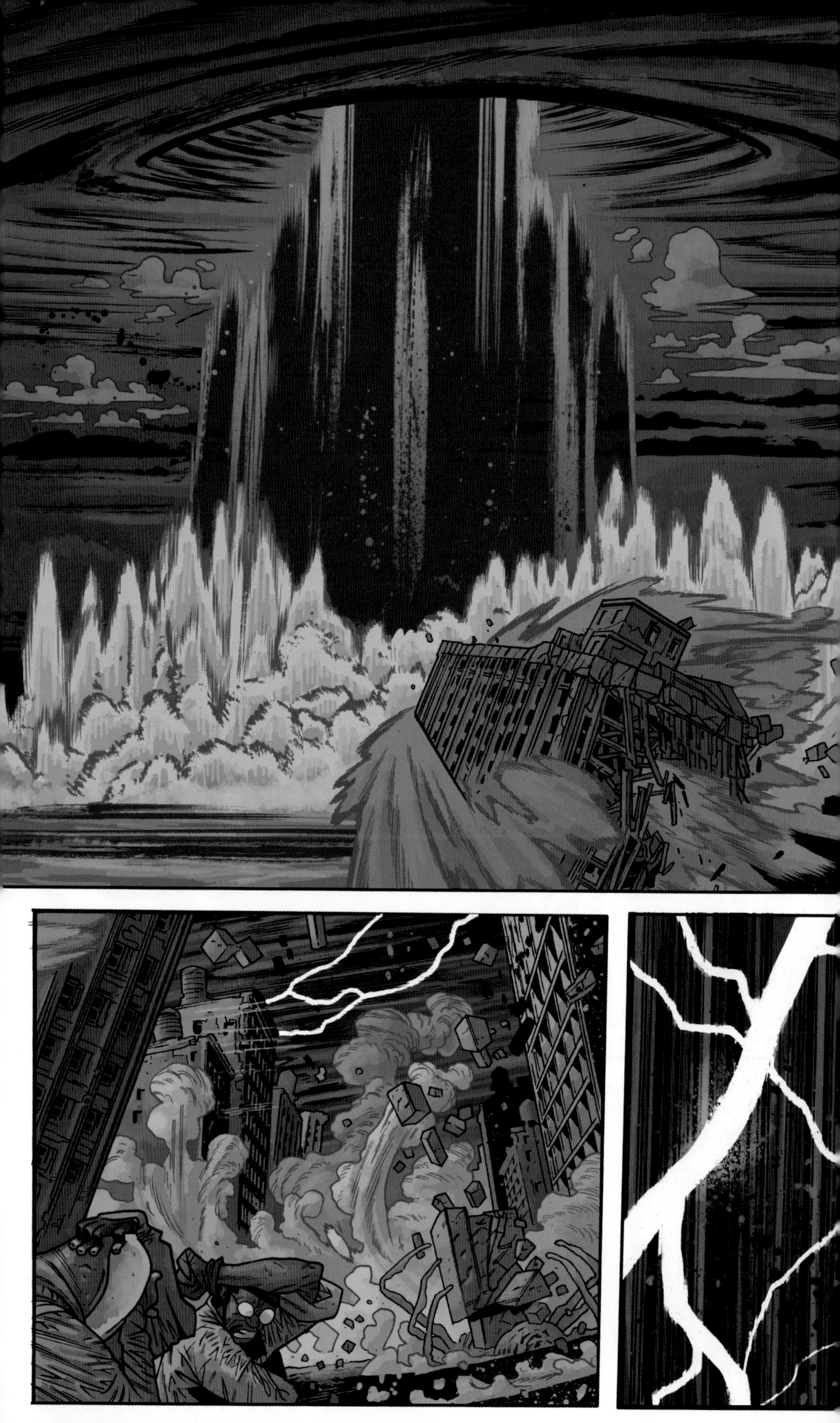

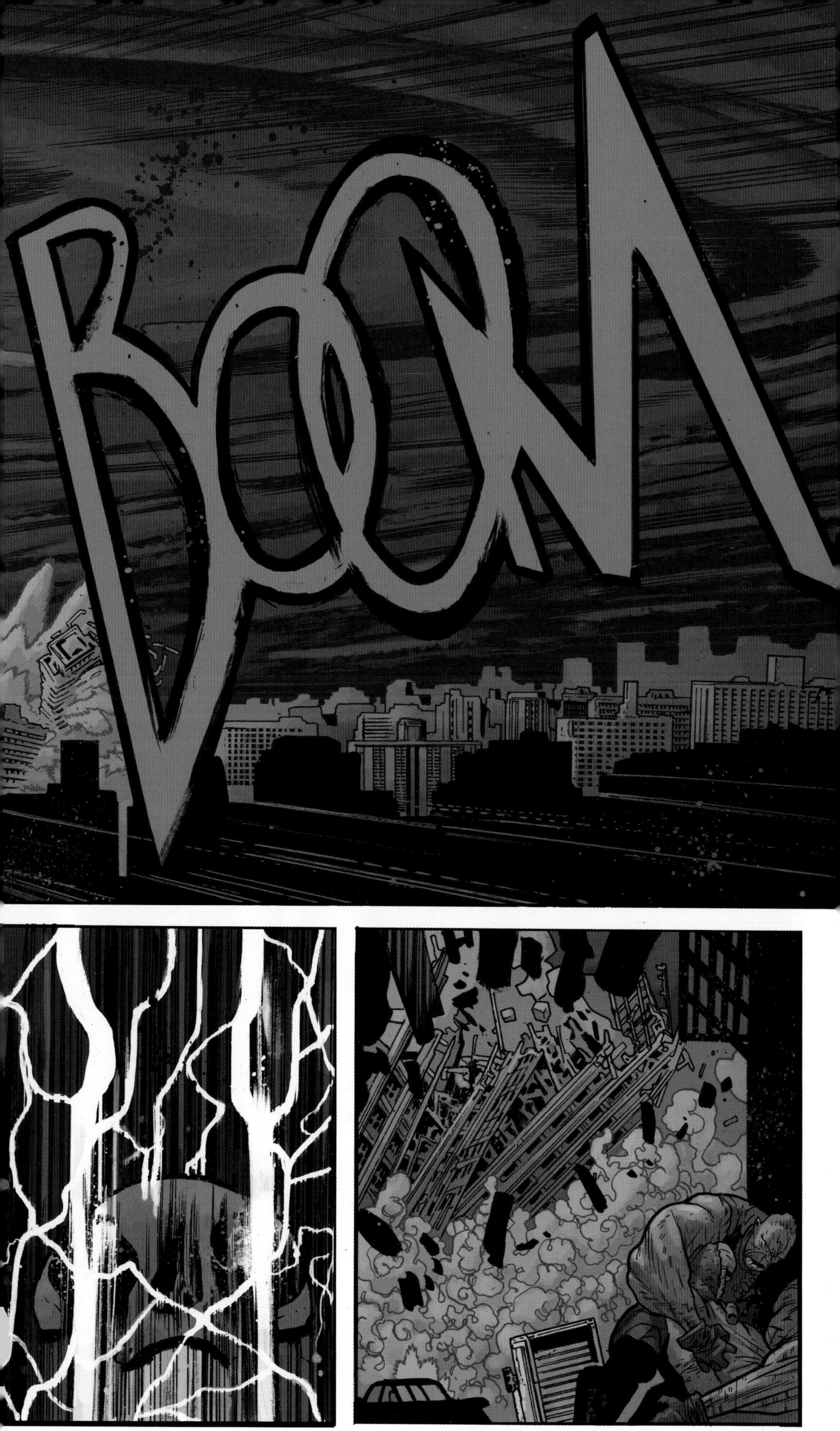
BOOM

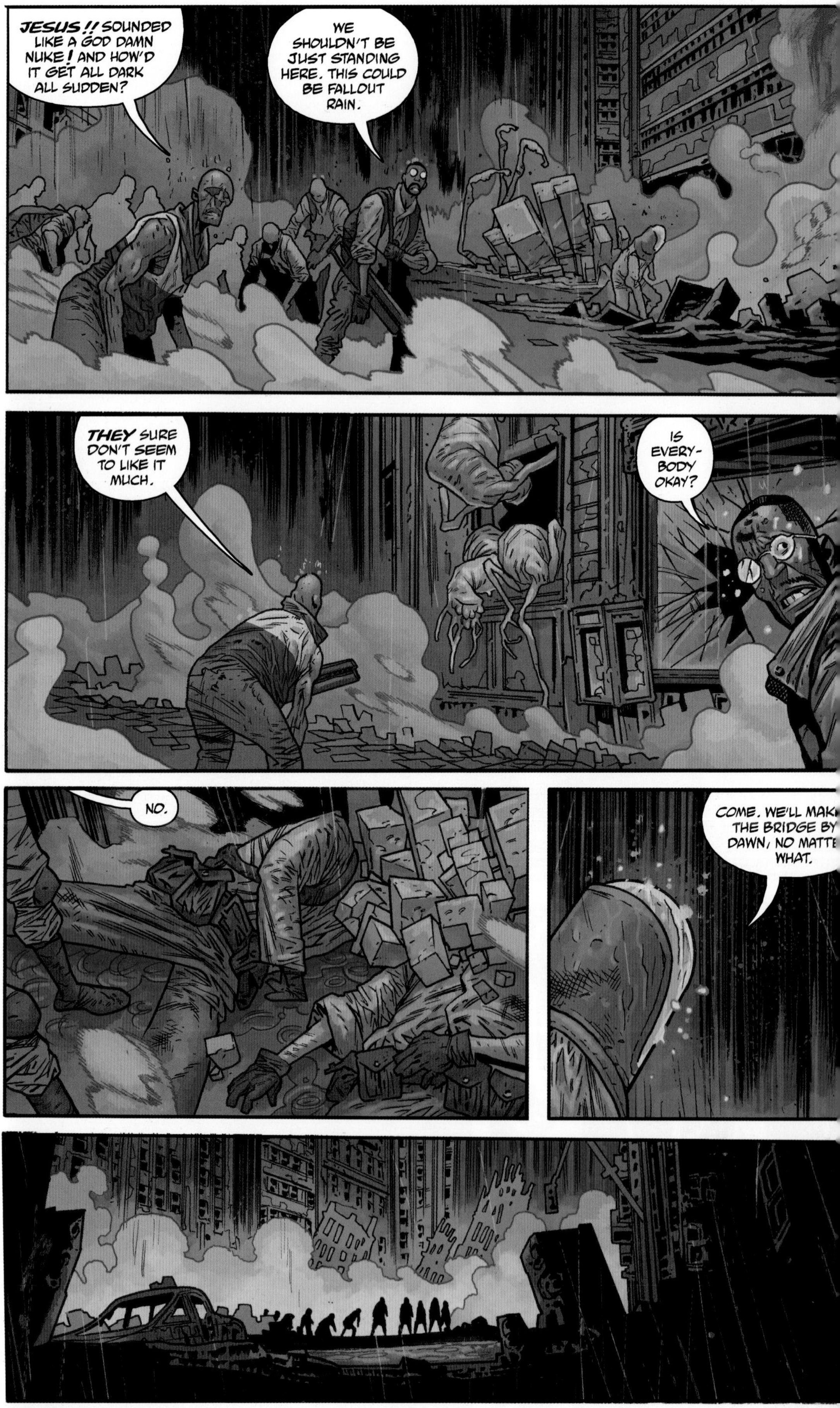
JESUS!! SOUNDED LIKE A GOD DAMN NUKE! AND HOW'D IT GET ALL DARK ALL SUDDEN?
WE SHOULDN'T BE JUST STANDING HERE. THIS COULD BE FALLOUT RAIN.
THEY SURE DON'T SEEM TO LIKE IT MUCH.
IS EVERY-BODY OKAY?
NO.
COME. WE'LL MAK THE BRIDGE BY DAWN, NO MATTE WHAT.

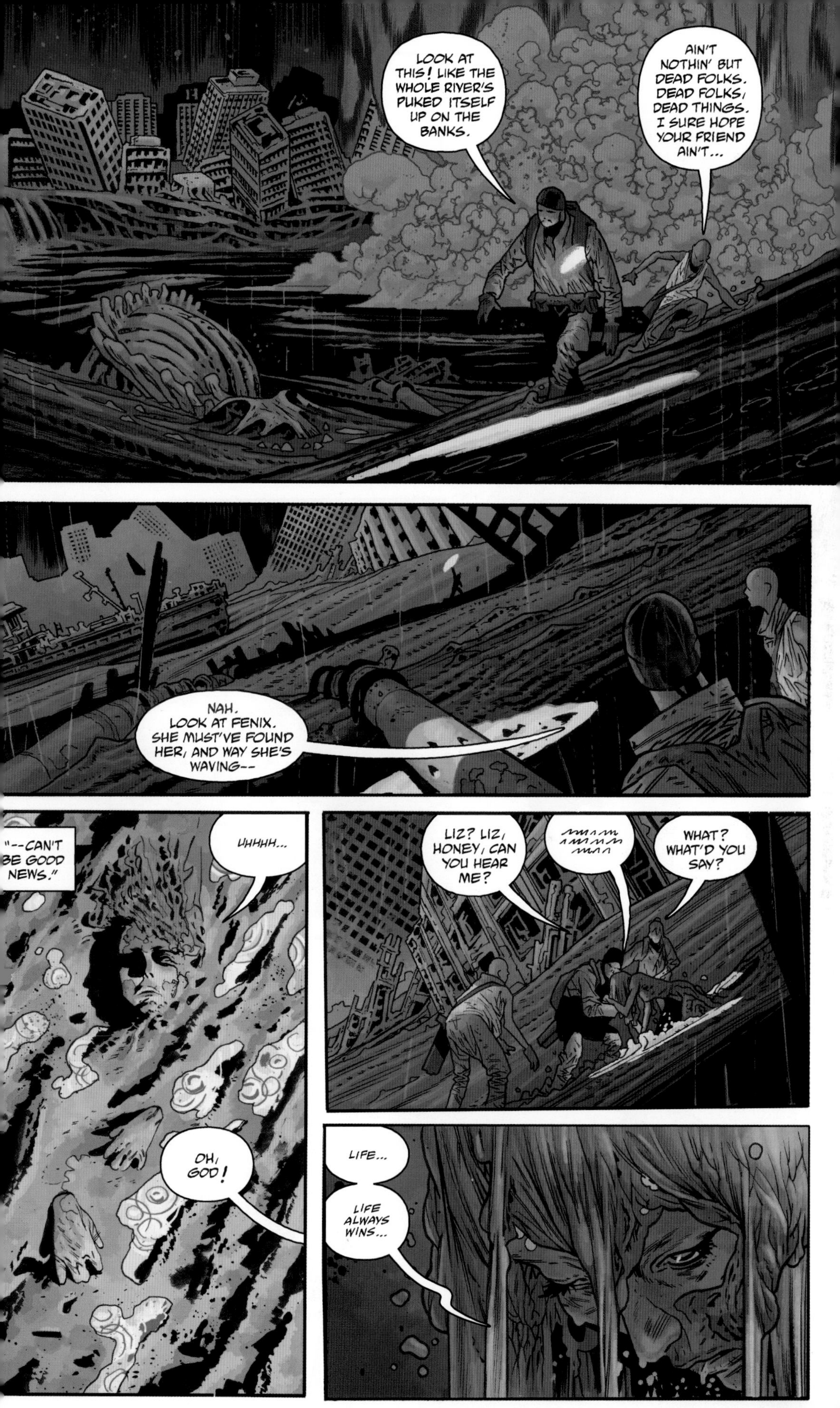
LOOK AT THIS! LIKE THE WHOLE RIVER'S PUKED ITSELF UP ON THE BANKS.
AIN'T NOTHIN' BUT DEAD FOLKS. DEAD FOLKS, DEAD THINGS. I SURE HOPE YOUR FRIEND AIN'T...
NAH. LOOK AT FENIX. SHE MUST'VE FOUND HER, AND WAY SHE'S WAVING--
"--CAN'T BE GOOD NEWS."
UHHHH...
OH, GOD!
LIZ? LIZ, HONEY, CAN YOU HEAR ME?
WHAT? WHAT'D YOU SAY?
LIFE...
LIFE ALWAYS WINS...

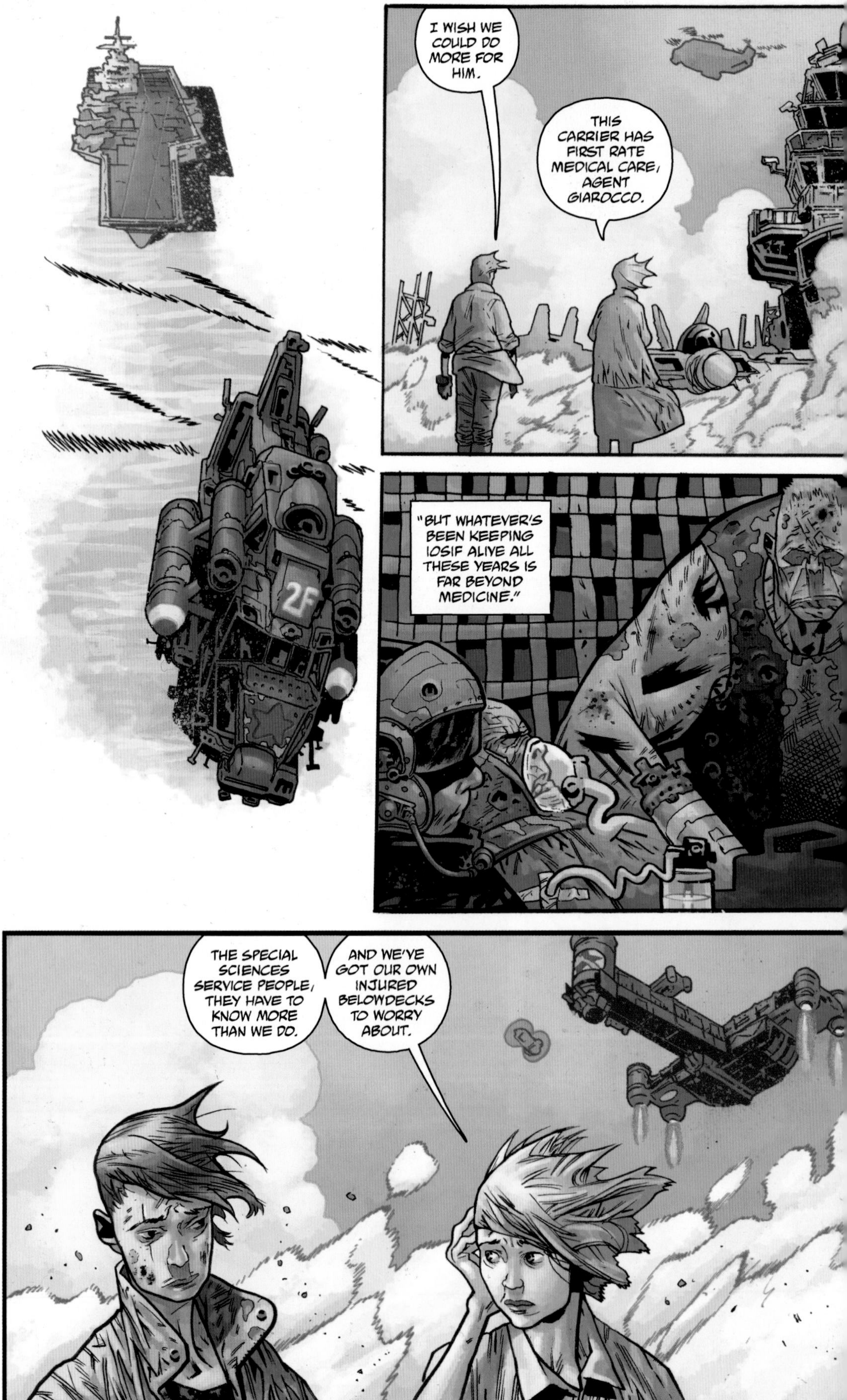

I WISH WE COULD DO MORE FOR HIM.
THIS CARRIER HAS FIRST RATE MEDICAL CARE, AGENT GIAROCCO.
2F
"BUT WHATEVER'S BEEN KEEPING IOSIF ALIVE ALL THESE YEARS IS FAR BEYOND MEDICINE."
THE SPECIAL SCIENCES SERVICE PEOPLE, THEY HAVE TO KNOW MORE THAN WE DO.
AND WE'VE GOT OUR OWN INJURED BELOWDECKS TO WORRY ABOUT.

HIYA, BRUISER! HOW YOU DOIN', BOY?

DON'T WORRY, FELLA. WE'LL BE BACK ON DRY LAND SOON.

YOU NEVER SAID YOU HAD NO DOG.

HONESTLY, I CAN UNDERSTAND FENIX'S MOTIVES. YOU ARE SUCH AN ASSET TO THE BUREAU, AFTER ALL. BUT *YOUR* ACTIONS--

WERE STUPID!

AND SELFISH. I WANTED TO BE THE HERO. I WANTED TO SLAY THE DRAGON, SAVE *EVERY-BODY*.

HAD I STUCK WITH YOU, TROXEL AND REIN WOULD STILL BE ALIVE.

YOU'RE THE HERO. YOU GOT PICHARD AND THE OTHERS OUT. *ALL* ALIVE.

ANGRY AS I AM AT YOU, ELISABETH, NOW THAT I'VE HAD TIME TO THINK ABOUT IT, I'M NOT SO SURE YOU DIDN'T PLAY A PART IN THAT.

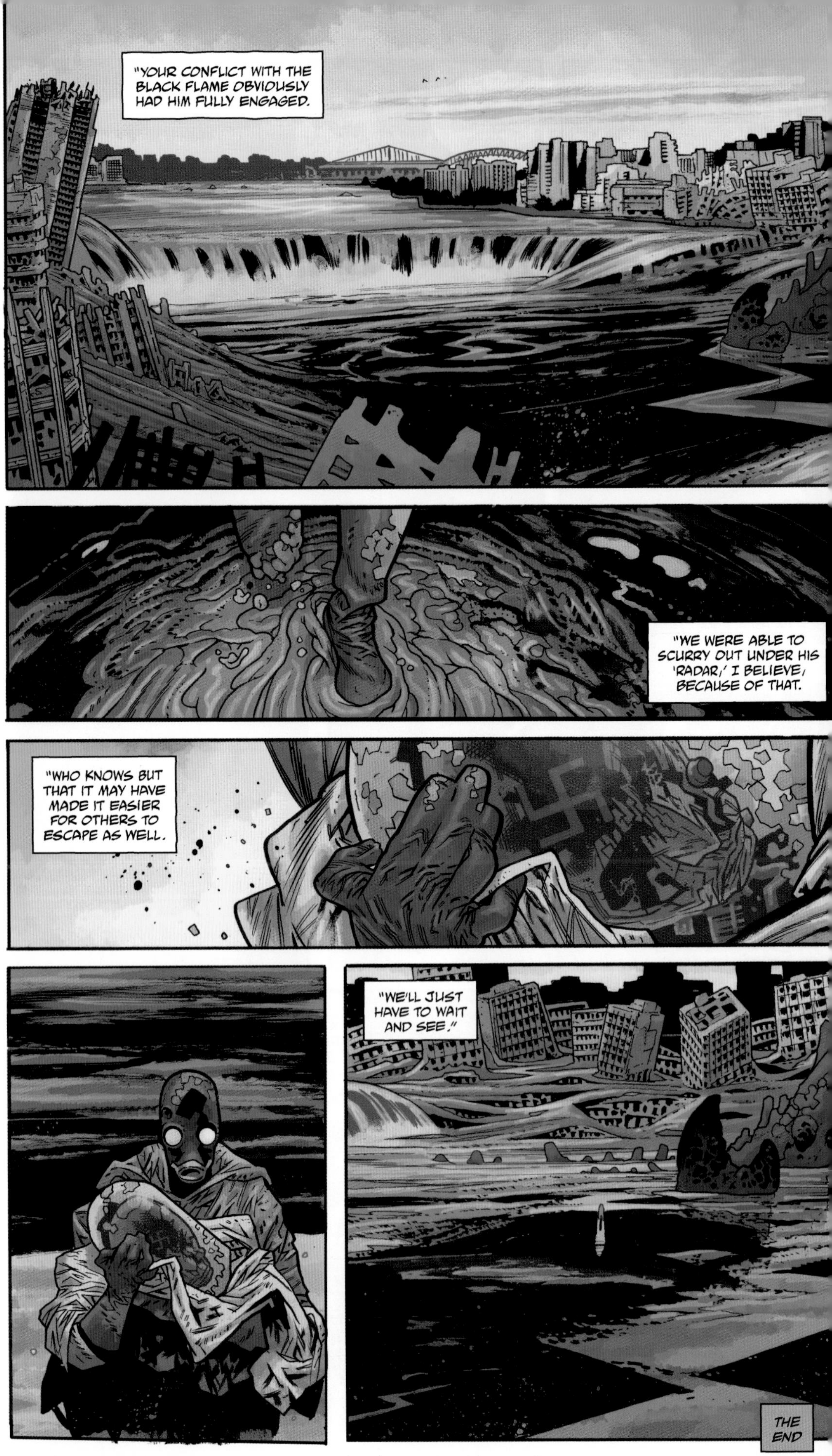
"YOUR CONFLICT WITH THE BLACK FLAME OBVIOUSLY HAD HIM FULLY ENGAGED.
"WE WERE ABLE TO SCURRY OUT UNDER HIS 'RADAR,' I BELIEVE, BECAUSE OF THAT.
"WHO KNOWS BUT THAT IT MAY HAVE MADE IT EASIER FOR OTHERS TO ESCAPE AS WELL.
"WE'LL JUST HAVE TO WAIT AND SEE."
THE END

B.P.R.D.

SKETCHBOOK

Notes by James Harren

LIZ

TIGHT. THIN LUCHADOR STYLE BOOTS

Liz! This series marks Liz's return to her formidable, fiery self.
The guys wanted her back in black and looking youthful again.

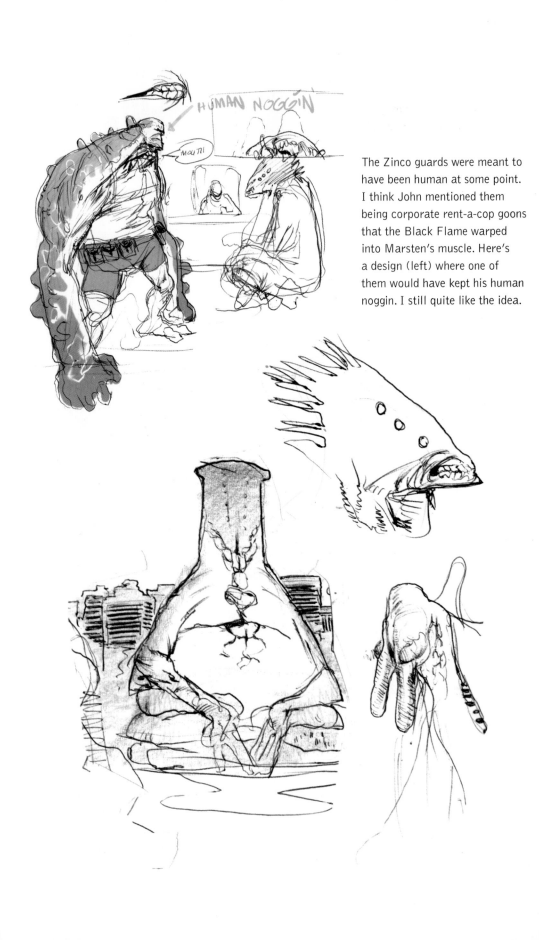

HUMAN NOGGIN

MOUTH

The Zinco guards were meant to have been human at some point. I think John mentioned them being corporate rent-a-cop goons that the Black Flame warped into Marsten's muscle. Here's a design (left) where one of them would have kept his human noggin. I still quite like the idea.

I did these guys early on when we were still developing the series. I remember drawing them after Mike dropped a photo on my Facebook page of a beetle swollen to the point of transparency with maggot larvae. He said this would be "right up my alley." I wasn't thrilled that he shared the photo right before breakfast, but he was absolutely right.

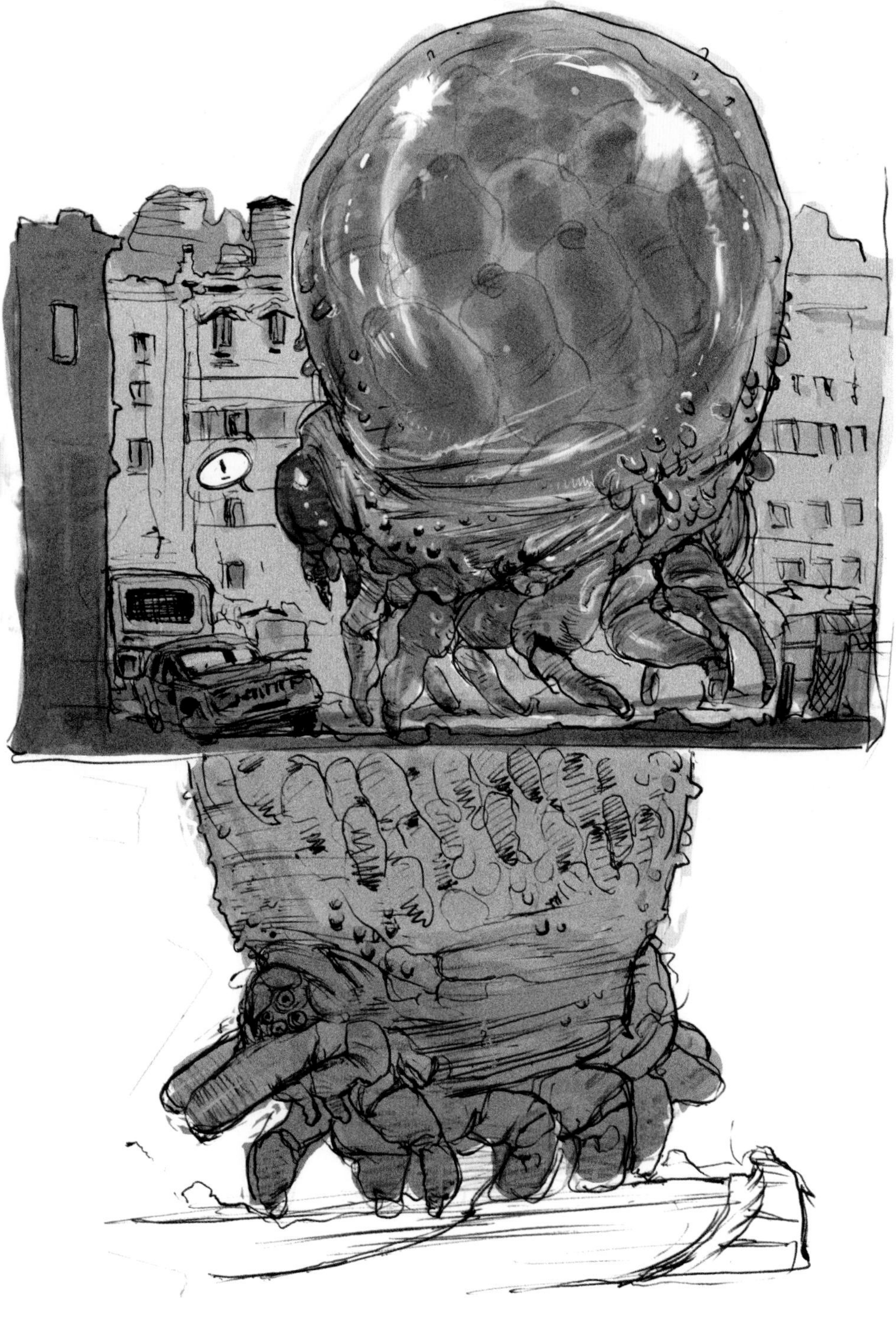

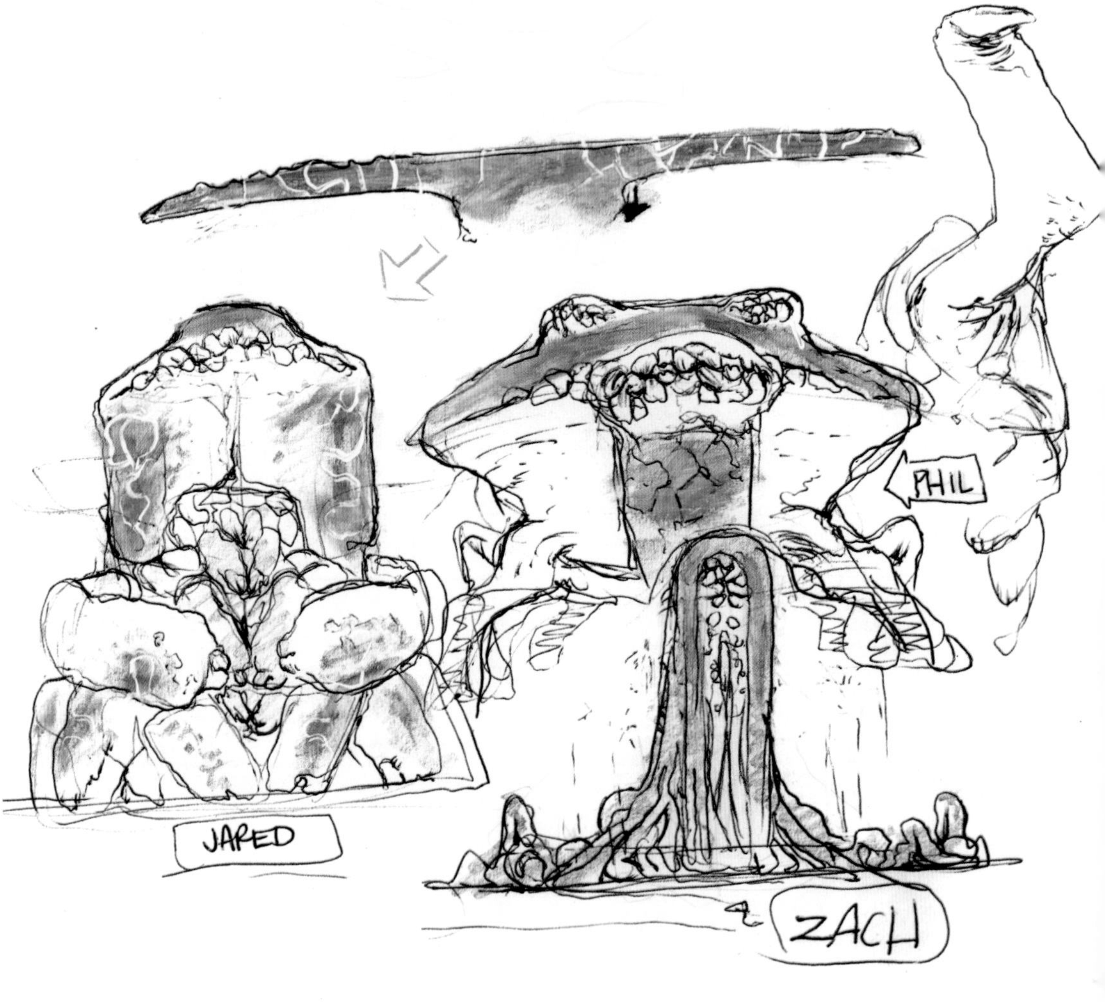
JARED
ZACH
PHIL

Some Ogdru ideas for that shot in chapter 1 when we first see the Manhattan skyline. I wanted it to make an impression, so I went a little overboard on ideas. Some of these guys might make their way into future series. Also, I was going through a strange period where I was designing them all with given names.

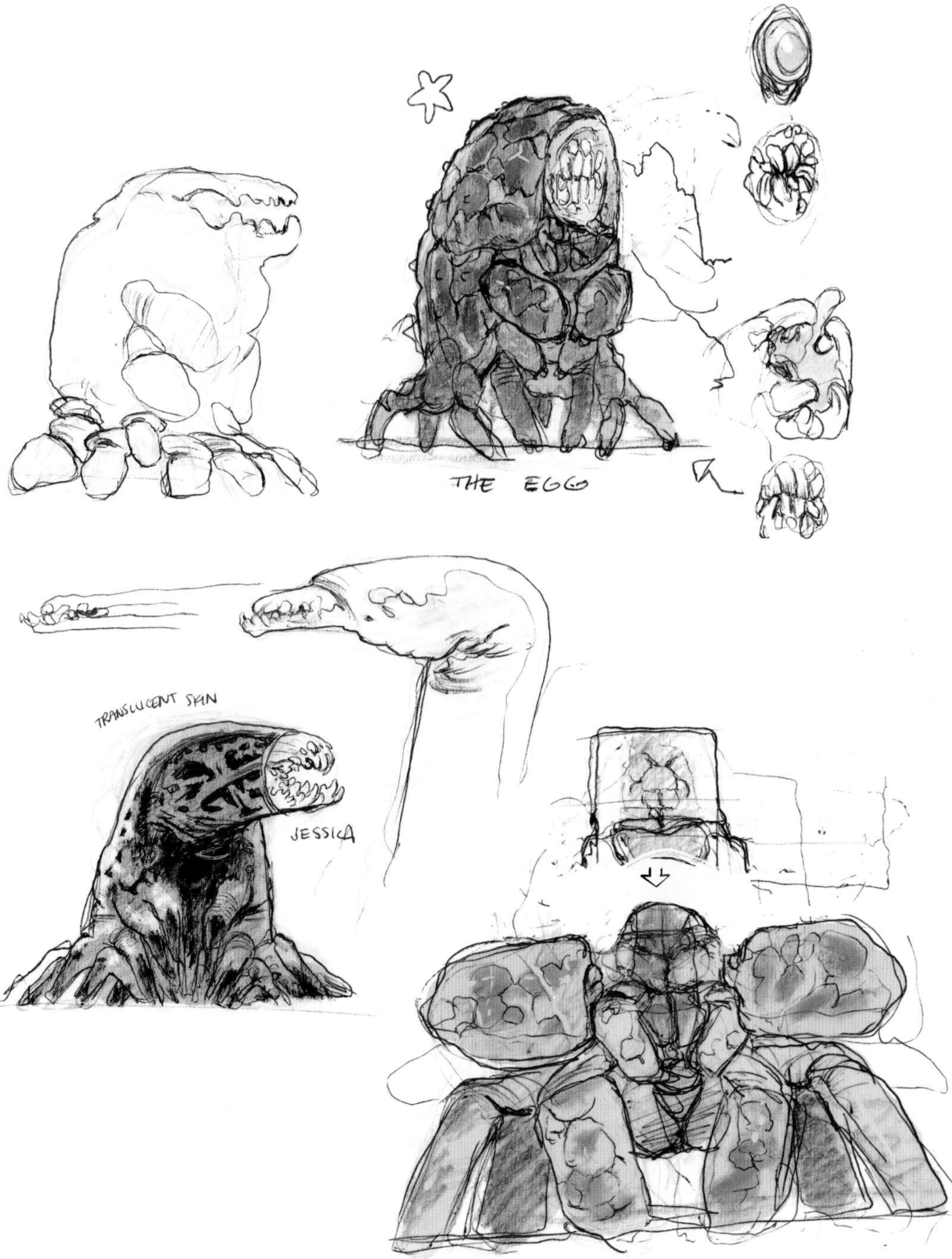
THE EGG
TRANSLUCENT SKIN
JESSICA

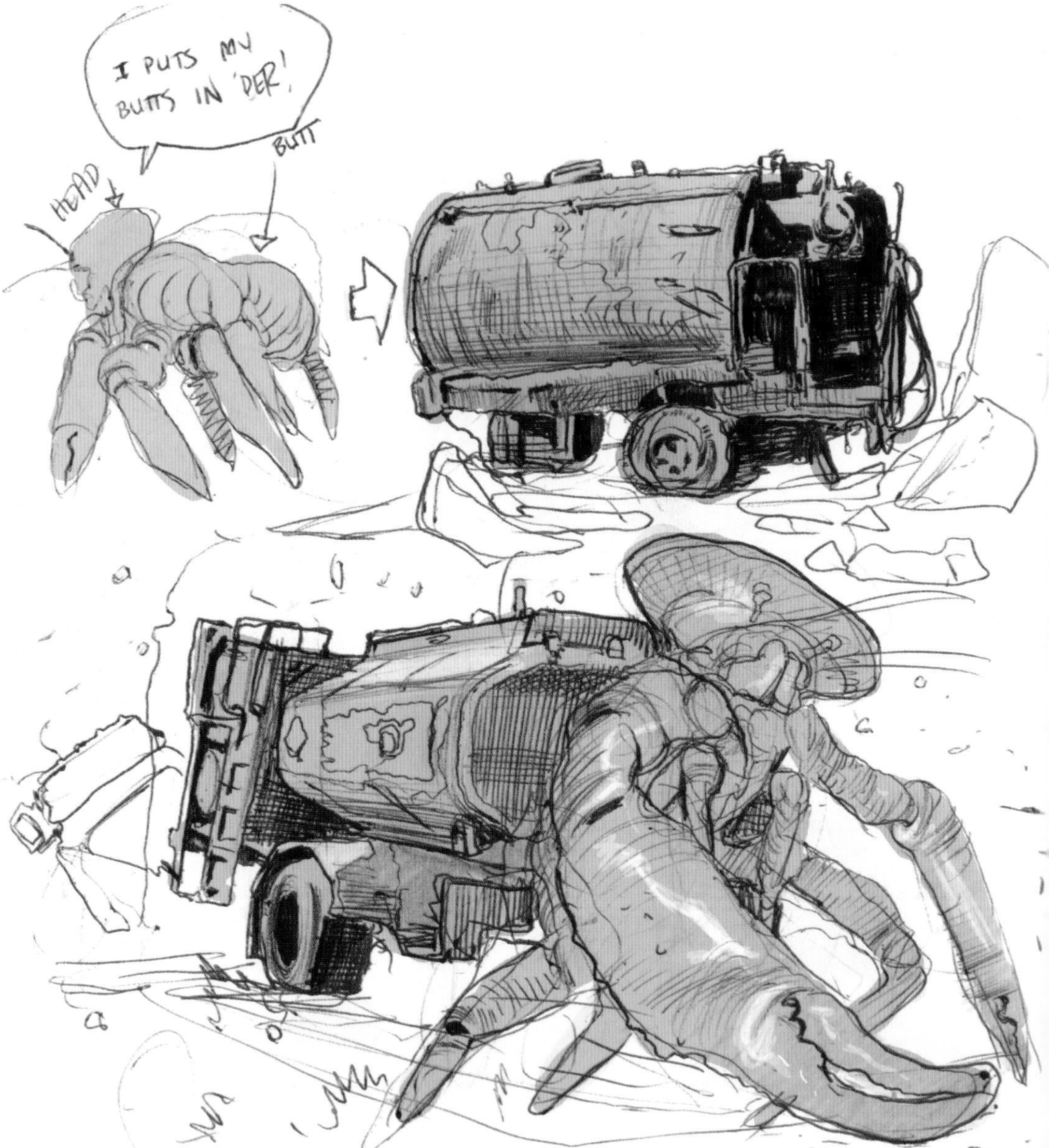
I PUTS MY BUTTS IN 'DER!
HEAD
BUTT

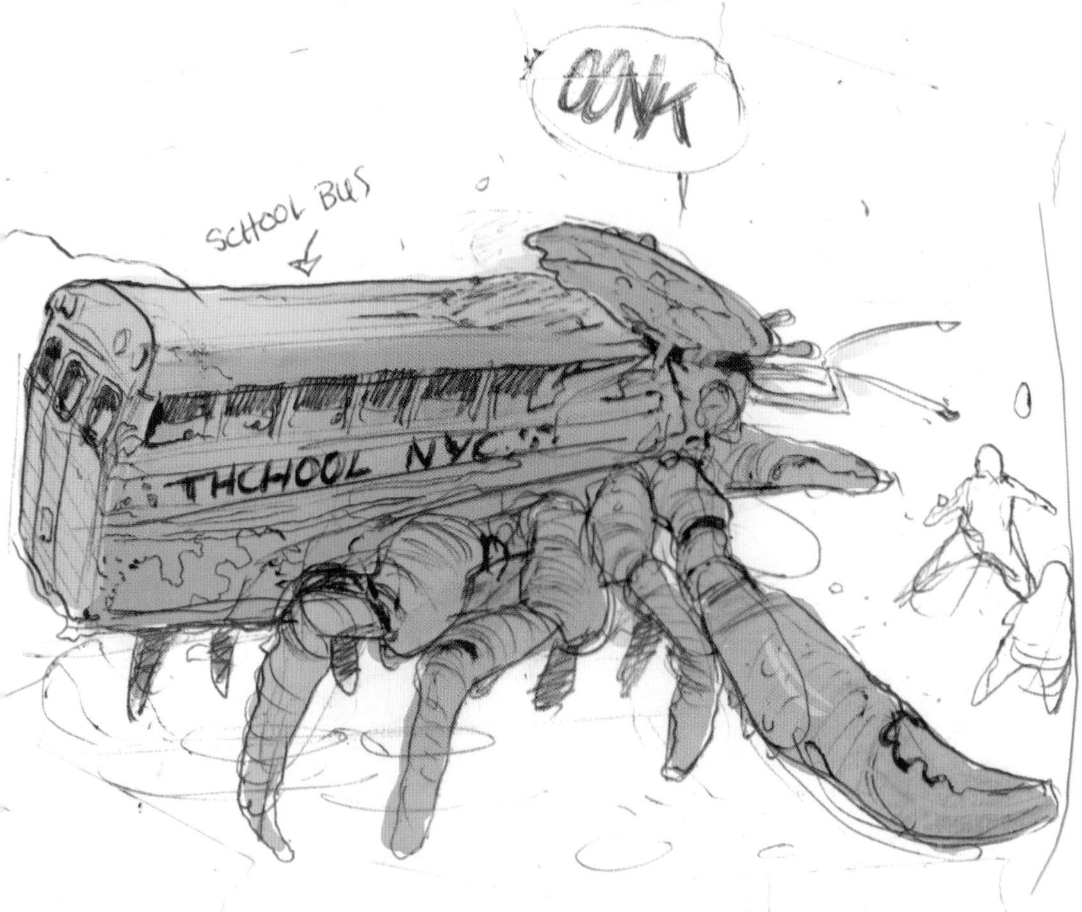
OONK
SCHOOL BUS
THCHOOL NYC

The crab! The script called for a crab monster inside the Holland Tunnel amidst garbage and semi-submerged cars. It was my idea (I think) to have him use some of the wreckage as a hermit-crab shell. This was a threshold guardian to our as-yet-unseen Manhattan, so I wanted him to be properly weird.

When I designed the new Black Flame for Tyler's arc, *The Return of the Master*, we were talking about him looking different for my arc. This is me going overboard and straying way too far from the original idea. In the end, I think we all agreed that we just wanted to see that first design in action.

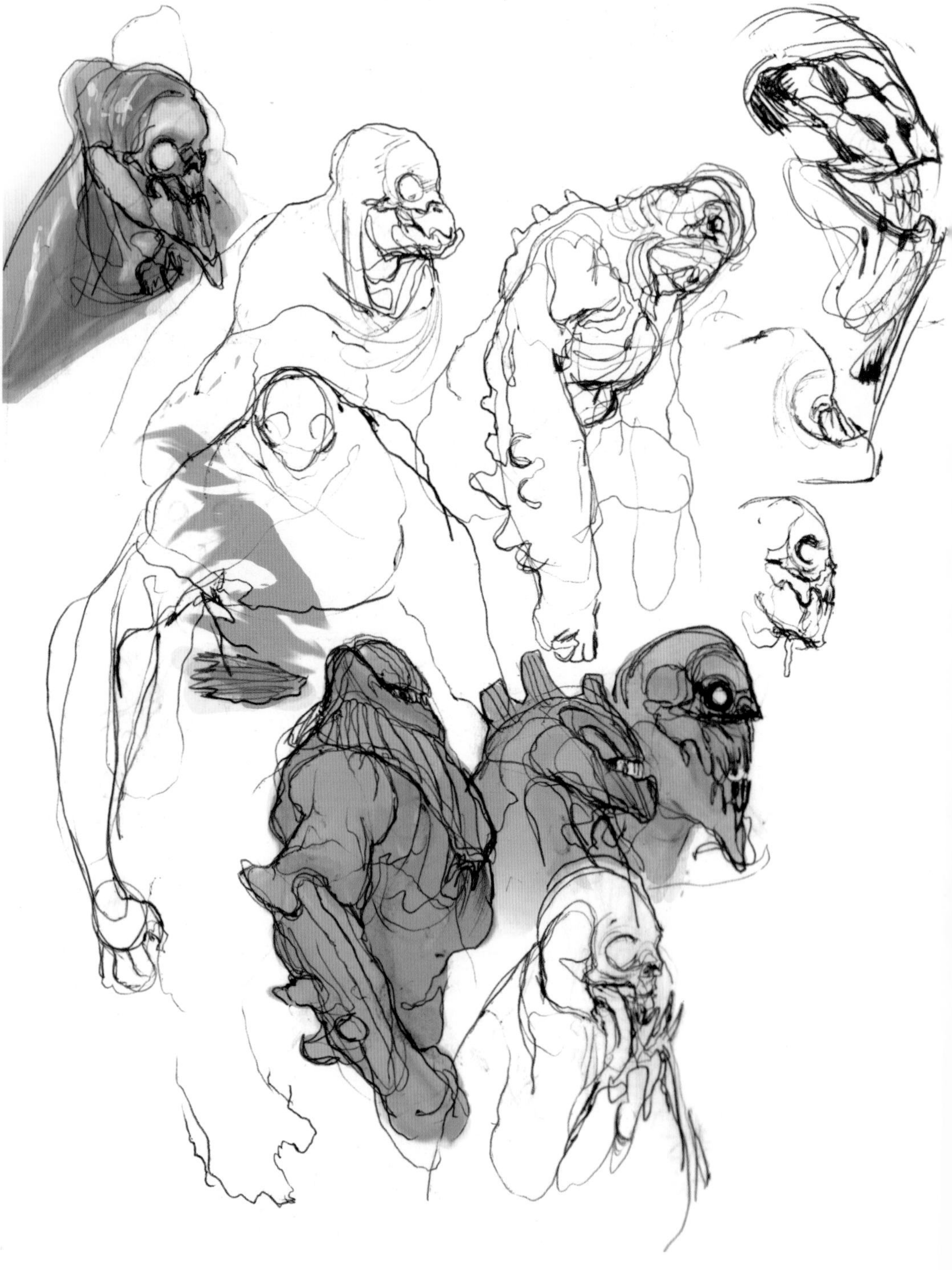

When I thought the Black Flame would have something close to armor, I really went down the rabbit hole for ideas (facing). I still like him having that stain down his chest to echo his suit-and-tie days as a corporate tycoon. But again, I was miles away from who and what the Black Flame is and has been in this series.

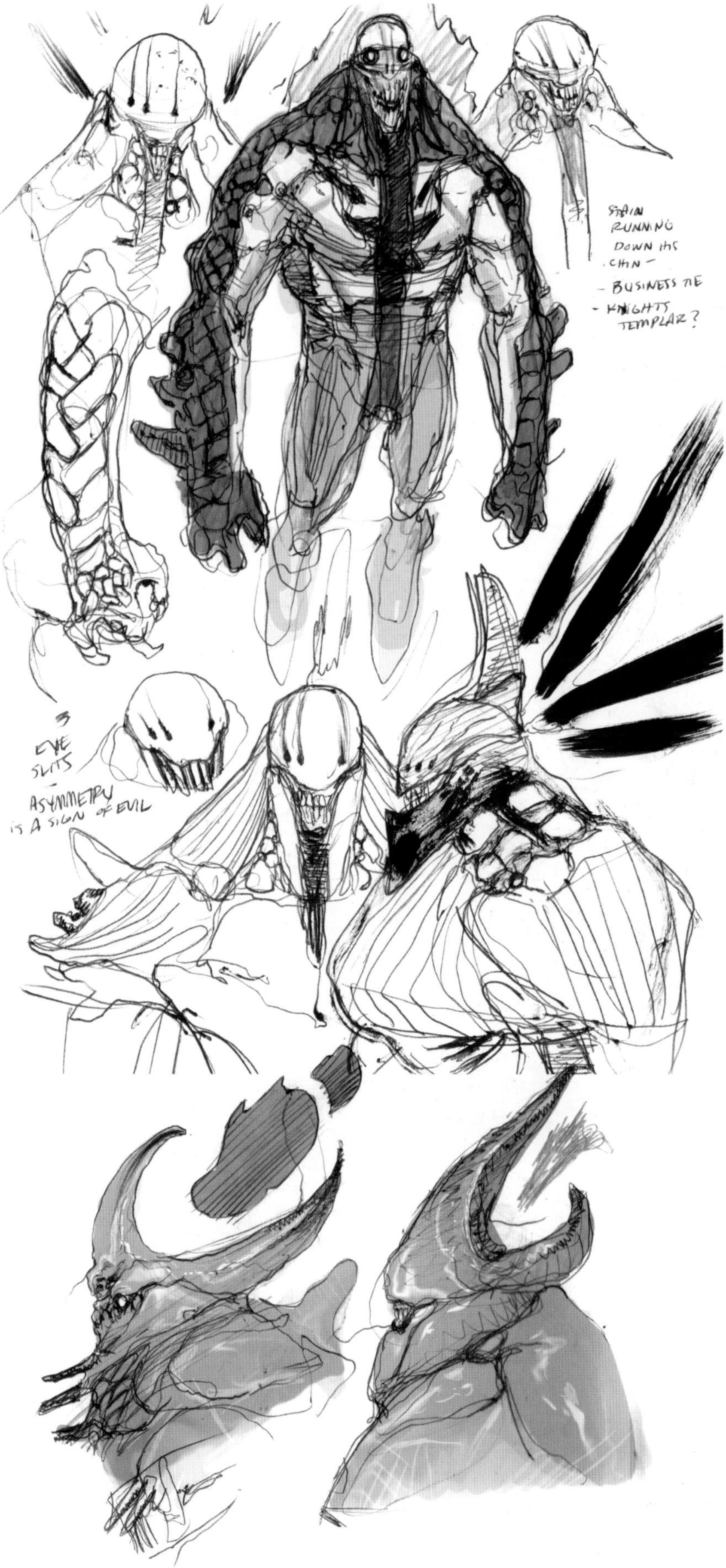
STAIN RUNNING DOWN HIS CHIN - BUSINESS TIE - KNIGHTS TEMPLAR?
3 EYE SLITS - ASYMMETRY IS A SIGN OF EVIL

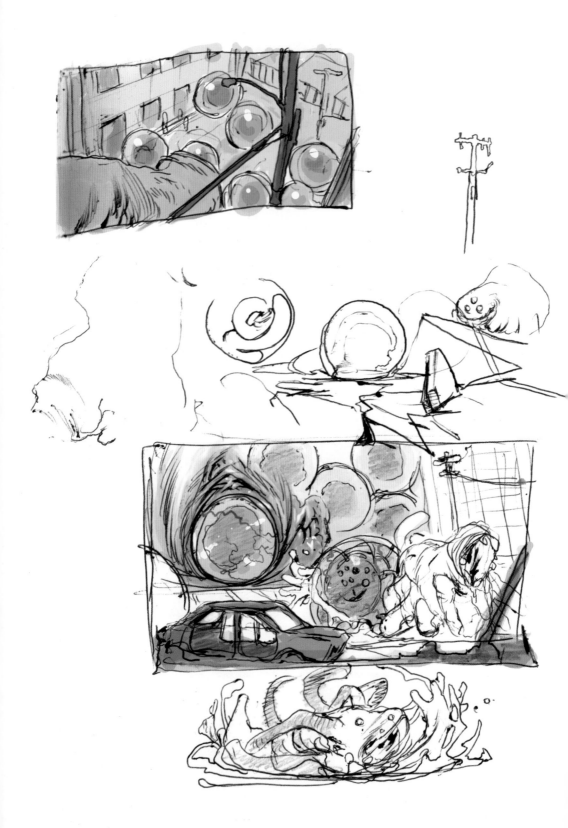

A couple of passes at some monster cloaca for chapter 3. They didn't have to tug my coat too hard for me to come up with this stuff.

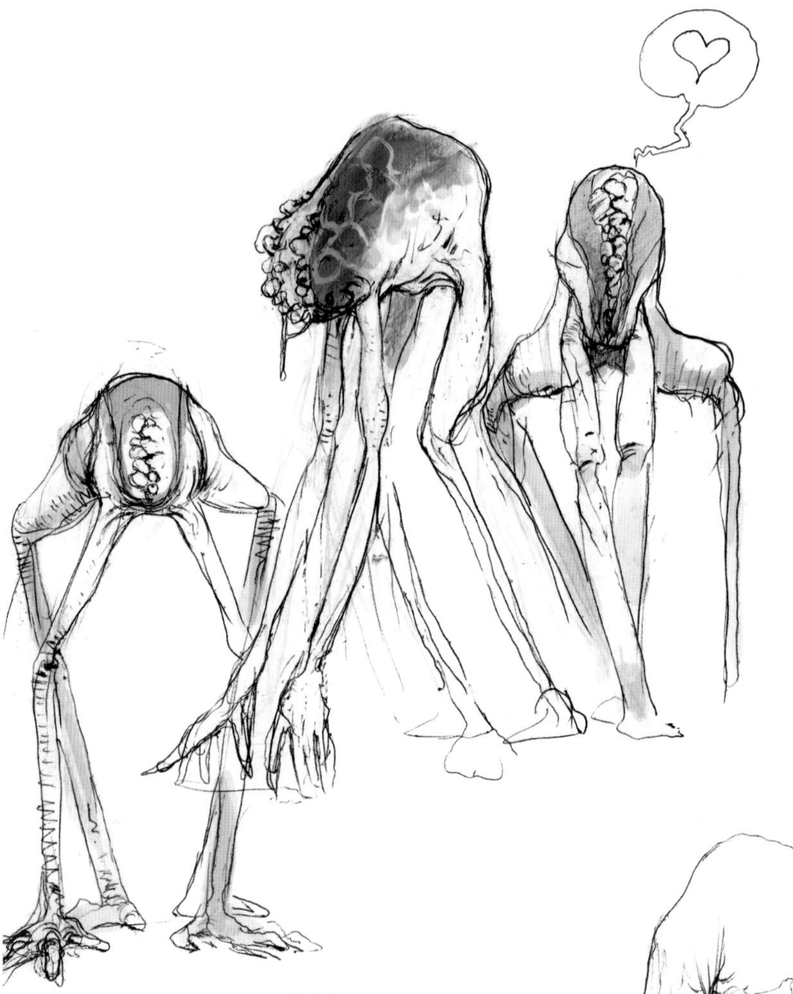
CRICKETS

The designs for the crickets had a lot of back and forth. I think the design idea was pretty open. The guys just wanted a swarm of something creepy that could fall between human and bat-faced monster in the way of scale. I knew I'd be drawing a lot of them, so I wanted their silhouette to be simple and recognizable both up close and in a churning mass.

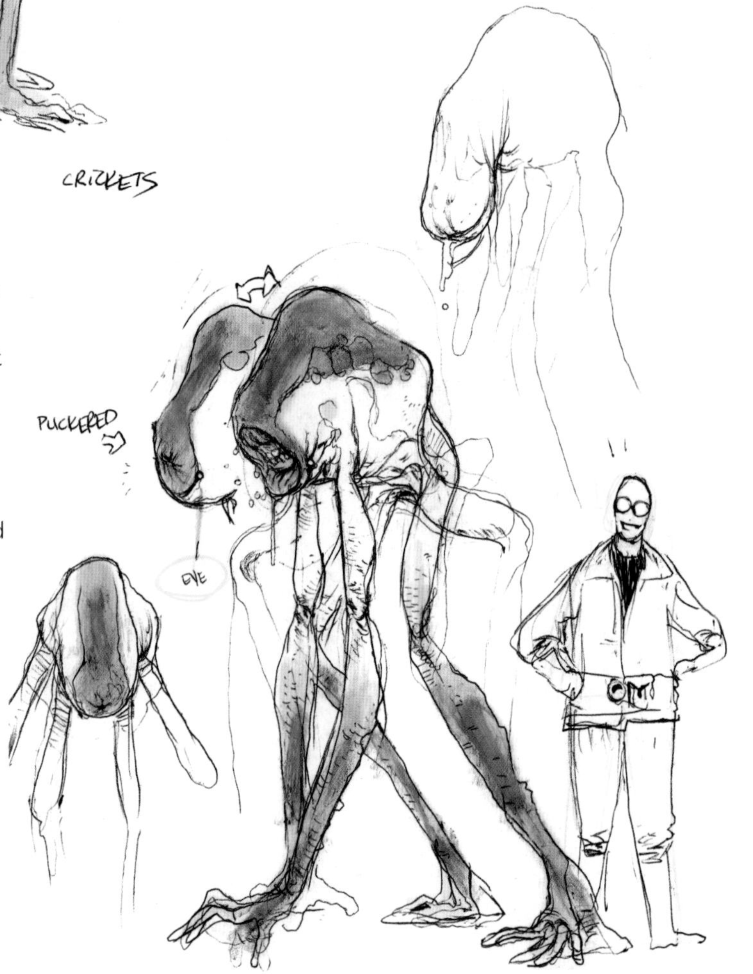
PUCKERED
EYE

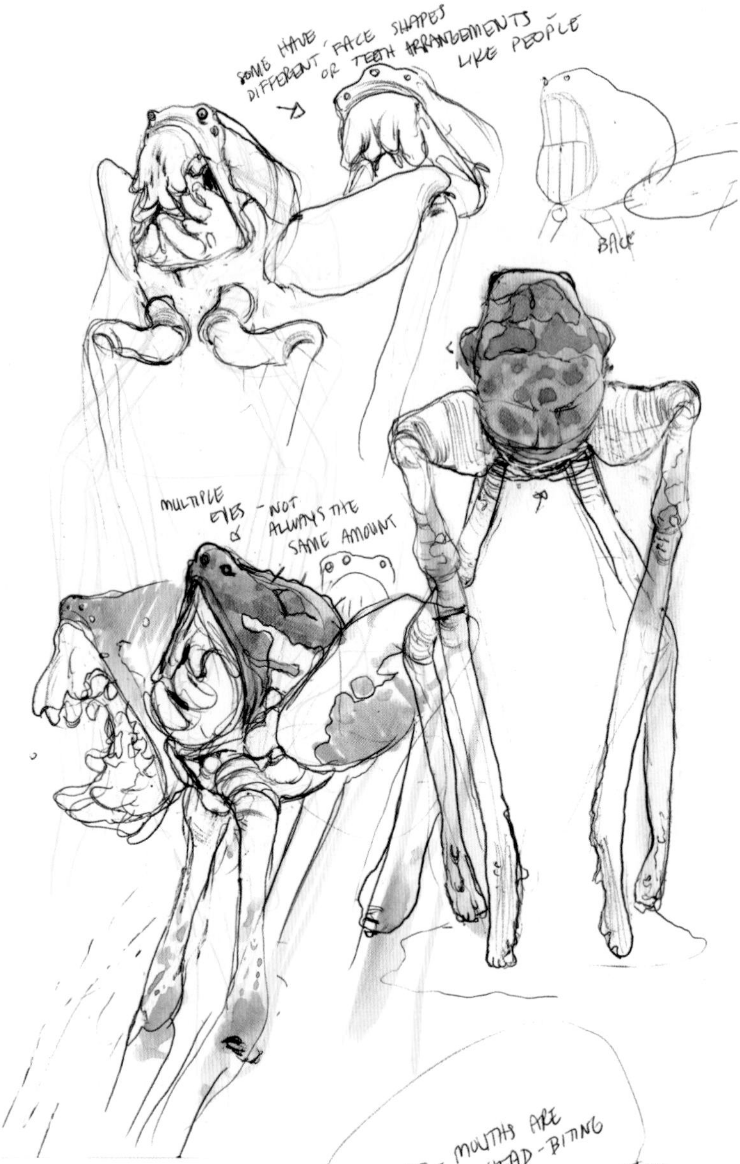
SOME HAVE DIFFERENT FACE SHAPES OR TEETH ARRANGEMENTS LIKE PEOPLE
BACK
MULTIPLE EYES - NOT ALWAYS THE SAME AMOUNT

This wound up being the design we went with. I thought the uniformity of those big dumb mouths would work great in a swarm. Like a mob of hungry, big-toothed idiots.

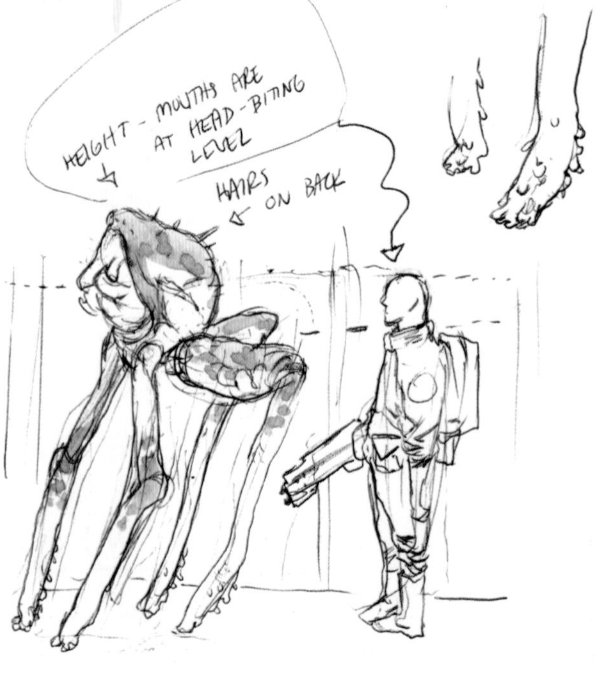
HEIGHT - MOUTHS ARE AT HEAD-BITING LEVEL
HAIRS ON BACK

Another swing and a miss. I didn't think this fella had enough personality.

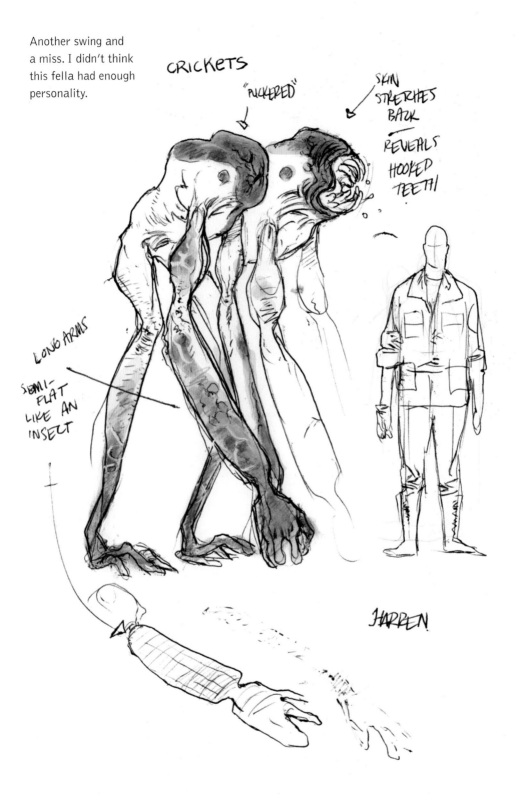

CRICKETS

"PUCKERED"

SKIN STRETCHES BACK REVEALS HOOKED TEETH!

LONG ARMS

SEMI-FLAT LIKE AN INSECT

HARREN

The following pages feature variant covers from the series, celebrating the 20th Anniversary since the B.P.R.D.'s first appearance in Hellboy: Seed of Destruction in 1994. Cover art by Mike Mignola, Richard Corben, James Harren, Ryan Sook, and Kevin Nowlan. Dave Stewart colored the first three images, and the artists colored the last two themselves.

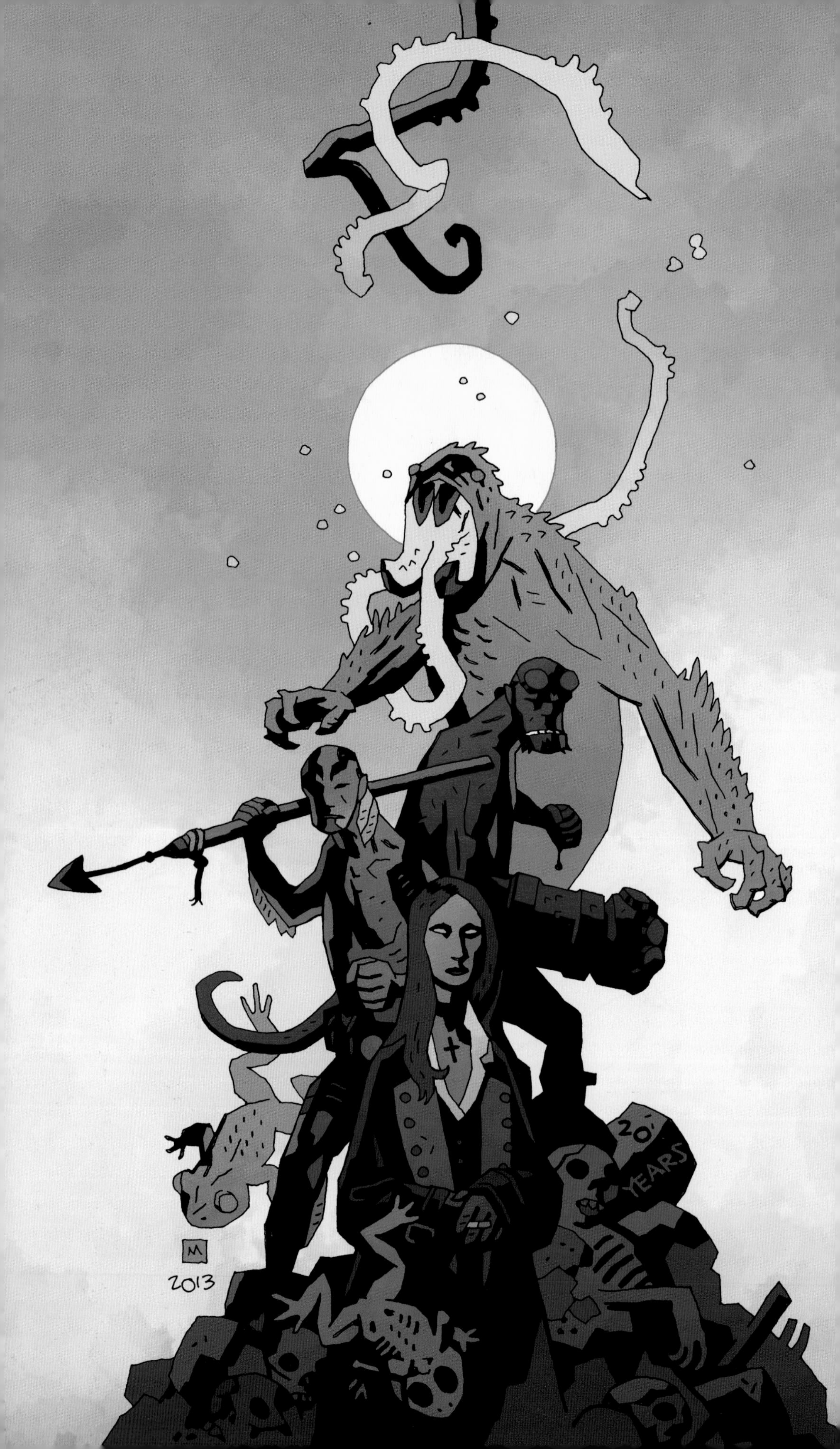

20
YEARS
2013

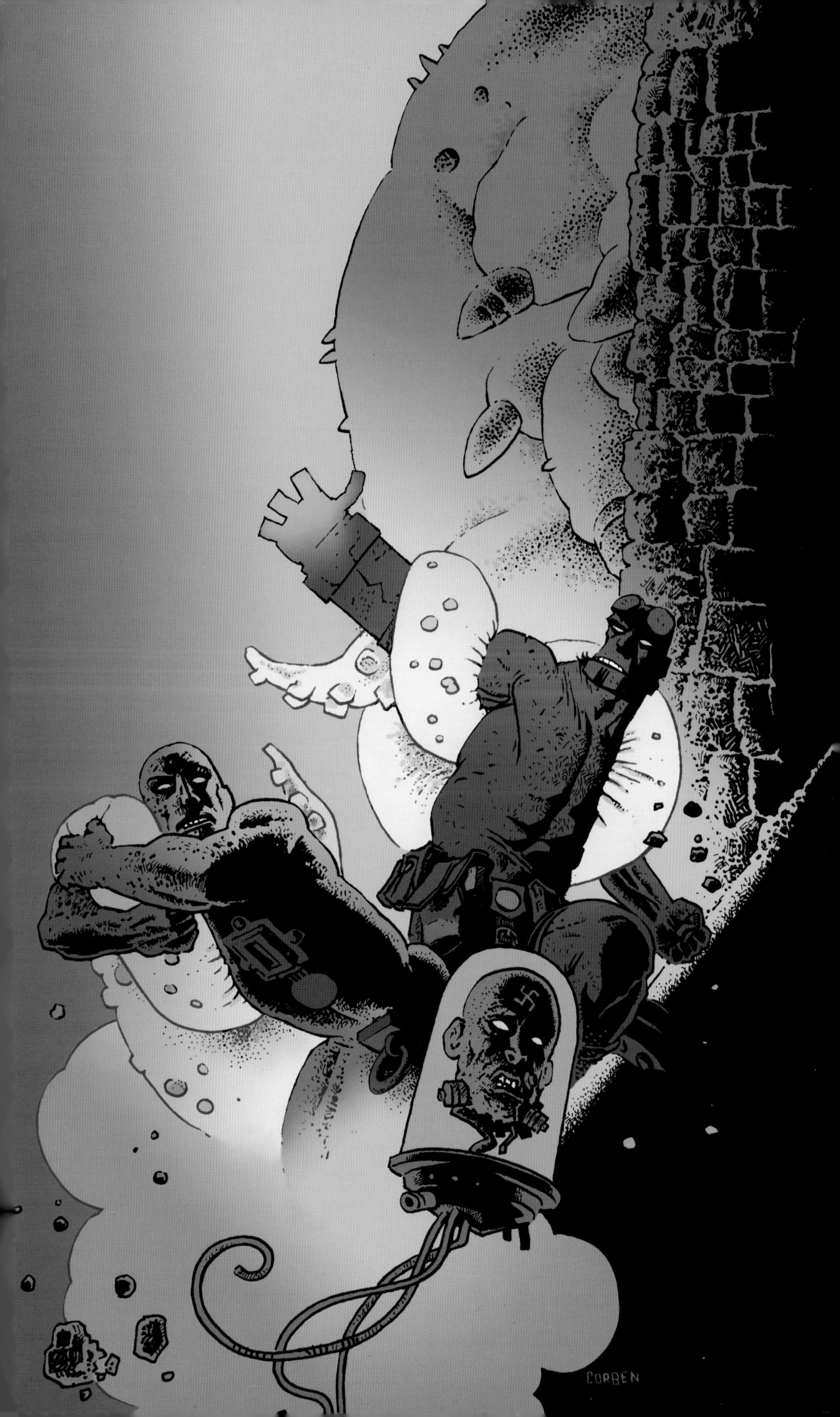
CORBEN

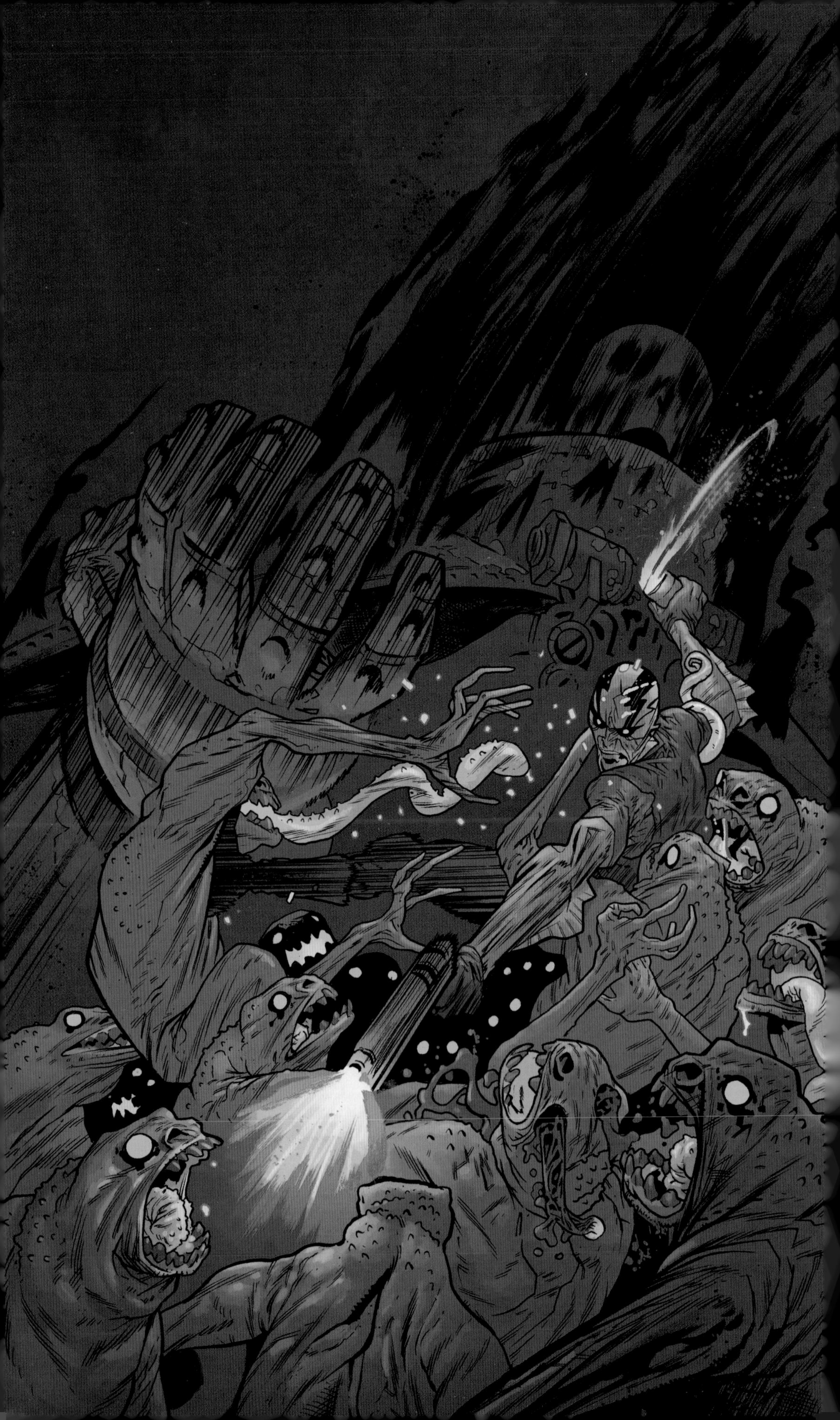